Rawdon Briggs Lee

A History and Description of the Modern Dogs of Great Britain and Ireland

Sporting division

Rawdon Briggs Lee

A History and Description of the Modern Dogs of Great Britain and Ireland
Sporting division

ISBN/EAN: 9783337324001

Printed in Europe, USA, Canada, Australia, Japan

Cover: Foto ©ninafisch / pixelio.de

More available books at **www.hansebooks.com**

A

HISTORY AND DESCRIPTION

OF THE

MODERN DOGS

OF

GREAT BRITAIN AND IRELAND.

SPORTING DIVISION: VOL. I.

(A NEW EDITION.)

BY

RAWDON B. LEE,

KENNEL EDITOR OF "THE FIELD," AUTHOR OF THE HISTORIES OF
"THE FOX TERRIER," "THE COLLIE," ETC.

THE ILLUSTRATIONS BY ARTHUR WARDLE.

LONDON:

HORACE COX,

"FIELD" OFFICE, WINDSOR HOUSE, BREAM'S BUILDINGS, E.C.

1897.

# PREFACE.

In the following pages an endeavour has been made to summarise the progress, and describe the Sporting varieties of the dog as they are at present known, and, I believe, appreciated, in the British Isles. Without losing any of the early history, my wish has been to introduce matter bringing the subject up to date; not only so far as the work of hounds and other dogs in the field is concerned, but as they are as companions, and when winning, or attempting to win, prizes in the show ring.

One or two new features have been introduced, or rather revived, the most important change being in connection with Mr. Wardle's illustrations. With three exceptions these are not portraits, although originally drawn from living examples. They are to be taken as typical specimens of the various breeds they represent. The reasons for this departure from modern custom will be obvious; and no doubt, for future reference, such pictures must be more useful than any portraits of individual dogs could be—dogs whose prominence before the public is more or less ephemeral.

The exceptions are the drawings of the Greyhounds, Welsh hounds, and Kerry Beagles. For the former, the extraordinary work of "Master M'Grath" and "Fullerton," could not be passed over; besides, they form an admirable example of two greyhounds, totally different in make and shape, equally good in the field. This is the first occasion upon which illustrations of Kerry Beagles and Welsh hounds have been published in a work of this kind. The drawing of the former is taken from a photograph kindly lent me by Mr. Clement Ryan, of Emly House, Tipperary, and is, I believe, quite successful in conveying an idea of what a Kerry Beagle is like. The Welsh hounds are portraits of specimens in the kennels of Mr. E. Buckley, of

Milford Hall, Newtown, N. Wales, and of the Hon. H. C. Wynn, of Rug, Corwen, N. Wales.

Following the precedent of other writers, a point scale is included in the description of each variety of dog. This is done, not with an idea that mere figures are of the slightest use in proving the excellence, or otherwise, of any animal, but because some readers, accustomed to such tables, might think the book somewhat incomplete without them.

I thank all who assisted in providing subjects for illustration and in giving valuable information that could not have been obtained except from owners who have made particular varieties of the dog a special study. To them I dedicate this work, as a slight return for their kindness and the interest they have taken in its publication.

RAWDON B. LEE.

Brixton, London, May, 1897.

CONTENTS.

CHAPTER I.
	PAGE
THE BLOODHOUND	1

CHAPTER II.
THE FOXHOUND	53

CHAPTER III.
THE STAGHOUND	109

CHAPTER IV.
THE HARRIER	121

CHAPTER V.
THE BEAGLE	133

CHAPTER VI.
THE OTTER HOUND	157

CHAPTER VII.
WELSH HOUNDS	173

CHAPTER VIII.
THE DEERHOUND	199

CHAPTER IX.

THE GREYHOUND 227

CHAPTER X.

THE WHIPPET 259

CHAPTER XI.

THE IRISH WOLFHOUND 269

CHAPTER XII.

THE BORZOI OR RUSSIAN WOLFHOUND . . 285

CHAPTER XIII.

THE GREAT DANE OR GERMAN BOARHOUND . 325

INDEX 347

ILLUSTRATIONS.

BLOODHOUND AND DEERHOUND.	*Frontispiece.*	
BLOODHOUND . . .	*Facing page*	1
FOXHOUNDS . .	,,	53
HARRIERS.	,,	121
BEAGLES .	,,	133
KERRY BEAGLES .	,,	153
OTTER HOUNDS	,,	157
WELSH HOUNDS .	,,	173
DEERHOUNDS	,,	199
GREYHOUNDS	,,	227
WHIPPETS	,,	259
IRISH WOLFHOUNDS . .	,,	269
BORZOIS	,,	285
GREAT DANES .	,,	325

CHAPTER I.

THE BLOODHOUND.

ALTHOUGH many writers have endeavoured to find the origin of the bloodhound in the Talbot of ancient days, there is no reason to believe that the former had as great a connecting link with the latter as the foxhound and other hounds, of both this country and of the Continent. We have been told of black Talbots, others white in colour, some tawny, whilst pied, or brown white and tan, specimens have repeatedly been alluded to. No doubt from these our ordinary hounds have sprung; but the heavier and more powerful bloodhound must have arisen from some other source. What that source was there is no means of finding out satisfactorily, and the origin of the bloodhound, like that of most other varieties of the dog, is likely to remain an unknown quantity.

In many particulars the modern hound resembles his progenitor of several hundred years ago, not in appearance perhaps, but in character and in aptitude for his peculiar kind of work, the latter at one period of our history being of a particularly useful character. He has been much used as a cross to improve the olfactory organs, the voice, and the size and strength of other hounds, particularly of otter hounds and foxhounds; but he has always had admirers who kept him for his own sake—because of his handsome and noble appearance, and because he was faithful and affectionate. Others encouraged him because he bore a vulgar and undeserved character for ferocity not attained by any other breed of dog.

Doubtless his name—"bloodhound," or sleuth-hound—had a great deal to do with this, especially as he had obtained a reputation for ability to find a man, be he either thief, political offender, or otherwise, by hunting the scent or line of his footsteps, as another hound would hunt the fox or hare, saving and excepting that he would not worry and attempt to eat his quarry. Having run him, as it were, "to ground," he would be contented with "baying" his man until his capture came to be effected. Certain authors, to gratify their own ends, or serve their own purpose, have repeatedly drawn upon their imagination in detailing, with an exactness worthy of a better cause, horrible scenes between bloodhounds and their "prey," ending in the death or serious injury of the latter. These stories originally arose from the "Southern States" of America when slavery was rife, and it is now positively stated that the hounds kept by the slave owners were not bloodhounds, but half-bred foxhounds—Virginian hounds—which were quite as loth as our modern hounds to attack a human being, although they might have hunted him to a tree or other place where he had taken refuge. Slaves, as a fact, were too valuable to be indiscriminately worried by bloodhounds, as some sensational writers have told us was of everyday occurrence.

The natural instinct of the bloodhound is to hunt man rather than beast. As a puppy, he may put his nose to the ground and fumble out the line of any pedestrian who has just passed along the road. Other dogs will, as a rule, commence by hunting their master, the bloodhound finds his nose by hunting a stranger. There are old records of his being repeatedly used for the latter purpose, whether the quarry to be found were a murderer or poacher, or maybe only some poor gentleman or nobleman whose political belief or religion was not quite in conformity with that of those bigots who happened to rule over him.

Early in the seventeenth century, when the Moss-troopers (but a polite name for Scottish robbers) invested the border counties of Cumberland, Northumberland, and Westmoreland, it was found that the ordinary means of arrest and punishment were insufficient to stop the raids of the thieves, so special provision was made that should, if possible, put an end to their depredations. The Scots were fleet of foot and active, and it was believed that the employment of bloodhounds would strike terror into the hearts of the marauders. The latter were to be pursued "with hot trod fragrant delect, with red hand (as the Scots termed it), with hound, and horn, and voice." Surely such a hunt as this was exciting enough, and the hard-visaged borderers would have little compunction in allowing their hounds to give full vent to their savagery.

The following is a copy of a warrant issued in September, 1616, to the garrison at Carlisle, giving orders as to the keeping of " slough dogs : "

Whereas upon due consideration of the increase of stealths, daily growing both in deed and report among you on the borders, we formally concluded and agreed, that for reformations therefor, watches should be set, and slough dogs provided and kept according to the contents of His Majesty's directions to us in that behalf prescribed ; and for that, according to our agreement, Sir William Hutton, at his last being in the country, did appoint how the watches should be kept, when and where they should begin, and how they might best and most fitly continue. And for the bettering of His Majesty's service, and preventing further danger that might ensue by the outlaws in resorting to the houses of

Thomas Routledge, alias Balihead, being nearest and next adjoining to the Marshes (he himself having also joined them— as is reported), order and direction were likewise given, that some of the garrison should keep and reside in his the said Thomas Routledge's house; and there to remain until further directions be given them, unless he the said Thomas Routledge shall come in and enter himself answerable to His Majesty's law, as is most convenient . . . . and that you see that slough dogs be provided according to our former directions, as this note to this warrant annexed particularly sets down.

The slough dogs to be provided and kept at the charge of the inhabitants, were as follows:

Beyond Eske, there is to be kept at the foot of the Sarke one dog; by the inhabitants the inside of the Sarke to Richmond Clugh, to be kept at the Moate one dog; by the inhabitants of the parish of Arthured, above Richmond's Clugh with the Bayliffe and Blackquarter, to be kept at Baliehead one dog.

Without quoting the whole of the warrant, it may be stated that six other "slough dogs" were ordered to be provided and kept at the expense of the following parishes, one dog in each: Newcastle, Stapleton, Irdington; Lanercost and Walton; Kirklington, Scaleby, Houghton, and Rickarby; and Westlinton; Roucliff, Etterby, Staunton, Stanix and Cargo, to be kept at Roucliff.

No doubt there was considerable difficulty in obtaining the levy or tax from the inhabitants to keep these hounds in condition fit to run down a man, and not hungry enough to eat him when they had caught him. In case of refusal to pay their dues to the sheriff or bailiffs appointed to collect the same, the defaulters were to be put into gaol till the amount was forthcoming. It would be quite interesting to note if such imprisonment was ever enforced. Whether this was so or not, I have not found any record to show, but it was said that the hounds proved very useful for the purpose for which they were provided.

The utilisation of bloodhounds in the above manner did not escape the notice of Sir Walter Scott. A King of Scotland, Robert Bruce, threw hounds off his track by wading down stream, and thus without touching the river bank contriving to ensconce himself, squirrel-like, in a tree. The great Wallace, too, was so sorely pressed by sleuth hounds that to save himself he slew a companion, whom he suspected of treachery, in order that when the creatures came up, they remained with the dead man whilst the living one escaped. Later the ill-fated Duke of Monmouth, who sought concealment in a ditch, after his defeat by the Royal troops at Sedgemoor, was discovered in his ignoble position by bloodhounds. Happily this was the last battle fought on English ground, and it seems strange that its cause, "King" Monmouth, should be so captured by means of a British hound. In 1795, two hundred bloodhounds were, under British auspices, landed in

Jamaica for the purpose of subduing a rising of the Maroons. Fortunately this canine importation struck such terror in the hearts of the rebels that they at once laid down their arms and the war came to an end.

However, long before Sedgemoor and the time of the border forays the bloodhound was used in this country. Gratius Faliscus, and Strabo, about the Christian era, mentioned the importation of dogs of this kind from Britain to Gaul, and Oppian immortalises in verse the Agassæos for their exquisite power of scent and great courage. These big dogs were obtained from Britain for the ignoble purposes of war. Afterwards they came to be used for hunting the stag and other large game, and from them are no doubt descended many of the fine hounds still to be found in the possession of our Gallic cousins.

Dame Juliana Berners, writing in her "Book of St. Albans," published in 1486, does not appear to mention the bloodhound, or sleuth hound, but the Lemor or Lymer was probably the same dog, and so called because it ran the line of scent, and not, as it has been asserted, because it was the custom to run it in a leash. Dr. Keyes (1570), mentions bloodhounds as having lips of large size, and ears of no small length. The learned doctor tells us how these hounds ought to be chained up in the daytime in dark places, so that they become bolder and more courageous in following the felon in the "solitary hours of darkness." He likewise describes them as being run in a leash which is held in the hand of the man in charge of the dogs. This was to enable the huntsman, shall I call him, to be up with the hounds when his services would be required. It seems from the same writer, that, in addition to hunting the footsteps of the felon, these dogs were also trained to hunt the cattle that might have been stolen, a purpose for which he says they were much used on the borders. This may have been so or not, most likely the latter, for a drove of stolen cattle would be easy enough to track without the aid of a keen scenting "slough dog," though he might be able to be of assistance in terrorising the thief if he were ambitious to try the strength and powers of his would-be captor.

From that period down to the present time, the bloodhound was mostly kept as a companion, and only occasionally has he been trained to "man-hunting," to the terror of the poacher and the evil-doer. For the latter purpose, he has proved of great service, and many stories are told of the extraordinary power a skilful hound may possess, through its faculty in sticking to the original scent, however it may have been crossed and re-crossed by either man or beast. Colonel Huldman mentions the capture of some poachers through the instrumentality of bloodhounds, who hunted the men for fully five miles from the plantation, in which they were committing their depredations. Another case is mentioned, where a sheep-stealer was discovered by similar means, though the hound was not laid on the man's track until his scent was at least six hours old. Another hound is said to have hunted for twenty miles a fellow who was suspected of having cut off the ears of one of his former master's horses, and the scoundrel was captured and treated according to his deserts.

The *Field* had the following not long ago:

" In 1854 Tom Finkle, an old superintendent of police, was stationed at Bedale, in Yorkshire, before the rural force was established. He was the owner of a bloodhound named Voltigeur. Old Tom was fond of company, and at that time sat for many a night in the public-houses along with the farmers and tradesmen. When he was wanted for anything particular at the police station, Mrs. Finkle would let Voltigeur loose with, " Go and fetch master," and, no matter where " master " was, either in Bedale or the neighbourhood, the hound was sure to find him; and the moment Finkle saw Voltigeur, the old superintendent knew he was required at the station.

"In the winter of 1854, or early in 1855, certain burglars broke into a house at Askern, and stole a quantity of silver plate and linen. The burglars, heard by the inmates of the house, had to decamp rather hurriedly, and a messenger was immediately sent to the police station to report the outrage. Old Tom was, as usual, with his companions at the Royal Oak, whilst his wife was in bed. The latter immediately got up and turned Voltigeur loose, with the order, "Go and fetch master." The hound was not long in doing his duty, and Tom, jumping off his seat, said to his friends, "I am wanted at home," and hurried there as quickly as possible. His wife reported the circumstances of the robbery to her husband, who at once called his constable and saddled his horse.

"The two then started off to the scene of the robbery, and after visiting the house and learning all particulars, they went outside. When in the grounds, Finkle said to Voltigeur, "Where are they? Seek 'em," and Voltigeur, putting his nose to the ground, took up the scent and went away at a nice pace, every now and then giving tongue. The night being calm, Voltigeur's voice was heard by many. The hound made out the line of the robbers on to

The Bloodhound.

the High-street leading from Boroughbridge to Catterick, and after going about three miles on the High-street he stopped suddenly at a small watercourse that ran under the road. The superintendent dismounted and looked under the bridge, where he found a bundle containing a quantity of linen and silver plate, part of the proceeds of the robbery. He waited there for a time until his man came up, then, remounting, ordered his hound on again. Voltigeur put his nose to the ground, and went back along the same road he had come for about a mile. Then through a gate he made his way to an outbarn and buildings.

" Here the bloodhound became more excited, and was baying and giving tongue freely as his owner and his man got up. The superintendent went to one door, and the constable to the other. The former demanded admittance, but all was still as death, and the doors fast. Tom looked about the buildings and found a crowbar, and was then soon into the barn, where he discovered two men concealed in the straw. They appealed for mercy, and prayed him to keep the dog off, and they would yield themselves up quietly. The prisoners were then secured and searched, and upon them was found the remainder of the stolen property. They were taken to Bedale, locked up for the night, next day brought before the magistrates and committed to the assizes, where they were sentenced to five years' penal servitude each, there being previous convictions against them. Voltigeur was of the Duke of Leeds' strain of bloodhounds, some of which were at that time kept at Hornby Castle."

A more recent instance showing in what manner bloodhounds may be of aid to the police is the following, which occurred not very many months since, but for obvious reasons the names and the locality are not mentioned. Early in 1896 a constable was out in the early morning, when about 6.30 a.m. he came across a couple of notorious poachers who were walking along a footpath through some fields. They, seeing the constable, called out in alarm as a signal to their companions, who were no doubt coming behind. Owing to the darkness, the latter escaped; but the constable took some rabbits and nets from the men he had met, for being in the possession of which under such circumstances, they were, later on, duly punished. At daybreak the constable, accompanied by a young bloodhound bitch, his own property, returned to the place, and was able to distinguish the footsteps of a number of men who had come out of a turnip field. They had separated, some going in one direction, others in another. The hound was put upon the tracks, and with her

The Bloodhound.

nose to the ground she hunted them across two fields, going straight up to sundry bags of game which had been hidden in a hedgerow. So far so good; but the constable was not yet satisfied, and he took his hound back to where she had originally been laid on the line. This time she went off in a fresh direction, and soon left the policeman some distance behind. He following up, ultimately found her standing at another hedgerow, where more bags of game were found concealed. These were secretly watched all day, but the poachers must have "smelled a rat," for none of themselves or their families came near. This is rather to be wondered at, for the bags were numerous and their contents valuable. At night the constable and the lessee of the shooting concealed themselves near the place where the first lot of game was discovered. Now they had not long to wait, for in about half an hour there came a sound of approaching footsteps, and two men appeared, who immediately appropriated the bags and their contents, which included nets and the usual poachers' paraphernalia. They were at once recognised, and, the spoil taken from them, were allowed to go. Summonses followed in due course, and when the case was heard a plea was set up that they had not taken the game themselves, but had been sent for it by their mates. Fines of 40s.

and costs were imposed, or, failing the payment, a month's imprisonment.

Now, in the above case a comparatively untrained puppy was found to be of great use; and had it not been for her the two men would never have been caught. There is no doubt they were members of the original gang, and had taken part in the capture of the game for which they were convicted.

The hound in question is one of our ordinary bloodhounds, such as win prizes on the show bench. She is by Chaucer ex Crony. Chaucer by champion Bono, from Beppa, by Beckford out of Bianca. Crony is by Dictator out of Dainty. Chaucer was bred by Mr. E. Brough, and Crony by Mr. T. W. Markland, whilst Mr. W. H. Cooper, of Hillmorton Paddocks, near Rugby, bred the bitch who was the heroine of the adventure.

A rather funny episode comes to us from a recent New York dog show, and it bears on the same subject. A Yorkshire terrier was stolen, a man was suspected, traced to the railway, where it was found he had taken a ticket for Baltimore. A telegram beat the train, and the fellow was arrested with the dog in his possession. However, in the meantime, a happy idea struck the lady superintendent of the show (this is an innovation which has not reached us yet), who put a bloodhound, called Queen of the

The Bloodhound.

West, on what were supposed to be the tracks of the thief. The hound made the line out right gallantly, and ultimately "ran her man to bay." Unfortunately for the lady superintendent, the hound had got on the track of an ordinary visitor to the show, who had little difficulty in proving his innocence, and after suitable apologies the hunted man went away satisfied, gratified probably that he had been constituted a hero without the pains and penalties which are so often attached to one who is out of the ordinary run of men.

But dog stories, like the yarns of fishermen and shooters, are apt to become rather monotonous than otherwise, to say nothing of the exaggerations that creep into them occasionally. However, the authenticity of the above interesting accounts are beyond reproach, hence deemed worthy of reproduction here.

Captain Powell, writing in 1892 on the convicts of Florida (London: Gay and Bird), gives some useful information as to the dogs used there in tracking such criminals as may attempt to escape. He says that, although bloodhounds were first used, they were found quite unfitted for the purpose, and at the present time foxhounds are utilised for manhunting in all the southern convict camps. These hounds are trained when young to follow the track of a man who is sent to run a few miles through the woods; and there is no difficulty whatever in so training them. Indeed, the author tells us that he has had hounds that were "natural man-hunters," and gives an instance where some puppies he was rearing at the time a convict tried to escape were put on his trail, and followed it until the man was captured. Captain Powell corroborates what I have already written, that it is a popular error to suppose that hounds attack a prisoner when they, as it were, run into him. When once the man is brought to bay, hounds are a great deal too wary to venture close enough to their chase to run the risk of a blow; in fact, they merely act as guides to the men who follow closely on horseback. The convicts and others have little or no fear of these hounds, and for a few cents any stranger in the locality can obtain one of the idle fellows, who are to be found everywhere, willing to be hunted by the pack. The human quarry usually divests himself of a greater part of his already ragged clothes, and, with a start of a mile or so, makes his way over a rough and wooded country until he finds a convenient place in which he can keep the hounds at bay.

At Warwick, in 1886, an attempt was made to hold trials of bloodhounds in connection with the dog show held there. These were, however, a

The Bloodhound. 17

failure, excepting so far as they afforded an inducement to owners of the variety to give a little time and trouble to working their favourites, which hitherto had only been kept for fancy purposes. A little later, similar meetings were held at Dublin, in the grounds of the Alexandra Palace, London, and elsewhere, but in no case could they be called very successful.

I had the good fortune to be present at two particularly interesting gatherings, that took place during the wintry weather of January, 1889, and maybe the following particulars, written at the time, give a better idea of the modern capabilities of bloodhounds than could be written now. It must be noted that the hounds mentioned were of the so-called prize strains, were "show dogs" in the modern acceptation of the term, and, excepting perhaps in ferocity, they would no doubt compare favourably with any hounds of the kind that lived fifty, a hundred, or more years ago.

Readers will no doubt be aware that, about 1889 and a little earlier, considerable commotion had been caused in the metropolis by the perpetration of some terrible crimes. The police arrangements were entirely futile, and the murderers still remain at large. The attention of the authorities was drawn to the fact that bloodhounds might be of use to them

C

in such a case. Mr. Hood Wright offered the loan of his hound Hector, but, owing to the fact that he required some indemnity in case his dog was killed or injured, Hector remained at home.

Mr. E. Brough was then communicated with, and he brought from Scarborough to London a couple of his hounds. They had several "rehearsals" in St. James's Park, where they acquitted themselves to the satisfaction of the Chief Commissioner of Police; but it may be said that, though the line of scent was repeatedly crossed by a strange foot, without throwing off the hound, when the same was done in the streets and on the pavement hounds were quite at fault. Indeed, to be useful in tracking criminals in a town very special training would be needed, and, personally, I believe that bloodhounds, even with that training, would be useless in our large centres for police purposes.

Under fair conditions any bloodhound will, in a few lessons, run the trail of a man a mile or two, or more, whose start may vary from ten minutes or a quarter of an hour, or longer. Some of the more practised hounds can hunt the scent even though it be an hour old, and we know that a couple of Mr. Brough's bloodhounds, early one summer's morning, hunted for a considerable distance the footsteps of a man who had gone along the road thirteen hours before.

This is, of course, exceptional, but, with a proper course of training during three or four generations, there is no reason to doubt that bloodhounds would be able to reliably make out the trail of a man who had gone three or four hours previously.

That hounds will ever be got to track a criminal, or anyone else, on the cold, damp flags continually passed over by pedestrians, as in the streets of London and other large towns, no one who understands them will believe. Such work they never have done, and never will do; nor do the owners themselves aspire to such excellence for their favourites. In country districts they may be of aid, but in towns, so far as appearances are at present, the apprehension of criminals must be left to the mental sagacity of the official biped.

Bloodhounds might be of use in smelling out any secreted article or a man in hiding.

In May, 1893, the dead body of a murdered child was discovered by means of Mr. Markland's well-known bloodhound Dainty. The inhabitants of the locality round about, had been horror stricken by what was known as the Wilmslow tragedy, and one of the missing victims could not for a long time be discovered. The hound we mention being brought to the place by the police, hunted about, went into the kitchen of the house where the tragedy had taken place, and ultimately made its way to the cellar. Here it marked under a coal heap, and, the coals being removed, a flag was found, and buried two feet below it was discovered the body of the child in question. Other hounds had previously been tried, but not one of them had shown such excellent olfactory organs as the old bitch Dainty. It was thought the body had been under the flag for eight to ten days. Similar cases could be given, but such discoveries might as easily be made by any terrier or other variety of the dog with ordinary scenting powers.

The bloodhound stands alone amongst all the canine race in his fondness for hunting the footsteps of a stranger; any dog will hunt those of his master or of someone he knows, and of a stranger, probably, whose shoes are soaked in some stinking preparation to leave a scent behind. The bloodhound requires nothing but the so-called "clean shoe," and, once lay him on the track, he hunts it as a foxhound would the fox, or the harrier or beagle the hare.

To proceed with the following description of man-hunting with bloodhounds:

The storm of Sunday had passed, and how deep the snow lay in the streets and in the country places on the Monday, are now a matter of history. The air was keen and sharp, made so by a brisk north wind which blew on the Monday morning, when we left Euston station for Boxmoor, where we were to see two couples of Mr. Brough's bloodhounds run in the open country without assistance of any kind, and under any conditions which might prevail at the time. Surely the surroundings could not well have been more unfavourable unless a rapid thaw, immediately following the snow, had made them so. At Boxmoor the country was thoroughly white. The snow lay on the ground to an uniform depth of about eight inches; where it had drifted, occasionally we were almost up to our knees. For a time the sky was fairly bright, but later a blinding shower of snow fell, which happily cleared off in about an hour's time. At our terminus we were joined by Mr. Holmes Pegler, who brought with him a dog hound named Danger, by Maltravers out of Blossom. This hound a few generations back can claim some of the old southern hound blood; but he shows not the slightest trace of this, being a good-looking black and tan animal, though not then in the best form, so far as health was concerned. He had very little preliminary training, and thus afforded fair evidence of what a bloodhound will do under adverse circumstances. Our small party—which included, in addition to the gentlemen already mentioned, three ladies in a sleigh, Dr. Philpot, and Mr. W. K. Taunton—made the best way along the lanes to the Downs, and, ascended them, on to the Sheep Hanger Common. Towards the summit we found ourselves on one side of a pretty valley, which even under its wintry garb looked quite charming, and afforded some idea of the beauty of the locality when summer blooms. However, before quite reaching the hilltop it was decided to give Danger a trial.

A man was selected for the purpose, and the course he had to run was pointed out to him. The thickly lying snow made locomotion very difficult, and as even now there came a recurrence of the storm, a comparatively short start was given. In seven minutes from the time the man had set off, Danger was laid on his track, and, picking up the line in an instant, went away at a quick rate along the hillside. We tried to run with the hound, but to do this in the deep snow and keep Danger in sight was impossible. After following him some six hundred yards or so, we had to make our way to the tiny knot of spectators on the hilltop, and once there saw that he had lost the line, after running it well for something less than half a mile. In making a cast round, he unfortunately struck the wind of the spectators, and came back to them. Nor did he seem very persevering in attempting to regain the scent, giving us the idea that in previous trials he had not been

The Bloodhound.

allowed to depend upon his own exertions to recover a lost trail.

Mr. Brough's hounds included Barnaby (one of the couple brought to London at the instance of the late Commissioner of Police) and Beeswing, with Belhus and Blueberry, their offspring. The two first named are well-known hounds on the show bench. Barnaby had run at the Warwick trials; the younger animals are fairly good looking, and their work was quite satisfactory. Blueberry was afforded the next trial, a stranger to her acting as the quarry, taking his route down the hill over sundry fences, going a semi-circular course of about a mile. After eight minutes' law the hound was unleashed, and had no difficulty in hitting the line, though snow was falling heavily. She carried it along at a good pace, quite mute, and, a little at a loss at one fence in the hollow, cast well around, re-found the line, and, without more ado, ran it out up to the man.

At one portion of this trial a labourer crossed the track, but the bitch stuck to her line, and was not thrown out for a moment. Without resting, the two couples of the Scarborough hounds had a quarry provided in Dr. Philpot. For some distance he made his way along the hillside, through scrub and stunted bushes, down to a hedge at the foot of the vale. Here there was a road, and, crossing this and a fence, the quarry ran up a bare field to a plantation. Skirting the wood for three hundred yards, another fence was reached, across this, along some bare ground, by the side of another hedge, to the foot of the hill where we stood. No better view of such a trial could be had. This course was quite a mile. As the four hounds were to start, they were slipped ten minutes after their quarry had gone. Barnaby, a little slow in commencing, was not long behind, and, with a fresh and cheerful burst of music, the little pack raced along at an extraordinary pace, considering the depth of the snow. A little hesitancy in the bottom, Barnaby made a cast forward, had "it" again, "his wife and children" flew to his note, and away they rattled up to the plantation.

The old dog's size and strength were useful in this deep going, and he led the way; but scent must have been good, for, without losing it again, they raced down the hill, and fairly caught their man before he reascended from the valley. A good trial in every way.

Possibly the prettiest hunt of the day was afforded by Beeswing and Danger, with Master Pegler to be hunted, and a ten minutes' start given him. These hounds did not at the first hit off the line, but, when fairly on the track, went through the scrub, down the hill to the foot road, and over the fence without a check. Some nice work was done in the bare field, especially where the quarry struck off at a sharp angle, and along by the fence of the plantation. They had no difficulty in making out the whole of the course, which we would take to be about three-quarters of a mile.

The final trial was run by the entire two couples and a half of hounds, and with fifteen minutes' law to the quarry. Now that the snow had ceased, the pack quickly went along the right line down the hill and over the first fence. In the middle of the second field, some quarter of a mile from the start, Danger seemed at a loss, and, turning back to his owner who was following as fast as the deep snow would admit, somewhat disconcerted the other hounds, as they turned round to the voice of Mr. Pegler, who called his hound up. Higher up the field Beeswing appeared to be the one that struck the scent again, her voice attracting her kennel companions, who rattled along the correct track up to a hedge which lay to the left. The quarry had skirted this boundary line, and made his way down hill to a couple of hay stacks, or, at any rate, stacks of some kind. He had doubled along the road here, but hounds found him without the slightest difficulty.

Hunting and shooting men know scent is one of the mysteries of nature. Here we were out on a day when one might reasonably expect that hounds would be unable to run a hundred yards without a check. Still, all these bloodhounds, with their quarry given from seven to fifteen minutes' start, hit the line, and took it along at a "racing pace," it may be called, when the ten or eight inches of snow are taken into consideration. The keen north wind, too, must have been against scent, and one of the best trials of all was run in a blinding snowstorm. Surely, then, these bloodhounds have olfactory powers of more than average excellence; at any rate, that Monday they proved to us their possession of such. The men who acted as quarry had no knowledge of these hounds, no strongly smelling concoctions were smeared over their boots; and, indeed, they had been standing over the shoe tops in snow during the whole of the time the trials were taking place. So the "clean shoe" must in the end have been sadly water soaked. These bloodhounds did all we expected them to do, even more, and we are quite prepared to see the same hounds, under more favourable circumstances, hunt a man's trail or footsteps, though they be two hours old. Running singly, each hound was mute; together they gave tongue, and their voices were very fine. It may be interesting to state that, in their earlier training, with slight exceptions, including a hound or two he worked in

Staffordshire about 1876, Mr. Brough's hounds have "run mute," whether hunting together or separately; but, working them with a noisy basset, they were tempted or encouraged to throw their voices, as they now do when hunting in company. Of course, bloodhounds vary in their voices, some being much more free in their use than others, and a bitch of Mr. Brough's called Brilliant was so fond of using hers, that, when running the line, she every now and then stopped, sat down for a few seconds, and poured forth the most charming melody, which she evidently enjoyed.

The trials arranged by the Kennel Club in 1889 were advertised to take place on the racecourse adjoining the Alexandra Palace on Wednesday morning, at 10.30. As it happened, when that hour was reached, the only one of the three judges present was Colonel Starkie, who a little later was joined by Lord Alfred Fitzroy. Then snow began to fall, few of the stewards were in the dog show, and the prospects seemed to favour an abandonment of the trials altogether. Up to 11.30 o'clock nothing had been decided upon, so Mr. Craven, with his couple of entered hounds, went home. Next it was officially stated that a decision would be come to at twenty minutes to one, and it was then resolved to hold the trials. The snow had by this time given place to rain; a cold, chilly wind blew from the south-west; and these combinations, with the addition of the wet, damp ground, upon which old snow lay three inches or more in depth, made the surroundings as unfavourable as they well could be.

Mr. Lindsay Hogg, in addition to the gentlemen already named, judged, but the duties were almost sinecures. Several tracks had been marked out by small flags, and, although these courses were said to be six hundred yards in length, they appeared considerably more—probably that distance straight away, with the run home additional. Each hound was allowed a track of his own, which extended along the racecourse for several hundred yards on the flat, over sundry lots of railings, winding round in the direction of a small plantation. The hounds had to pass this, and then enter the road on the run home.

The latter portion of the track was along the same line by each man who acted as the quarry, thus making the trials more difficult tests for the hound; though those that ran first must necessarily have had the advantage, as the latter part of the road was less foiled by one or two men than it would have been by half a dozen. Two stakes were provided, the one for the "clean boot," the other for the "not clean boot." The latter in this instance

The Bloodhound.

meant that the shoe soles of the man acting as quarry had been rubbed with horseflesh, the only material at hand for the purpose. As a fact, the second stake never ought to have been arranged, and it is by no means to the credit of a bloodhound that he should require such assistance; the status of the trials was thus reduced to the commonplace " hound dog " trails, so popular in the rural districts of the North of England. As matters progressed, the bloodhounds actually hunted the clean boot better than they did the soiled one, and we would suggest that in future, when the " not clean boot " is to be run, terriers rather than bloodhounds should be utilised for the work.

However, in due course one of the keepers out of the show was despatched as quarry, with a start of ten minutes, during which time he traversed more than three-fourths of the course. Then the first hound, Mr. B. C. Knowles's Koodoo, was slipped. She struck the line immediately, but lost it after going about a hundred yards, and, casting round, hit the scent of some of the spectators, and, failing to persevere, was called up.

Mr. W. J. Scott's Hebe III., a smart bitch, likewise picked up the line quickly, and, running it a little too much to windward, was at a loss for a moment. She cast well, and without assistance struck the scent, and kept it until she turned the corner at the plantation and out of sight of the spectators. For a time Hebe tried to regain the lost line, and looked like doing so until catching the wind of a labourer, and rather startling him by making his passing acquaintance. She failed to finish her task.

Mr. R. Hood Wright's well-known Hector II., who had performed well at the trials in the grounds at Warwick Castle two years before, and now nearly eight years old, was, after the stipulated five minutes, put upon the line. He did not start with so much dash as the bitch had done, carried his head nearer the ground, and ran the exact line the quarry had taken. This he did well, and the manner in which he leaped those railings the man had climbed, and ran under those he had crept through, interested the spectators not a little. There was no mistake as to the correctness of his nose up to the plantation; but here, where the quarry had turned, the hound was at fault. He cast about till striking the line again, and was hard on the track of the man on turning into the road home. This he stuck to until near the goal, when he became somewhat disconcerted, no doubt striking the wind of the spectators as he approached them. His trial was very nicely run.

The Bloodhound.

Mrs. Danger's Jaff was absent, and Mr. E. Brough's Blueberry strangely refused to run, though what we saw of her work on Monday proved her an excellent bitch, and her owner considered her about his best. Mr. Brough's Barnaby, mentioned earlier on, went quicker along the line the runner had taken than Hector had done, and, like him, cleared or went under the railings according to the mode the quarry had adopted. Just before reaching the plantation Barnaby lost the scent, but cast to the right and left until it was struck again. He, too, was a considerable time out of sight behind the plantation, but on reappearing in the road he was running the line of the man, which he continued much as Mr. Wright's hound had done, failing to quite come up to the winning post for similar reasons.

Dr. Hales Parry's Primate was absent, so the end of the stake was reached, there being four of the nine entries that failed to meet their engagement. The judges awarded the prizes as follows: First, Mr. R. H. Wright's Hector II.; second, Mr. E. Brough's Barnaby; third, Mr. W. J. Scott's Hebe III.; the fourth, of course, being withheld. There was little to choose between the first two, for both ran excellent trials, considering the unfavourable surroundings, and afforded ample proof, even to the incredulous, that the bloodhound will hunt a man without even smelling any part of his person or clothes until laid on the track of his footsteps.

The second stake is of no account whatever, being that already alluded to, where the men acting as quarry had their shoe soles smeared with raw horseflesh. It was, however, thought that three competitors of the five entries would run well, so the time was taken, and Koodoo, who did badly on the "clean boot," now ran a brilliant course at a good pace, going the distance, including a check behind the wood, in five minutes. Hebe III. and Hector II. both began well, but, losing the line at about three-fourths the distance, failed to regain it, and were called up. They were awarded equal seconds, Mr. Knowles's Koodoo taking premier honours.

So much for the bloodhound trials; and now, when writing in 1897, they appear to have been entirely discontinued, at any rate so far as public exhibitions of them are concerned.

With the introduction of dog shows the general public were enabled to see how far the bloodhound survived, and the early exhibitions held at Birmingham always included two nicely filled classes of this dog, which many persons believed to be almost extinct.

"Stonehenge," writing in 1869, says:

Until within the last twenty-five years, or thereabouts, the blood-hound has been almost entirely confined to the kennels of the

The Bloodhound.

English nobility; but at about that distance of time Mr. Jennings, of Pickering, in Yorkshire, obtained a draft or two from Lord Feversham and Baron Rothschild, and in a few years, by his skill and care, produced his Druid and Welcome, a magnificent couple of hounds, which he afterwards sold, at what was then considered a high price, to Prince Napoleon for breeding purposes. In the course of time, and probably from the fame acquired by these dogs at the various shows, his example was followed by his north-country neighbours, Major Cowen and Mr. J. W. Pease, who monopolised the prizes of the show bench with successive Druids, descended from Mr. Jennings' dog of that name, and aided by Draco, Dingle, Dauntless, &c., all of the same strain. In 1869, however, another candidate for fame appeared in Mr. Holford's Regent, a magnificent dog, both in shape and colour, but still of the same strains, and, until the appearance of Mr. Reynold Ray's Roswell in 1870, no fresh blood was introduced among the first-prize winners at our chief shows. The dog, who died in 1877, maintained his position for the same period almost without dispute, and even in his old age it took a good dog to beat him.

About 1860, Lord Bagot, of Blithefield, near Stafford, had some very fine hounds, and was successful with both the dogs and bitches he put on the benches at the National Show in Curzon Hall.

Coming down to the present time, there are perhaps more admirers of the bloodhound than at any previous period of its history. Dog shows have, no doubt, popularised him; and, well cared for and well treated, made a companion of instead of being kept chained in a kennel or in a dark cellar, he has lost most of his natural ferocity, and is quite as amiable as any other variety of the canine race.

D

Colonel Cowen, until his much lamented death in 1895, kept a hound or two at Blaydon, near Newcastle; Mr. E. Brough, near Scarborough, is perhaps our greatest breeder; but good bloodhounds are also to be found in the kennels of Mr. H. C. Hodson, Lichfield; of Dr. Sidney Turner, Sydenham; of Mr. R. Hood Wright, Frome; of Miss F. E. Woodcock, West Norwood; of Mr. Walter Evans, Birchfield, Birmingham; of Mr. A. Bowker, Winchester; of Mr. A. O. Mudie, Herts; of Mr. F. Gibson, Hull; of Mr. J. Kidd, Dundee; of Mr. T. H. Mangin, Lymington; of Mr. F. de Paravicini, Oxford; and of Mr. M. H. Hills, near Birmingham.

Here mention must be made of the pack of bloodhounds, kept over twenty years ago by the late Lord Wolverton, who hunted the "carted" deer with them in Dorsetshire, in the Blackmore Vale country. These hounds, or most of them, originally came from Captain Roden, New Grove, co. Meath, who, about 1864, obtained several hounds, a couple or so coming from Hinks, of Birmingham, the well-known dealer. They were sold by Lord Wolverton to Lord Carrington, who had them but a single season, during which he showed sport in Buckinghamshire. From here they went into the kennels of Count Le Couteulx de Canteleu, in France (author of that excellent work, "Manuel de Venerie Française," a portion of which originally appeared in the *Field* in 1872), where they have been useful in hunting both wild deer and wild boar, and in crossing with many French varieties of the hound.

Prior to this, Mr. Selby Lowndes had several couples of bloodhounds in Whaddon Chase, where occasionally they had a run after deer. One of his hounds, named Gamester, bore a great reputation as a man-hunter, and on more than one occasion was useful in capturing thieves. This hound appears to have been a waif from some other kennel, for he was purchased from a hawker for £10, the latter using him as a protection, and to run under his van.

Then it is said, bloodhounds have been owned by the verderers in connection with the New Forest in Hampshire, but they were known as Talbots, and most of them were smaller than our modern hounds. Mr. T. Nevill had a small pack at Chilland, near Winchester, dark coloured hounds — black St. Hubert's they were called. A well-known writer in *Baily's Magazine*, gives a long description of them. It was said they would hunt anything, from "the jackal and the lordly stag, to the water-rat and such 'small deer.'" However, of late, bloodhounds have not proved so satisfactory as foxhounds for hunting deer, but, as stated further on, Mr. C. H. Wilson, master of the Oxenholme staghounds, is using the former as "crosses" to improve the voice of hounds, which have of late degenerated considerably in that respect. Bloodhounds will not stand rating, have to be kept free from excitement, allowed to hunt in their own slow, quiet way, and the excitement and "thrusting" of modern large fields are all against seeing the staid bloodhound at his best. At the present time there is no pack of bloodhounds kept in this country for hunting purposes; still, with the many admirers of the race, there is little fear of the strain being allowed to become of the past.

Thus our bloodhound has, in reality, suffered less from a craze to breed for certain exaggerated features than some other dogs have done. He is still a fairly powerful and large hound, with great thickness of bone, well sprung ribs, and considerable power behind. I rather fancy that, like most large-sized dogs, he fails more in his loins and hind legs than elsewhere, nor does he, as a rule, carry so much muscle as a foxhound. No doubt, in head and ears he has much improved since the time he was kept for the public good at the expense of the inhabitants on the Scottish borders.

Some of our modern English bloodhounds have been simply extraordinary in what are technically called "head" properties. Perhaps the finest hound in this respect was Captain Clayton's Luath XI., a

The Bloodhound. 37

fawn in colour, a huge specimen of his variety, weighing over 106lb., but unfortunately spoiled by his execrable fore legs and feet. On the contrary, Mrs. Humphries' Don, that once did a considerable amount of winning, excelled in fore legs and feet, but was weak and straight in his pasterns; a very plain-headed hound, always much over estimated. Mr. E. Nichols had a dark-coloured hound, called Triumph, that excelled in head and ears, and perhaps there has been no better hound in this respect than Cromwell, by Nestor—Daisy, and bred by Mr. W. Nash in 1884. The head properties of this hound were so fine that on his death, in 1892, a model was taken of them by Sir Everett Millais, who had Cromwell in his kennels at the time. But here a list cannot be given of all the excellent bloodhounds that have made their appearance of late years, the dog-show catalogues afford a better selection than I could supply here, and the owners of the kennels named on a preceding page are certainly to be complimented on the progress they have made with the bloodhound, notwithstanding the difficulty to be surmounted in rearing the puppies.

Mr. Edwin Brough, no doubt the most experienced breeder of the present day, believes the modern bloodhound to be much speedier on foot than in the old days of the Mosstroopers, and there are now, in

1897, more really good bloodhounds to be found in this country than has ever been the case. Perhaps Bono, Bardolph, Burgundy, Barbarossa, Brunhilda, and Benedicta, from the Scarborough kennels, generally have never been excelled; and now, in 1897, the two latter, as Bono and Bardolph had done earlier on, often win the special cup awarded to the best dog in the show. Mr. H. C. Hodson's Rameses, Rollick, Romeo, and Rubric are all hounds of high class, and the names of several others equally good could easily be mentioned, including Mrs. Heyden's South Carolina, Mrs. C. Tinker's Dimple, and Mr. Bowker's Berengaria.

The pedigrees of our present bloodhounds have been well kept during the past generation or so, and their reliability in the Stud Book is undoubted.

The late Mr. J. H. Walsh ("Stonehenge") appears to have had a prejudice against the temperament and character of the bloodhound, formed evidently by a very savage and determined dog of Grantley Berkeley's, called Druid. Whether modern dog shows have been the means of improving this hound's temper, and making him as amiable and devoted a friend as any other dog, I cannot tell; but, that he is so, no one who has ever kept the variety will doubt. Bring a bloodhound up in the house or stable and use him as a companion, and he

The Bloodhound.   39

will requite you for your trouble. He is gentle and kind, less addicted to fighting than many other big dogs; he is sensible, cleanly, of noble aspect, and in demeanour the aristocrat of hounds.

Of course, there are ill-conditioned dogs of every variety, but the average bloodhound will develop into as good a companion as any other of his race; he may be shy at first, but kindness will improve him in this respect. In hunting, he is slower than the foxhound, but more painstaking than are the members of the fashionable packs. He dwells on the quest a considerable time, seemingly enjoying the peculiar sensation he may derive through his olfactory organs, and will cast on his own account; the latter, a faculty that ought not to be lost, though in many hunting countries, where a good gallop is considered more desirable than the observation of hound work, the master or huntsman assists the hounds, rather than allows them to assist themselves.

The lovely voice the bloodhound possesses need not be dilated upon by me, and moreover, he has a power of transmitting that "melody" to his offspring to an unusual extent. I fancy that our modern otterhound owes something of his melodious cry to some not very remote crosses with the bloodhound; and if I mistake not, the late Major Cowen found this strain of "Druids" useful in his well-known Braes o' Derwent foxhounds. Mr. C. H. Wilson, master of the Oxenholme staghounds, is crossing his foxhounds and harriers with bloodhounds, in order to restore the voice and music which in a great measure had been lost in breeding for pace.

If asked to recommend a large dog as a companion, I should certainly place the bloodhound very high on the list, possibly on a level with the St. Bernard, and only below the Scottish deerhound And in one respect he is better even than the latter; for he is not nearly so quarrelsome with other dogs. Not very long ago, a bloodhound was running about the busy streets of Brixton daily; he never snarled at a passing cur or terrier, and was the favourite of every little boy and girl in the neighbourhood. Had their parents known that the big black and brown creature their children were petting and stroking on the head was a bloodhound, the ferocious dog of story books and history, what a scene there would have been. And still more recently it is no uncommon sight to see a lady and her maid accompanied by three couples of bloodhounds enjoying themselves on one of our most frequented suburban commons. Here the big hounds romp and enjoy themselves and seem to be under better command than the collies and terriers, with which all such districts abound.

The Bloodhound.

Sir E. Landseer, the animal painter, thoroughly appreciated the bloodhound, its staid manner, its majestic appearance. He, with Mr. Jacob Bell, kept hounds of his own, and all know how he immortalised them on canvas. His " Sleeping Bloodhound," now in the National Gallery, was a portrait of Mr. Bell's favourite Countess, run over and killed in a stable yard. It was after her death she was painted, forming the subject, "A sleep that has no waking." Grafton, in the popular picture, " Dignity and Impudence " was a bloodhound considered to be of great merit in his day, now he would be regarded as a very ordinary specimen.

Mr. Brough, writing in the *Century Magazine*, some few years since, goes at considerable length into the training of bloodhounds, which is best done by allowing the hound to hunt the " clean boot," rather than one smeared with blood or anything else. He says:

" Hounds work better when entered to one particular scent and kept to that only. Mr. Brough never allows his hounds to hunt anything but the clean boot, but begins to take his pups to exercise on the roads when three or four months old, and a very short time suffices to get them under good command. You can begin scarcely too early to teach pups to hunt the clean boot. For the first few times it is best to let them run some one they know; afterwards it does not matter how often the runner is changed. He should caress and make much of the pups and let them see him start, but get out of their sight as quickly as possible and run in a straight line, say two hundred yards up wind on grass-land, and then hide himself. The man who hunts the pups should know the exact line taken, and take the pups over it, trying to encourage them to hunt until they get to their man, who should reward them with a bit of meat. This may have to be repeated several times before they really get their heads down; but when they have once begun to hunt they improve rapidly and take great delight in the quest. Everything should be made as easy as possible at first, and the difficulties increased very gradually. This may be done by having the line crossed by others, by increasing the time before the pups are laid on, or by crossing roads, &c. When the pups get old enough they should be taught to jump boldly and to swim brooks where necessary. When young hounds have begun to run fairly well it will be found very useful to let the runner carry a bundle of sticks two feet or two feet six inches long, pointed at one end and with a piece of white paper in a cleft at the other end. When he makes a turn or crosses a fence he should put one of these sticks down and incline it in the direction he is going to take next. This will give the person hunting the hounds some idea of the correctness of their work, though the best hounds do not always run the nearest to the line. On a good scenting day I have seen hounds running hard fifty yards or more to leeward of the line taken. These sticks should be taken up when done with, or they may be found misleading on some other occasion. The hounds will soon learn to cast themselves or try back if they over-run the line, and should never receive any assistance so long as they continue working on their own account. It is most important that they should become self-reliant. The line should be varied as much as possible. It is not well to run hounds over exactly the same course they have been hunted on some previous occasion. If some hounds are much slower than the rest it is best to hunt them by themselves, or they may get to "score to cry," as the old writers say, instead of patiently working out the line for themselves.

It is a great advantage to get hounds accustomed to strange sights and noises. If a hound is intended to be brought to a pitch of excellence that shall enable him to be used in thoroughfares, he should be brought up in a town and see as much bustle as possible. If he is only intended to be used in open country, with occasional bits of road work, this is not necessary. Bloodhounds give tongue freely when hunting any wild animal, but many hounds run perfectly mute when hunting man. This is, however, very much a matter of breeding. Some strains run man without giving tongue at all; others are very musical."

In America they have established a bloodhound club adopting their standard from that which was formulated and published in an earlier edition of this volume. Strange as it may appear, after all the bloodhound stories and the slaves, America had to come to us for bloodhounds, and I believe the first couple sent over were from the Scarborough kennels in 1888. These were bred from by Mr. Winchell, Mr. Brough, and others. More, however, were imported, with the present result. Thus it is not likely that club members or others have discovered any pure bloodhounds in Virginia or in any other of the Southern States.

Not long ago some correspondence took place in the *Field* with regard to what were called "Bavarian mountain bloodhounds." From a photograph of a group forwarded to me, I had no difficulty in coming to the conclusion that these hounds were "bloodhounds" but in name, being undersized and without any of that dignity of expression and general character which form such distinguishing features in

The Bloodhound. 45

our modern dog. Indeed these Bavarian hounds possess even less bloodhound type than the "Kerry beagles" illustrated on another page. The Bavarian hound is used for deer hunting in the mountains and forests, and is said to run mute until he has brought his game to bay, nor will he then worry or attempt to eat the quarry. In height he is from 19in. to 20in. at the shoulder, and is mostly brown or liver and tan in colour.

The points of the bloodhound are numerically as follows :

	Value.		Value.
Head	20	Back and ribs	10
Ears and eyes	15	Legs and feet	15
Flews	5	Colour and coat	7½
Neck	5	Stern	5
Chest and shoulders	10	Symmetry	7½
	55		45

Grand Total, 100.

Some little time ago Dr. Sidney Turner and Mr. E. Brough compiled and carefully drew up the following " Points and Characteristics of the Bloodhound or Sleuthhound."

" *General Character.*—The bloodhound possesses in a most marked degree every point and characteristic of those dogs which hunt together by scent (Sagaces). He is very powerful, and stands over more ground than is usual with hounds of other breeds. The skin is thin to the touch and extremely loose, this being more especially noticeable about the head and neck, where it hangs in deep folds.

"*Height.*—The mean average height of adult dogs is 26in., and of adult bitches 24in. Dogs usually vary from 25in. to 27in., and bitches from 23in. to 25in. ; but in either case, the greater height is to be preferred, provided that character and quality are also combined.

"*Weight.*—The mean average weight of adult dogs, in fair condition, is 90lb., and of adult bitches, 80lb. Dogs attain the weight of 110lb., bitches 100lb. The greater weights are to be preferred, provided (as in the case of height) that quality and proportion are also combined.

"*Expression.*—The expression is noble and dignified, and characterised by solemnity, wisdom, and power.

"*Temperament..*—In temperament he is extremely affectionate, neither quarrelsome with companions nor with other dogs. His nature is somewhat shy, and equally sensitive to kindness or correction by his master.

"*Head.*—The head is narrow in proportion to its length, and long in proportion to the body, tapering but slightly from the temples to the end of the muzzle, thus (when viewed from above and in front) having the appearance of being flattened at the sides and of being nearly equal in width throughout its entire length. In profile, the upper outline of the skull is nearly in the same plane as that of the fore-face. The length from end of nose to stop (midway between the eyes) should be not less than

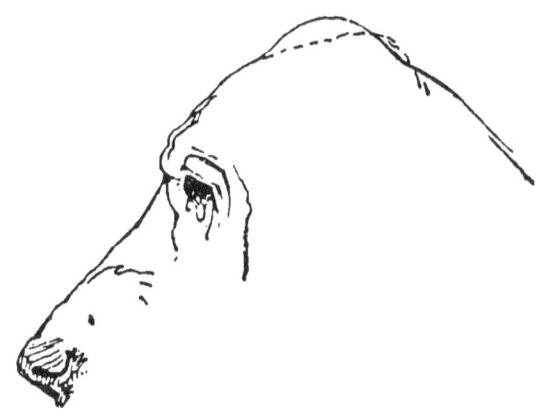

THE DOTTED LINES SHOW A FAULTY PEAK.

that from stop to back of occipital protuberance (peak). The entire length of head from the posterior part of the occipital protuberance to the end of the muzzle should be twelve inches or more, in dogs, and eleven inches or more in bitches.

"*Skull.*—The skull is long and narrow, with the occipital peak very pronounced. The brows are not prominent, although, owing to the deep-set eyes, they may have that appearance.

"*Fore-face.*—The fore-face is long, deep, and of even width throughout, with square outline when seen in profile.

"*Eyes.*—The eyes are deeply sunk in the orbits, the lids assuming a lozenge or diamond shape, in consequence of the lower lids being dragged down

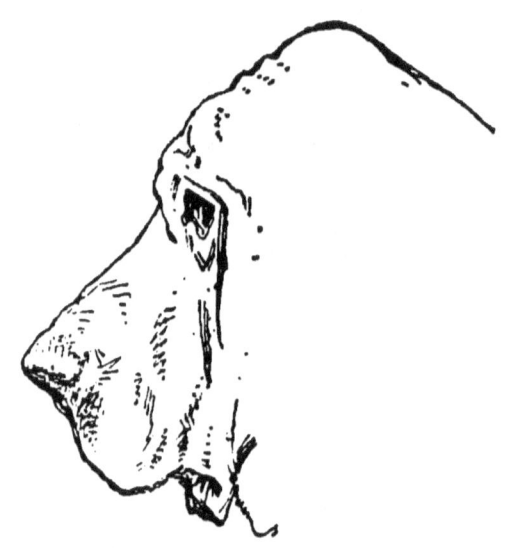

and everted by the heavy flews. The eyes correspond with the general tone of colour of the animal, varying from deep hazel to yellow. The hazel colour is, however, to be preferred, although very seldom seen in red-and-tan hounds.

"*Ears.*—The ears are thin and soft to the touch, extremely long, set very low, and fall in graceful folds, the lower parts curling inwards and backwards.

The Bloodhound.

"*Wrinkle.*—The head is furnished with an amount of loose skin, which in nearly every position appears superabundant, but more particularly so when the head is carried low; the skin then falls

into loose pendulous ridges and folds, especially over the forehead and sides of the face.

"*Nostrils.*—The nostrils are large and open.

"*Lips, Flews, and Dewlap.*—In front the lips fall squarely, making a right angle with the upper line of the fore-face; whilst behind they form deep hanging flews, and, being continued into the pendant folds of loose skin about the neck, constitute the dewlap, which is very pronounced. These characters are found, though in a less degree, in the bitch.

"*Neck, Shoulders, and Chest.*—The neck is long; the shoulders muscular and well sloped backwards; the ribs are well sprung; and the chest well let down between the forelegs, forming a deep keel.

"*Legs and Feet.*—The forelegs are straight and large in bone, with elbows squarely set; the feet strong and well knuckled up; the thighs and second thighs (gaskins) are very muscular; the hocks well bent and let down and squarely set.

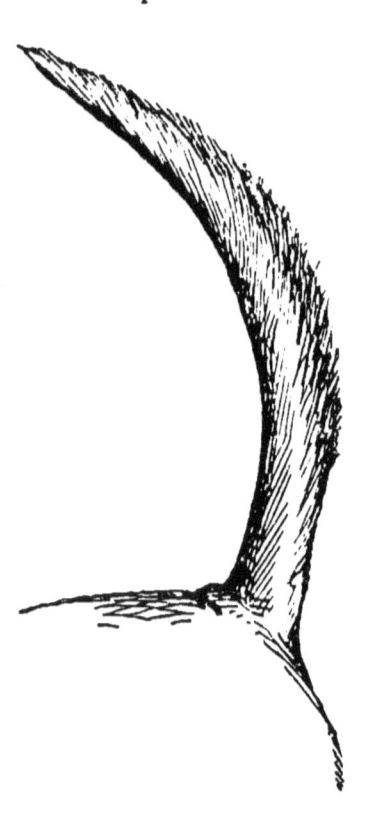

"*Back and Loin.*—The back and loins are strong, the latter deep and slightly arched.

"*Stern.*—The stern is long and tapering and set on rather high, with a moderate amount of hair underneath.

"*Gait.*—The gait is elastic, swinging, and free, the stern being carried high, but not too much curled over the back.

"*Colour.*—The colours are black and tan, red and tan and tawny, the darker colour being sometimes interspersed with lighter or badger-coloured hair, and sometimes flecked with white. A small amount of white is permissible on chest, feet, and tip of stern."

There is little or nothing more to be said of the modern bloodhound. That many writers have given him an evil character, for which there was no justification, none who are acquainted with him will deny. Whether in his kennel or in the house, on the show bench or in the country, he is always the same noble, sensible creature; rather indolent perhaps, but a faithful companion, and interesting as an object of admiration. He is a difficult dog to rear, being delicate in his infancy, but once over distemper and other dangers of puppyhood, he is as hardy as most, and certainly about the least troublesome of all big dogs. Still, the pure bred hounds cannot be recommended as watch dogs, for they are not fond of barking at and making known the presence of strangers; and one of their admirers says that his favourite hound would rather " bay the moon " than by his voice proclaim the approach of bad characters—burglars, or such like. A story came to us the other day that a convict escaped from one of the Florida penitentiaries and got well away before the hounds were put upon his line. He, however, discomfited the creatures in a cunning manner, for, providing himself with a quantity of pepper, he strewed it on his track. This not only quite prevented the hounds following him, but, it is said, pretty nearly killed one of the best of them, who persevered for a considerable time longer than his comrades in endeavouring to make out the scent of the fugitive.

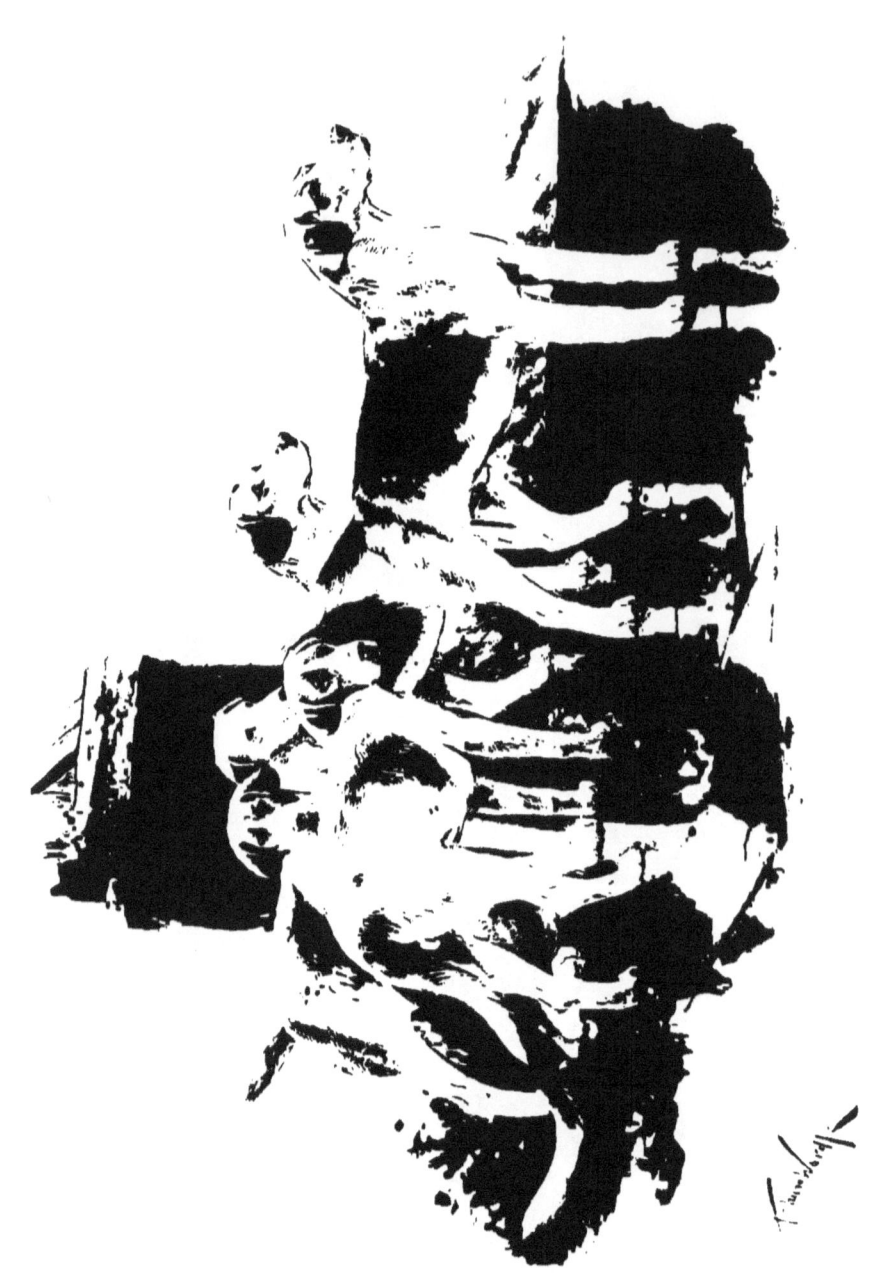

CHAPTER II.

THE FOXHOUND.

THE most perfect of his race is the foxhound—perfect in shape, in pace, in nose, in courage. Not one of his canine companions is his equal, for in addition to his merits as a mere quadruped, as a hound he is the reason for the maintenance of expensive establishments, for the breeding of high class horses, and generally for giving an impetus to trade and causing a "turnover," without which the agriculturist might starve and the greatness of our country be placed in peril. Our bravest soldiers have been foxhunters; our most successful men in almost every walk of commerce have had their characters moulded in the hunting field, or later in life have regained their shattered health by gallops after hounds across the green meadows of the Midlands or along the broad acres of Yorkshire.

At the present time there are about 200 packs of foxhounds hunting regularly in the various districts of Great Britain, and I am well within the mark when I estimate the cost of keeping up the kennels, including hounds, food, wages of hunt servants, masters' expenses, &c., at over three million pounds per annum. Nor do these figures attempt to cover the ordinary expenses disbursed by those hunting men who have not hounds of their own, the cost of their horses, their keep, and other items. What in addition these amount to cannot well be ascertained, but he will be a bold man who attempts to deny that foxhunting, as one of our national sports, possesses a place in the economy of the State. Special trains on our great railway system are repeatedly run to fashionable meets of foxhounds. Some large hotels are to a considerable extent supported by customers who visit them because of their contiguity to foxhound countries. We have been called a nation of shopkeepers —a nation of foxhunters would have been more appropriate. One way and another the expenditure upon this healthy amusement during each successive season may be reckoned in millions of pounds sterling, and still there are so called humanitarians who decry the sport as a discredit to our country. Lord Yarborough estimated the cost of hound keeping at over four and a half millions yearly, and estimates that 99,000 horses are engaged therein. Again it is said that in Yorkshire alone over twenty packs of hounds, including harriers and otter hounds, hunting there, are kept up at a cost of not less than 600,000*l*. per annum. Of course such figures, in the absence of carefully compiled statistics, can only be approximate. Some few years ago, a well known master of hounds (Lord Middleton) found it necessary to appeal to his country to support him in continuing the hunt by subscription, he stating that his family had spent over 100,000*l*. on the sport.

"The fox was made to be hunted, and not to kill geese and lambs," said a sporting farmer to me one day, "and he likes it too," continued the good agriculturist, "or would he take such long rounds as he does when he could lurk and skulk about and thoroughly baffle hounds whenever inclined to do so?" Maybe our good red fox does like to be hunted; at any rate, when bedraggled and beaten he seldom looks sad and pitiful, and the hunter loves him as much as he does his pack; and why should he not love him and hunt him at the same time? The most kindly of all men, Izaak Walton, implies that an angler should love the worm with which he baits his hook, and no one decried such sympathy, excepting, perhaps, the cruellest men, or those of the Lord Byron type.

Foxhounds have for more than three hundred years been carefully bred and reared for hunting purposes, and for that length of time the sport has been carried on in England pretty much on the same lines as now, taking into consideration the change in our mode of living and in the cultivation of the land. But long prior to this period, foxhunting was a fashionable pastime, and Edward II. had a huntsman named Twici, who, early in the fourteenth century, became an author and an authority on sport. He said :

> Draw with your hounds about groves and thickets and bushes near villages; a fox will lurk in rude places to prey upon pigs and poultry, but it will be necessary to stop up earths, if you can find them, the night before you intend to hunt; and the best time will be about midnight, for then the fox goeth out to seek his prey . . . The best time for hunting a fox is in January, February, and March, for then you shall but see your hounds hunting . . . Shun casting off too many hounds at once, because woods and coverts are full of sundry chases, and let such as you cast off be old and staunch hounds, which are sure. . . Let the hounds worry and kill the fox themselves, and tear him as much as they please.

And so proceeds the ancient royal huntsman, who doubtless enjoyed his sport in those times with as much gratification as do we ourselves at the present day.

Although thus early there were hounds similar to those of modern times, they were not kept entirely for the purpose of hunting the fox, and to be actually perfect in work they should not be entered to any

The Foxhound.

other quarry. There is some amount of uncertainty as to the earliest date when hounds were kept solely for the chase of the fox. I quite agree with that painstaking and researchful writer, Mr. W. C. A. Blew, who, in his new edition of "Notitia Venatica," ascribes the earliest date to a few years prior to 1689; for at that time the Charlton Hunt in Sussex, conducted by Mr. Roper, who managed the hounds for the ill-fated Duke of Monmouth and Earl Grey, hunted the fox. Particulars of this appear in the fifteenth volume of the "Sussex Archæological Collection." In 1750 the Charlton were called the Goodwood.

In the *Field* of Nov. 6, 1875, there is an illustration of an old hunting horn, at that time in the possession of Mr. Reginald Corbet, master of the South Cheshire hounds. On it there is the following inscription: "Thomas Boothby, Esq., Tooley Park, Leicester. With this horn he hunted the first pack of foxhounds then in England fifty-five years. Born 1677, died 1752." Here is another early date, and where could be found plainer proofs, though some writers have thrown discredit on them because they thought it possible these hounds occasionally hunted any out-lying deer that might be doing damage to the farmer's crops. As well say some of our modern harriers are not harriers because, when the legitimate chase is scarce, they have a day or two with the "carted" deer.

There was a very interesting old hunting story Lord Wilton writes, in his "Sports and Pursuits of the English," that, not until 1750 were hounds entered solely to fox; but against his statement must be placed that of Charles J. Apperley, who died in 1843, and is favourably known under his *nom de plume* of "Nimrod." He says that an ancestor of Lord Arundel of Wardour had a pack of foxhounds at the close of the seventeenth century, thus about coeval with the Sussex and Leicestershire already named; and the same reliable writer proceeds to say that, remaining in the same family, they hunted in Wiltshire and Hampshire until 1782, when they passed to Mr. Meynell, a name historical in foxhound annals. Another such pack was that of Mr. Thomas Fownes, who was hunting from Stapleton in Dorsetshire very early in the eighteenth century; but the Charlton Hunt and Squire Boothby's hounds had before this been entered to fox, and, with our present knowledge, with them must rest the credit of being the earliest packs of foxhounds in this country.

Mr. Fownes' pack went to Mr. Bowes, of Streatlam, Yorkshire; and the Belvoir hounds kennelled at Belvoir Castle, near Grantham, with Sir Gilbert

Greenall as their master, are lineally descended from those alluded to by Lord Wilton. Since these early times and up to the present, every care has been taken, and no expense spared, to produce a foxhound as near perfection as possible, in order to follow the calling which finds such favour in our land. Squire Osbaldeston, Colonel Thornton, Mr. John Musters, Lord Henry Bentinck, and others of a past generation owned hounds that, either collectively or individually, could not be surpassed. With so much attention given to them, it was no wonder a great writer on the subject arose, and in 1810 we have Peter Beckford's *magnum opus*, which, so far as it goes, has had no rival in its complete description of the foxhound, its work and management. And what he wrote of him is equally true to-day, for no hound or dog has changed so little in appearance and character during a century, as the foxhound. There have been no crazes for fashionable colour, or for head formed, or ears hung, on purely fanciful principles. Hunters wanted a dog for work, they soon provided one, and have kept and sustained that animal for the purpose.

The duties a foxhound has often to undergo are of the most arduous description; he is repeatedly on his legs for eight or ten hours at a stretch, often galloping a great portion of that time, or may be doing more laborious work in the thick coverts, or even walking on the hard road to or from the meet.

Though not bred with great precision and with such care for pedigrees, as is the case with fashionable packs, there are lightly built hounds hunting in the mountainous districts of Cumberland and Westmorland whose stamina must be phenomenal. Their country is the roughest imaginable, up the mountains and down the vales, edging precipices and scaling deep, dangerous passes. Every season these hounds have a run that may last into the teens of hours, beginning soon after daybreak and not ending when stars have studded the heavens and hunters are left far behind. A few years back hounds were heard in full cry at ten at night, and next morning stragglers found their way home to the kennels, others turning up a day or two later. Some had to be looked for, having become "crag bound," *i.e.*, clambered down to a projection in the rock from whence they could not return. During such runs, owing to the rough country, hounds do not go the pace of ordinary foxhounds, but they possess greater patience in working out a cold line, and are perfect in making casts on their own account. The latter a most necessary gift when they are at fault

The Foxhound.

and no one near to assist them in hitting off the lost line, for this hunting at the lakes is done on foot—horses could not follow, nor mules either, where men and hounds have to go.

In March, 1892, the Coniston hounds, the Rev. E. M. Reynolds, master, had an extraordinary run in the neighbourhood of Troutbeck and Kentmere. They were either dragging or hunting for over ten hours, in a terribly rough and wild country, and their fox, dead beat and only just in front of them, had his life saved by a severe storm —the like of which is only known in the Lake district—coming on, and effectually driving both hunters and hounds off the mountains into the valley. Although the finish was not far from kennels, the hounds had been out for thirteen hours before they were safe at home again.

A notable run was that of the Mellbrake, in February, 1896. Drawing Withop Woods, which skirt the shores of Bassenthwaite Lake, they roused four foxes. The pack, small as it was (twelve and a half couples), divided into four, three of which, after very good hunting runs, killed their foxes; the fourth lot went right away out of sight and hearing, and, although hounds turned up at their kennels towards night, it was not ascertained whether they had killed their fox or not. Hounds were entirely left to themselves, as it is too rough a country to ride over. Probably the longest and most severe run on record is that told by Mr. John Crozier, for over fifty years master of the Blencathra. This was in 1858. The fox was started soon after noon on Skiddaw. He tried to shake off his pursuers by travelling in a ring several times, but finding that of no avail, he took to the lowlands, going by Millbeck to Applethwaite, past Crosthwaite church, through Portinscale village, along Cat Bells, through Borrowdale, and over the mountains into Westmorland. Still keeping to the south-west, fox and hounds by midnight were at Black Hill, where shepherds heard them marking the fox at the earth. The men went to the place, but under cover of the darkness reynard got away towards Broughton-in-Furness, in Lancashire. The hounds were found next morning lying asleep near Coniston Crag, in Lancashire. The distance in a straight line from Skiddaw to the place where the hunt ceased is thirty-five miles, but at least another fifteen must be added for the many deviations, thus making a run of fifty miles over the roughest part of the Lake district.

Here is another good hunt on the hills: One Friday in November, 1896, the Coniston hounds met near Stock Ghyll Force, Ambleside, to try for a fox that had been doing mischief near Strawberry Bank. A drag was soon found, which led into Skelgill Wood, from whence hounds went away on a strong line. The course taken was over the shoulder of Wansfell, down past the Old Grove, and away up the valley towards the "Highest House;" but before reaching this point the fox swung to the left, crossed the Kirkstone road, and went over the highest point of the Red Screes. Thence he made down to Cayston, where he ran completely round the head of Scandale on the wall, a manœuvre by which he got rid of his pursuers for some time. But the huntsman and others coming up, hounds were cast forward to High Pike, where he was again unkennelled among the crags. Making at once for the highest point, he crossed close to the " stone man " on the top, and then sinking the hill went down into the Vale of Rydal. The day was now growing cold and stormy, and scent was not good, but hounds persevered at a fair pace, driving him through Hart Crag on to the top of Fairfield. Here a bitter gale was blowing, and bringing up a thick mist. There was neither seeing nor hearing, and all the followers of the hunt could do was to collect all the stragglers they could, and set their faces towards home. Meanwhile some eight or nine hounds drove their fox away on to Helvellyn, and late in the afternoon they were heard coming down into Wythburn. Here they crossed the road close to their game, and in a short time recrossed it, climbing again a little way up Helvellyn. After a somewhat long check they were heard, for it was now too dark to see, running very hard; and then all was still. A search, with the aid of lanterns, for the fox proved fruitless, but hounds were got together, and kindly put up by the landlord of the Nag's Head at Wythburn, the well-known hostelry close to the foot of Helvellyn. There have no doubt been longer runs than this, but few higher, as hounds went over the very tops of Red Screes, High Pike, and Fairfield, and were not very far from the summit of the mighty Helvellyn.

Other more fashionable packs have had extraordinary chases in their day, over a flatter country, and where hounds were going hard and fast the whole of the time. The Duke of Cleveland's run near Borough Bridge in 1738, which lasted from a quarter to eight in the morning until ten minutes to six in the evening, deserves to be a record. Other runs of almost equal duration are still talked about, but with a good country, fast hounds, and bustling the latter on by hard riding, to say nothing of the late hour of meets, hunting runs are not of such a lengthy duration as they were years ago. Mr. Vyner tells

The Foxhound. 65

us of one with his hounds, in which the first eleven miles were covered over pretty rough ground in about fifty-three minutes, which must be taken as something quite extraordinary, when fences and one thing and another are taken into consideration. Such a run in the open cannot be placed side by side with the "trail" hunt of Colonel Thornton and others, to which allusion is made later on.

In the days of our great-grandfathers hounds met at eight o'clock in the morning; now, excepting in cubbing time, and, in a few exceptional countries, the hour of noon has been reached ere huntsmen and hounds appear on the scene. We have a luxury in our modern sport—not to its improvement—that our ancestors could never have even dreamt of.

There is a tale of a Northumberland hound, descended from Colonel Thornton's Lounger, by reason of his excellence called the Conqueror, that ran a fox single-handed for eighteen miles, and killed him in the end. A doubtful story rather. Another hound of the gallant colonel's had been running riot in covert, and on making her way out, evidently on a strong scent, the whip gave her a cut with his crop, which unfortunately struck out her eye, which lay on the cheek. This did not stop the plucky bitch, for, with her nose to the ground and hackles up, she raced along the line, and in the end was first in at the fox's death, though in the latter part of the run the pack had got on terms with her. Thus she did not kill single-handed, as the story is so often told.

In 1887, Comrade, a well known hound for "trail hunting," was with her owner, Mr. J. Irving, Forest Hall, Westmorland, in an allotment adjoining his house. A fox jumped up in front of them, and, although the going was rough and hilly, and three inches of snow lay on the ground, the bitch never lost sight, and after a grand course of more than a mile, pulled her quarry down in gallant style. A fine healthy fox, too, he was. This "trail hunting" is a favourite diversion in the north of England, and special strains of lightly-built foxhounds are used for the purpose. The line is generally run over an uneven country, and may extend for any distance between four and a dozen miles. Hounds are started from the same place, and the one coming in first, having completed the course, which was laid with fox's entrails, bedding, or some other strong scenting matter, wins the prize. A good hound will usually occupy less than three minutes in covering a mile. At a gathering in Rydal Park, Westmorland, in 1895, where most of the best hounds in the country competed, the course of about nine miles, over rough ground, mostly on the hills, was covered by the leading hound in forty-five minutes. At Newby Bridge, at the foot of Windermere, in 1896, at a trail promoted by Mr. Newby Wilson, a course of ten miles was run in a little over thirty minutes, though, in mentioning these records of hound pace, it must not be forgotten that the distance is not always exactly measured, nor are the times so carefully taken as is the case in foot and bicycle racing. These hounds run almost or quite mute.

The match at Newmarket, in 1792, between Mr. Meynell and Mr. Smith Barry, was perhaps the first means taken to ascertain the pace of foxhounds, though almost a hundred years earlier hunting had been followed. Blue Cap and Wanton, who came in first and second, ran the course of about four miles on Newmarket Heath in a few seconds over eight minutes, but these hounds had been specially trained for the purpose. However, Colonel Thornton's celebrated hound Merkin, whose portrait appears in Daniel's " Rural Sports," ran a heat of four miles, which she completed in seven and a half minutes. She was afterwards sold for four hogsheads of claret and a couple of her whelps when she was bred from. In comparing the time of this race with that in Rydal Park, the difference of the courses must be taken into consideration, and it is extremely likely that Merkin would have cut her feet to pieces and been placed *hors de combat* had she run over the hills and rocks surrounding Rydal Hall. Trail hunting is a common amusement in the north, and good hounds for the purpose are of great value. About four years ago there died a noted trail hound named Mounter, a Lancashire dog, who during his career had won ninety-seven first prizes at such meetings, many of them of considerable value. At the present time trail hunting is gaining in popularity in the north of England, where it is encouraged by the squires and others, who in many cases keep crack hounds of their own, and in others subscribe handsomely for the prizes which are offered periodically. One of the features at Grasmere (Westmorland) sports, usually held in August, is the trail hunt, and early in the season one of equal note is held during Cartmel (Lancashire) races, and affords more pleasure to the natives than do the galloping horses.

Perhaps the following letter from the *Field* with regard to the pace of hounds may not be without interest: "This subject has interested me a good deal during the past twelve months, for the following reasons: We have in this part of the country, as you probably know, a number of 'hound trails,' the most important of which—our dog Derby—takes place at the celebrated Grasmere sports.

"In August, 1894, I purchased a trail hound

The Foxhound.

puppy, aged 14 months, for the purpose of trying my hand at training a hound myself to compete with the knowing ones, and thereby also increase the interest in this really pretty sport, by watching my own hound running among the others. In this way I have seen a good deal of this sport, and remarked the extraordinary speed attained by these hounds over hilly and often very rough ground. The usual time occupied in running one of our trails is from twenty-three to twenty-eight minutes, the line being circular so as to permit of a view, and to enable the finish to take place as near as possible to the start.

"Now when you come to discuss the length of the trail, even with the men who have run it (and who of necessity are intimately acquainted with the ground), they will give you the most varied estimates of the distance covered. You will be told seven, eight, nine, or even ten miles. Only the week before last there was a report of one of our trails in a local paper: 'Distance, nine miles; time, twenty-three minutes.' The time given was correct, but in my opinion the distance was vastly exaggerated. I therefore determined to measure with a chain the course on the fells over which my hound, in company with two or three others (one, Mr. Stanley le Fleming's Rattler, a first prize winner at Grasmere), has been regularly run when exercising.

"The time generally occupied in running this course is twenty-five to twenty-six minutes, and the fastest time in which the leading hound has ever done it is twenty-four minutes and thirty seconds. The distance, when measured with the chain, turned out to be 6 miles 975 yards. This gives a speed of fifteen and a half miles per hour over a pumping course—very different from an ordinary foxhunting country, of course—but with a scent more than breast high.

"The course is certainly hilly, as the following will show: On completing 1 mile 570 yards they have climbed 1250ft.; in the next 1 mile 710 yards they descend 100ft.; during the next 1450 yards they first ascend a further 100ft., and then descend 400ft.; the next mile requires 400ft. to be climbed, when they run a mile on comparatively level ground, and descend the 1250ft. again in the last mile. It is practically all grass, with a few roughish places, and they surmount twenty-one stone walls averaging 5ft. 6in. in height.

"Last June I bought from a midland pack a foxhound bitch by Lord Galway's Harkaway (89), dam out of Firefly (86), and dam's sire Belvoir Weathergage, the reason given for parting with her being that she was too fast for the pack. After a good deal of perseverance we got her to run our paraffin and aniseed trail with evident delight, and we then put her into strict training, and ran her with the others. Over the course described above, she never came within three minutes of the other hounds, giving her speed at the rate of fourteen miles an hour.

"As we did not consider her fast enough, I have lent her to my neighbour, the Rev. E. M. Reynolds, master of the Coniston Foxhounds; but the other day, in company with Mr. Chas. H. Wilson, master of the Oxenholme Staghounds, we ran the four trail hounds a measured mile, straight. First of all upwind on the sands, against a very strong head wind. Time occupied, two minutes thirty-two seconds. We then ran them down wind on the grass. Time, two minutes twenty-five seconds. No fences or obstacles of any kind either time."

Foxhounds soon take to hunting game other than their legitimate quarry, more quickly adapting themselves to the change of scent than one would imagine. For years they have hunted the boar and stag in various countries all over the world, and the wolf likewise. Two years ago Mr. F. Lowe took a draft of hounds from various packs over to a friend in Russia. He says:

"During our stay we had a trial with the foxhounds in an inclosed park, to see how they would tackle a wolf. On the first day the new hounds did not at once seem to understand it, but they soon owned the line, and we had a fairly good burst; and, if we had been so minded, could have killed Mr. Wolf. On the second day we had made up our minds to have blood if the foxhounds could break him up, which my host seemed to doubt. I gave them a cheer or two as they began to feather on the line, and away they went in grand style. Fred Payne, of the Fitzwilliam, would have been delighted with the advancement of Rambler's education; and the Atherstone were likewise well represented. The music became a roar, and it was very quickly a case of from scent to view and 'who-whoop!' The pulling to pieces was quite after the English view of the thing; though the quarry was perhaps a bit tougher, and they did not seem to care about making a repast of him."

In addition to his qualifications of speed and nose the foxhound has a peculiar homing faculty, developed to a remarkable extent. Hounds have been known to return to their kennels from remarkable distances. One draft that had been sent from the Holderness into Kent were discontented with their new quarters, and had almost reached their old kennels before their absence from their fresh kennels had been discovered. A Cumberland hound returned from Sussex to its old home, evidently preferring the mountains of its native county to the downs of the southern one.

There is an old huntsman in the English Lake district, Tommy Dobson by name, who runs the Eskdale pack. He is a bobbin turner by trade, but manages to keep a lot of excellent working hounds and terriers together, the farmers and some landowners in that wild district giving him so much a head for the foxes he kills. He hunts on foot, for no horse could follow where he goes. Repeatedly he has long runs; his hounds get lost for a time, but they usually arrive at their kennels the day following the hunt. Dobson is a keen old sportsman, and may be the sole survivor in England of a class of men that can never be replaced. He kills twenty foxes or so in the season, much to the pleasure of the shepherds and farmers in this wildest part of our Lake district, who paid him so much per head from a fund provided for the purpose. Now that Dobson has well passed his three score years and ten, although he still hunts as of yore, ample provision has been made for him when he feels inclined to rest from the perils of the chase.

"Trencher fed" packs of hounds are not so numerous as once was the case, though such are still to be found. They get their name from the fact that they are not kept in kennels, but individual hounds have separate homes with the supporters of the hunt, and are regularly got together each morning a hunt is to take place. This is as a rule not much trouble, for, hearing a blast or two of their huntsman's horn, here and there hounds make their way to their master, very much on the same principal that the "bugle call" rouses the soldier from his bed and draws him to the place of muster. Packs of this kind are, as a rule, not so extensive as our leading ones, which repose in kennels dry and airy, and arranged on the most modern principles. One of the oldest packs in the country is the "trencher fed" Staintondale, located between Whitby and Filey in Yorkshire. Until recently this pack had, for upwards of 200 years, been hunted by a farmer and supported by farmers. Now the master is a Scarborough gentleman, but he works his hounds on the same old lines his predecessors had done before him. At the close of the day there are no kennels in which to house the pack, so each hound has to make its way home as it best can; and, says a recent correspondent, after the day's work is over, " As we reach different points along the road, first one hound and then another, at a word or sign from the huntsman, leaves us, and, leaping a gate or stile, trots leisurely to its home across the fields, with many a pause and backward glance at the old huntsman and the

The Foxhound.

companions it loves so well. If the hound lives in a remote part of the country, a piece of the fox's skin is tied round its neck as a sign that a kill has taken place. Sometimes two or three hounds living in the same direction are dismissed together, and at times they have a journey of eight miles to make alone. This incident forms, perhaps, the prett'est of any seen during the day."

A highly-esteemed writer on hunting, whose familiar *nom de plume* "Brooksby" is known throughout the world, writes :

"The essential talents of a foxhound are to be found in his power of nose, drive, and tongue. It is not to be expected that every member of a pack shall possess these in equal degree, but the strongest combination makes the best pack. And, as such characteristics are mainly the product of careful breeding, the family likeness that belongs to a high class pack of foxhounds will probably pertain not only to their appearance, but to their work in the field. All foxhounds should draw covert well, *i.e.*, perseveringly and closely—a faculty that is the result partly of education, partly of natural courage. It by no means follows that a thin-skinned, highly bred hound will not face briar, thorn, or gorse. On the contrary, his pluck, even at the cost of blood and wound, will often take him where his coarser coated relative would not dare to enter. Yet, though a whole pack may be seen busily waving their sterns as they push their way through bracken and furze, it is generally one of only two or three hounds—often almost invariably the same one—who first rouses the fox. An extraordinary instinct appears to belong, now and again, to some special hound, who has the gift, as he or she enters covert up the wind, of raising the head as if to take stock, and then making straight for the fox's lair. This is probably to be credited to exceptional power of nose. But to whatever source it may be due, huntsmen will bear me out in testifying to the frequent existence of such faculty.

"Again, it is generally some single hound—or one of only a few—who puzzles out the line down a road, when all the others are helpless and mystified. A huntsman, of course, soon gets to know upon which of his hounds he can place reliance; and, indeed, at such time he generally looks anxiously for old Bonnyfield or Sarah to help him out of the difficulty. No *greater* difficulty, by the way, exists than in the arrival upon a cold, scentless road, unless it be in coming to the junction point of four, any of which his fox may have followed. (Memo.—If there be one occasion more than another on which the field should render assistance to a huntsman by remaining perfectly still, it is when he is confronted by four cross-roads.)

"The development of character in a pack of foxhounds (we can best speak of them *en masse*, though the evolution is but the combined training of a hundred pupils), depends so much upon the influence and sympathy of the individual huntsman that we often see a pack temporarily made, or marred, in a very few seasons. The confidence and eager obedience which hounds show to their huntsman is evident from the time he calls them out of covert for a flying start, to the supreme moment when, every effort of their own being exhausted, he has the opportunity of carrying them to the line of their sinking fox, and there leaving them to run, with hackles up, to the death. By the reliance and readiness evinced by a pack of hounds in their huntsman, you may best take the measure of his talent for getting them to hunt. Foxhounds are very keen critics.

"Their fox away, down a quiet cool breeze, it is not less than marvellous how quickly eighteen couples of hounds will force their way through brake and thicket and thorn, to the man they trust. Fifteen couples will be with the horn, in, perhaps, sixty seconds; the other three couples ere sixty acres are crossed, though they have to dive and dart through twice sixty sets of galloping hoofs. For in the vital urgency (as accepted, at all events, in the shires) of starting close on your fox, it pays not—nay, is held hardly to be justifiable—to wait for every hound. Such practice, besides involving loss of valuable time, might, perhaps, induce the stragglers to believe that after all there was no hurry, and that next time they can afford to come forth more leisurely still. There is little fear now that, if worth their salt, they will soon reach the front, whatever difficulties they may have to encounter. And herein is evidenced another instance of the drive and courage of a foxhound.

"Eighteen couples all together—or at least with a front some ten couple broad, the rest in a cluster in close and vociferous attendance—the horn pushed back into its case; one scream of encouragement and delight from the ruddy, deep-mouthed, huntsman; fifty good fellows riding as near abreast of each other as the nature of the country will allow—this is the old picture; and this is what many a man will tell you has brought him in touch with Paradise. Ah, those sheep have been over the line! Steady, gentleman, steady! Now you shall see the drive of a foxhound, as we draw rein to give them time and room; and the huntsman stands mute, with a silence more eloquent than any immature exposition on his part. To the right they swing wide—a twenty acre cast. To the left they swing back, making good their ground in a longer sweep still. Then up go their heads as they gallop back—every old hound in the field knowing to a yard the spot where last the line was felt. Sit still, Jim, sit still! They haven't half done. Your talent is not wanted yet awhile. Old Nabob and Ravisher are already feathering forward. Out ring their tocsin notes. Ye'et, old fellows, well done. They have the situation in a moment; they dash past the crowded flock; gain the unfoiled ground, and the scent in full power, as they reach the fence—and the glad pursuit goes on as merrily as before.

" But the dash of the earlier minutes has sobered down. Their fox has made all use of the moment's breathing time to put further distance between himself and those terrible voices. Travelling down wind—as ninety-nine times out of a hundred he will when pressed—he finds the clamour of pursuit growing fainter; and now, though sorely strained— almost burst, as the term goes—by his first efforts, he has time to pull himself together, and carefully to avoid any sign of danger in his path. Thus he sheers off from a plough team, whisks aside from a hedgecutter, and doubles for his life from a sheep-dog. Now it becomes a question on the part of hounds—not of drive, but of nose—not of dash, but of patience; and this is a time when consideration on the part of the field is again absolutely essential. You would not rush up from either side upon your setter when at point. Why, then, try to baffle a much more excitable animal, when he, too, is working to his best ability, and needs, above all things, not to be driven or hurried. Yet, as the pace slackens, the rearguard come up, and, if allowed, will of a certainty over-run the van, and over-ride the hounds. Now is the master wanted—if hounds are to have a chance. Then will come out their faculty of nose, their instinct of hunting, their patient unravelling of a skein to which—nine times out of ten—they hold a better clue than can be suggested by the cleverest huntsman. Yonder it is, down a wet, chilly furrow! Mark that rogue Ramilies yonder—silent, though running hard! Mark him for the draft, Jim; or hang him, if you like, to-morrow! Hark forward to Prompter, my beauties! He'll tell you all about it. Now we are on the grass again. Now they are storming ahead; and we'll unbutton his waistcoat yet. Never mind that holloa, Jim. There are more foxes than one running about the country. I told you so. They've left it behind. And look at their bristles. See old Marigold go to the front. That means blood, for a thousand. Ten minutes more,

The Foxhound.

and they race into view. The young ones are speediest at sight. But 'tis for Hector, the cup dog of two summers ago, to grip and to hold. Fifty minutes and a six mile point. Who-hoop! my beauties! Every hound up. And the blood of Belvoir Weathergage to be found in at least ten couples."

The largest packs of foxhounds are, as a rule, divided into dogs and bitches, each sex running separately and distinctly on different days. The "ladies," as they are mostly called, are said to be the smarter in the field, and to possess dash and casting powers in greater perfection than the "dogs." In some few of the big packs dogs and bitches are run together, being matched according to size as nearly as possible. The dog hounds are, of course, the bigger of the two, and run from 23 to 24 inches at the shoulder, the bitches being from one to two inches or so below that standard. One of the smallest pure foxhounds that ever ran with hounds was the Blue Ransom, of the Pytchley, and said to be about $17\frac{1}{2}$ inches, whilst the giant of the race, the Warwickshire Riddlesworth, was 27 inches. At the present time our most extensive packs are the Blackmoor Vale, with 90 couples of hounds; the Badminton, formerly the Duke of Beaufort's, 75 couples; the Belvoir, 64 couples; the Puckeridge, 62 couples;

whilst the Berkeley, Crawley and Horsham, South Berks, Fitzwilliam, and Mr. Garth's have each 50 couples of running hounds in kennel. Other packs number anything between the nine couples of the Coniston to the 58½ couples of the Oakley, and the 55½ couples of the H.H. (Hampshire).

For a hundred years or more, it has been, and still remains, though some packs now discountenance it, the custom to "round" the ears of foxhounds, which is neither more nor less than shortening their aural appendages, to prevent the latter getting torn in covert, or in going through or over the fences. This is done at about four months old. Most hound puppies leave the kennels, after being taken from the dam, to be located, "walked" with the farmers and other friends of the hunt. Here they are fed well and wax strong until the time comes round, during April and May, for them to return to the kennels, to be properly entered with the cubs in the autumn.

The occasion is utilised for a "show of the puppies." Prizes are awarded, silver tea and coffee pots and such like "useful pieces of furniture" dear to the farmers' wives and daughters. A pleasant day is spent; the Master gives a luncheon, and he "toasts" and is "toasted" in return.

The hounds each year drafted to make room for the puppies are usually the perquisite of the huntsман, and they may go to other kennels, or become squandered over distant parts of the universe, where they form a connecting link with "home." Or they may go into the hands of some dealer or other, who finds a ready market for them to an enterprising theatrical manager, who seeks to add to the truthfulness of some country scene the increased attraction of a "scratch pack." During the past few years foxhounds have repeatedly appeared on the stage in our leading theatres, where, to the sound of the horn of the "super" and the clash of the orchestra, or the strains of "John Peel," their reception has been such as any *débutante* might have envied. But a stage hound's life behind the scenes cannot be a happy one, nor are their exercising grounds, through the thronged streets adjoining our great thoroughfares, so healthy as a roll on the grass in the Pytchley pastures.

As to the "rounding" of the ears, "Stonehenge" believed it useful in "preventing canker either from foul blood or mechanical injury . . . The sole use of an abnormally large ear, as far as I can see, is to aid the internal organ of hearing, and it is only found in hounds which depend upon co-operation for success—that is to say, that hunt in packs. In this kind of hunting, the ear is required to ascertain what is given out by the tongues of the leading hounds, so as to enable the tail of the pack to come up; but whether or no 'rounding' diminishes the sensitiveness of the organ of hearing, I am not prepared to say. It is, however, admitted by physiologists that the external ear aids by the sense of hearing, and as this large folding ear is confined to hounds hunting in packs, which, as above remarked, depend upon hearing or co-operation, it is reasonable to suppose that the hound's large ear is given to him to aid this kind of hunting; and, if so, it is by no means clear that 'rounding' is an unmixed good."

Foxhounds on the bench of ordinary dog shows are more a rarity than otherwise, though, whenever they do appear in such an odd position, always prove an attraction. In Yorkshire some attention was given to special exhibitions of foxhounds about twenty-five years ago, but they never appeared to quite take hold of the Tykes, and were allowed to lapse, the last of them being a large gathering that took place on Knavesmire, in 1877. Following this came the establishment at Peterborough, that is held in June, and it has so grown under its excellent management, that it now must be recognised as one of the institutions of our land. At Peterborough Hound Show, Masters, Huntsmen, and Whips, meet as on a common threshold, and they talk of their prospects, admire the hounds, and criticise the

The Foxhound.

awards in the most friendly spirit imaginable A day at Peterborough is one that hunting men look forward to as a kind of connecting link between that time when hounds race on a burning scent, and when they are the pets of the household. Almost all the best foxhounds of the day are to be seen at Peterborough Show, and no prospective Master should miss the gathering; few of the present Masters do so.

Already I have mentioned the odd price for which Merkin was sold, but it seems rather strange that whilst comparatively useless dogs of a purely fancy breed occasionally bring from £500 to £1000 apiece, a whole pack of foxhounds may often be purchased for the latter sum, or even for less. There are hounds that a master would not sell at any price, but if he would there could scarcely be the demand for them at such enormous figures as a terrier, a sheep dog, or a St. Bernard will often command. Mr. Corbet bought that crack pack the North Warwickshire for 1500 guineas, but John Ward paid 2000 guineas for the same hounds when they went into his hands. Mr. Osbaldeston knew what he was about when, in 1806, he purchased the Burton for 800 guineas; but when the "Squire's" hounds came to be sold at Tattersall's in 1840, they realised 5219 guineas (Sir Reginald Graham said 6400 guineas), which may be taken as the best on record for a pack of foxhounds. Some of them went back to Mr. Harvey Combe, and Lord Cardigan bought ten couples to remain in the Pytchley country. Against this may be set the modest item of 15 guineas which twenty-one couples of the Haydon hounds brought at auction in 1884; but this lowly record was beaten in 1895, when the Forest of Dean foxhounds were sold for a five pound note. There were fourteen couples of hounds here. Ten couples of Mr. Osbaldeston's realised 2380 guineas. Then, in 1845, Mr. Foljambe's hounds sold for 3600 guineas; Lord Donerail's, in 1859, for 1334 guineas; Mr. Drake's, 2632 guineas; and, in 1838, Ralph Lambton paid Lord Suffield 3000 guineas for his highly-bred hounds. These are, no doubt, the most unusual prices ever made for foxhounds. In 1867 the Wheatland hounds were sold at Tattersall's in different lots for £750. In May, 1894, twenty-four couples of entered hounds, four and a half unentered, and sundry litters of puppies—the Herts and Essex—sold at Rugby for 675 guineas; and in 1896, Mr. Vaughan-Davies' pack realised at Aldridge's, in St. Martin's-lane, 139 guineas for nineteen and a half couples of entered hounds, and 58 guineas for seven and a half couples unentered. Yearly, at Rugby, drafts are sold by auction almost

The Foxhound. 87

at any price, varying from a sovereign to £10 a couple. These figures will give some idea of the value of a pack of hounds at the present day.

"Stonehenge" jocularly remarks: "Nose combined with speed and stoutness have always been considered as the essentials for the foxhound, but of late years, owing to enormous fields which have attended our leading packs, and the forward riding displayed by them, another feature has been demanded, and 'the supply' in the 'grass countries' has been obtained in a remarkable manner. I allude to the gift peculiar to our best modern hounds of getting through a crowd of horses when accidentally 'slipped' by the pack. This faculty is developed to a very wonderful extent in all packs hunting the 'Shires,' varying, of course, slightly in each, and it is no less remarkably absent in certain packs otherwise equal to the Quorn and its neighbours, or even superior to them." I may say that through force of circumstances this valued gift of self-preservation has lately been exhibited by Her Majesty's and some other packs within easy railway distance of our great metropolis.

Allusion has already been made to the eminent French author on Venerie, le Comte de Canteleu, and the accompanying translation of a letter from his pen will, I think, be of interest:

"I have a perfect knowledge of the foxhound, and I am also fairly well informed as to the packs where the best blood is to be found. There are also plenty of packs of otter hounds infused with the blood of my old Griffons crossed with other breeds. I supplied a number of hounds to the otter hound pack belonging to Mr. Waldron S. Hill, Murrayfield House, near Edinburgh, from whence a good many of my hounds were scattered over England for otter hunting, to Wales amongst other places. Moreover, during the war of 1870 I sold Mr. Waldron S. Hill seven or eight hounds, the result of a cross with the wolf. I think, I remember, he told me he sold them to go to North America for cariboo hunting.

"I have a high opinion of the strength, endurance, and stamina of the foxhound. But then why does he last so short a time? When seven or eight years old he is completely used up, whereas the French hounds of former days (my own Griffons for instance) would last eleven or twelve years. The best quality of the foxhound, apart from his health, is his determination to capture the quarry and to burst him at the finish of a run. Unfortunately he cannot keep up the pace in our forests, which are so full of thick thorns, and he is apt to lose the line of an animal emitting a very slight scent; then, not having a very good nose, he cannot recover it. Another point is that no attention in the training of hounds in England has ever been given to the question of 'change,' which is of so great importance to us. And so it is that, excepting for wild boar hunting, the foxhound, which is so apt to change his animal, is not much used in France.

"When by good luck a foxhound is discovered that guards 'change,' he is, as a rule, perfection, and with a finer nose than any of his sort.

"I should just like to show you now an old Saintongeois of mine which I use for the wild boar. He will hunt yesterday's drag of an animal, often twelve or fourteen hours old, and will unharbour his pig at a distance of six to nine miles. The rest of the pack (foxhounds, and, nevertheless, very good ones, selected for me by Mr. Merthyr Guest out of his own kennels), following the old hound in complete ignorance, and going from right to left on the line without being able to own it until the arrival of the hound at the midden of the boar. The poor old fellow is covered with wounds, and the only wonder is that he has not been killed ten times over.

"I expect to see a great improvement in the English foxhound as regards voice, fineness of nose, and the quality of 'change,' because people in England have been buying many of our Saintongeois and Vendée hounds, and certainly the English hounds we are now receiving are more suitable for our purpose than formerly. It will not, however, do to go too fast, because unless able to acquire hounds of the very highest stamp, the result will be to produce cross-breds with less stamina than our old breeds. Recollect that with my Griffons, so staunch and hard, I have hunted old wolves over fifty miles from find to finish, and on several occasions both my own horse and that of my huntsman have died from the severity of such runs.

"In my opinion the English buy too many of the Vendée hounds; they would do far better to acquire those of Saintonge and Haut-Poitou, which are much superior to the Vendées, a breed which has been subject to such a variety of bad crosses that one never knows what will be the result. And finally, the hounds that really guard change are the St. Hubert's (or bloodhounds), the Saintongeois, and the Poitevins."

The following is from an article by Mr. G. S. Lowe, that appeared in the *Field* some half-dozen years ago, and as it deals more fully with our present strain of foxhounds and their pedigrees (there is a foxhound stud book now) than I could, there is excuse for its republication:

"The casual observer in the hunting field might

not be inclined to appreciate the laudations bestowed upon certain hounds in almost every pack. Hounds run very much in one form, and a huntsman of, say, forty years' experience might call up hounds to his memory to number in the aggregate several thousands, though in speaking of any exquisites he will refer to two or three only that, according to his idea, were incomparable. The faults of even good foxhounds must be, therefore, numerous—far more so, I expect, than the casual observer could detect, as faultless hounds, it would appear, crop up in the smallest proportions in the lifetime of a huntsman. Mr. Osbaldeston was generally in a position to have the best of hounds only, as in the heyday of his career, at any rate, he had an immense pack, hunted his own hounds six days a week, and, in the style in which he rode over Leicestershire and other countries, it can be fairly asserted that he was never separated from them. It is said that he depended on his hounds with a flying fox, speaking very little to them, but observing all they did, and in strong gorse he went in with them himself, and could make them hunt like spaniels. With all this experience, though, Osbaldeston had one hound out of the many he had to do with, of which he would speak with exceptional regard up to the very time of his death. I remember it was told me that a friend met the veteran in a billiard room, years after he had given up hunting, and, the conversation drifting into matters of the chase, the squire got upon the line of Furrier, and there was no getting him off it. He expatiated on the merit of this hound as the best ever bred; and it must be remembered also that, when Osbaldeston bred hounds, he supported his opinion by breeding from this hound to such an extent that he could take a pack into the field made up entirely of Furrier's progeny.

"Harry Ayris lived, I think, sixty years with the Fitzhardinge pack, and in an interview with him about fifteen years ago, when the old fellow was over eighty, I put the question straight to him as to the best hound he had ever seen. 'Cromwell,' was the ready reply, 'and no man ever hunted another like him.' It was difficult, then, to get Harry Ayris off the line of Cromwell; and it was no easier task to make the late John Walker believe that a better fox-hound had ever been bred than Sir Watkin Wynn's Royal. Lord Henry Bentinck had several favourites, and, for the benefit of those after him, he left a written record, showing how these particular hounds excelled their fellows. This is in manuscript still, I believe; but I am perfectly assured that the leading hound breeders of the day have seen it, and hence the great leaning of late years towards the pack that

The Foxhound. 93

came originally from Lord Henry's benches. One might go considerably further back, to quote how Mr. Corbet is said to have spoilt his pack by excessive in-breeding to Trojan; and how Sir Thomas Mostyn committed the same mistake by appreciating the blood too much of a famous bitch called Lady. It is sufficient, however, to note that this sort of allegiance to certain hounds has had a marvellous effect on hound breeding, and that such hounds can be regarded as landmarks through a veritable maze of pedigrees ranging over half a century. No animal of any sort whatever has been bred to in the same persistency as can be traced to the Osbaldeston Furrier; he was the best hound of his day, in the opinion of an experienced authority; and that opinion was followed by such hound breeders as the late Mr. Foljambe, the late Lord Henry Bentinck, and the late Mr. Parry, besides a host of others, not excepting those who attended to the well-being of the almost classical packs of Belvoir, Brocklesby, Fitzwilliam, and Badminton.

" There have been hounds in considerable numbers that could boast of temporary reputations, but they have not secured lasting fame; and I should be inclined to limit what might be called the standard favourites to a dozen since the days of the Osbaldeston Furrier. Others may be inclined to differ from my selections, but they will catch my meaning if they will trace recent pedigrees to their sources, and will regard such hounds as are seen at the Peterborough show. It is seen that during years of breeding there has been no loss of size and bone, to begin with—no loss of quality, as shown in clean necks and shoulders, and general carriage; and, if looks can be taken for anything, there can have been no loss in pace, or in such qualities of shape that suggest power and stamina. Hunting men of various countries can decide whether foxhounds are not as good or better than they have ever been; but a very strong feature in maintaining the qualities and characteristics of the foxhound has been the system of keeping several celebrated foxhounds in view when going in for high breeding. Mr. Parry, so long associated with the Puckeridge, had two hounds called Pilgrim and Rummager, both entered in 1840, and the latter was a great-grandson of the famous Furrier, whilst Pilgrim was descended from another celebrity known as the Belvoir Topper. With this couple of hounds Mr. Parry stamped his pack, as they were always kept in view, as it were, and before Mr. Parry left off hound-keeping his kennel had a very high reputation for blood. Of late years whole packs have been established from the Belvoir Senator, and others have been benefited in a similar degree, through holding to the Burton Dorimont line, the Drake Duster, the Wynnstay Royal, the Grove Furrier, or the Berkeley Castle Cromwell.

" To come to the notable twelve that have been, and may still be, esteemed as 'landmarks' of hound breeding, I should, of course, name the Osbaldeston Furrier, a Belvoir-bred hound, as he came in a draft from the ducal kennels, and was by their Saladin out of their Fallacy, and thence going back to Mr. Meynell's hounds of 1790. It has been stated that Furrier was not so much a perfect working hound as a hard runner, as he was inclined to be jealous and impatient on a cold scent; but he was the leading hound in every fast thing, and he never did wrong when holding that important post of honour. He was the sire of Ranter, and to that hound Mr. Foljambe was principally indebted for the Furrier blood, as his Herald and Harbinger, entered in 1835, were by Ranter. Herald was the sire of Wildair, sire of Wild Boy, sire of Modish, the dam of The Grove Guider. Harbinger and Herald appear several times in Barrister's pedigree, as, for instance, he was by Rambler, son of Roister, son of Captive, a daughter of Herald's; and the dam of Rambler again was Dorothy, her dam Dowager, by Songster, a son of Sybil by the Osbaldeston Ranter. The sire of Roister again was Render, son of Riot, by Ranter, and it is therefore not difficult to trace several lines of Furrier in the Grove Barrister, a hound well in the memory of all breeders of the present day. The Fitzwilliam claim a line to Furrier, chiefly through Hardwick, a hound entered in the Milton kennels in 1843, by Mr. Drake's Hector out of Goldfinch, her dam Frenzy, by Fatal, son of Ferryman, son of Furrier. Hardwick was the sire of Handmaid, the dam of Hardwick of 1851, and the latter sire in turn of Hercules and Harbinger. There was another double Furrier cross in the Fitzwilliams, as their Hero and Hotspur were by the second Hardwick out of Ransom, by Mr. Foljambe's Roister.

"Another famous line from Furrier, and through the same kennels as the above, is traced to the Burton Dorimont, a hound spoken of in Lord Henry Bentinck's diary as a thoroughly good foxhound. He was got by Roderick by Mr. Foljambe's Roister, named above as out of a Herald bitch. There was a double cross of this sort in Dorimont, as his dam Daffodil was out of Dairymaid by Driver, son of Harbinger, brother to Herald, and a third cross to Furrier might even be traced through the Belvoir Chaser. There is Dorimont blood in the Fitzwilliam kennel, as Dagmar and Daphne were by him; and their Selim of 1869 was out of Dagmar, and Selim is the sire of Balmy, Bloomer, Remedy, and others on the Milton benches, that have been bred from. Dorimont is largely represented also in the Oakley kennels, and, if I am not much mistaken, Sailor, a sire of note at the present time, from Lord Portsmouth's kennels, traces directly to him. At any rate, I know there was a good deal of the blood in Mr. Lane-Fox's kennel through a hound called Damper; and very few kennels, I expect, are without the strain. Dorimont was a branch from Furrier, but I should accept him as one of the corner stones of the stud book amongst my twelve selections.

"The Drake Duster is another not to be forgotten by anyone who has ever thought of breeding hounds. He was entered in 1844 by the late Mr. Drake, so long associated with the Bicester, and he was got by Bachelor out of Destitute, the former running into Mr. Warde's sort, and the latter to the Belvoir. The last named famous kennel got many good returns of their own blood from Duster, as Siren, the dam of Singer, was a daughter of his, and Singer was the sire of Senator. The most important line of the day is therefore due in a measure to the Drake Duster, as it can well be said that every kennel in England has gone in more or less for the Senator strain, and if there was anything to complain about, it was a fear that too much of it might be infused into some channels by way of in-breeding.

However, the oldest huntsmen, the late Jack Morgan amongst others, have assured me that for dash and drive there has been nothing like them, and it was a characteristic with all hounds straining from the Belvoir Singer that they were veritable tyrants on the line of a sinking fox, and savages at a death. There was a hound in Lord Poltimore's called Woldsman, by Comus, out of a bitch nearly sister in blood to Siren, and he had to be coupled up as soon as possible at a kill, as he was not particular about mouthing another hound in his fury; and two sons of his, afterwards with the Bicester, and their descendants again, were just like him. Another great descendant from the Drake Duster was the Belvoir Guider, a son of the former, out of Gamesome, by General. To Guider must be credited the foundation of Lord Portsmouth's pack, as his Lincoln and a host of valuable bitches, bred from in due course, gave to the Eggesford pack its high reputation. Guider also left his mark with the Bramham Moor and Sir Watkin Wynn's; but his stock has not been so widely distributed as the Senator's. Senator was entered in 1862, and, like Duster, he was out of a bitch called Destitute, the dam also of Render, and she was by Sir Richard Sutton's Dryden, by Lord Henry Bentinck's Contest. Besides the field qualities noticed above as belonging to the

Senators, all are very beautiful hounds that strain from that line. Very perfect necks and shoulders I have ascribed to them, and they are invariably full of quality, whilst their colours are, as a rule, perfection—the Belvoir tan, and hare-pied hue blended.

"I spoke of Lord Henry Bentinck's Contest in the above remarks relating to the dam of Senator, and that relationship alone might entitle him to be selected among the celebrated twelve to be considered as a pillar of the hound stud book. There is, however, something else to boast of to the memory of Contest, as he was the sire of Harry Ayris's favourite Cromwell, and the blood of the latter runs through the Badminton, the Croome particularly, through Lord Coventry's Rambler, and it is also largely represented in the Quorn, besides, as a matter of course, being mixed up in all the Berkeley Castle pedigrees. Cromwell was bred from at Berkeley Castle in the same sort of proportion as Furrier was used by Osbaldeston, as the entries during his lifetime show, and he was noted for getting excellent workers.

" The beautiful colours of the Senators may not be due to Contest, as I think I have been told that he was a grey-pied hound, and Cromwell was that colour, as I have seen his skin. The goodness of Contest, however, is explained in his noble owner's diary, as, if there was one particular favourite with Lord Henry more than another, it was Contest, considered by him to be the best of foxhounds in any part of a run; and, as in the case of Mr. Corbet's Trojan, Contest was an extraordinary wall and gate jumper. His blood can be traced to the three good-looking sisters that made up the two couples of the Warwickshire in the older bitch class at Peterborough—namely, Factious, Fair Maid, and Faultless, as Archibald, their sire, was out of a bitch by Lord Coventry's Rambler.

"I have mentioned the Osbaldeston Furrier, the Grove Barrister, the Drake Duster, the Burton Dorimont, the Belvoir Guider, the Belvoir Senator, the Burton Contest, and the Berkeley Castle Cromwell in this article as the most celebrated foxhounds to be traced to throughout all records. This makes up eight out of my proposed party of twelve; and I have no hesitation in giving as additions the Burton Regulus and the Wynnstay Royal. It would be impossible to enlarge too much upon the good such hounds have done; and it would be impossible to say which of the two has influenced high breeding most. Royal is represented to a large extent at Belvoir, Badminton, Mr. Garth's, the Bramham Moor, and numerous other kennels; whilst the Burton Regulus, besides adding much to the con-

The Foxhound.

tinuance of the high prestige belonging to Lord Henry Bentinck's pack, now mostly identified as the Blankney, is credited with a vast amount of merit contributed to the Badminton, Berkeley Castle, the Fitzwilliam, the Quorn, and the present Burton pack. It now becomes a little difficult to name two more, and I think the honour might fall on the Badminton Flyer of 1839, as he gave the Fitzwilliam Feudal to the hound world; and the latter was the sire of Foreman, sire of Forester, sire of Furrier; and so we can finish up as we started with a Furrier, in the hound of that name, held in so much esteem by the late Hon. George Fitzwilliam and George Carter, and the ancestor now of a very big tribe."

The Foxhound Stud Book, already alluded to, first published in 1865, appearing periodically, and edited by Sir Cecil Legard, is a useful and careful compilation.

The points and description of the foxhound are as follows:

	Value.		Value.
Head	15	Elbows	5
Neck	5	Legs and feet	20
Shoulders	10	Colour and coat	5
Chest and back ribs	10	Stern	5
Back and loin	10	Symmetry	5
Hind quarters	10		
	60		40

Grand Total **100**.

1. The *head* (value 15) should be of full size, but by no means heavy. Brow pronounced, but not high or sharp. There must be good length and breadth, sufficient to give in the dog hound a girth in front of the ears of fully 16in. The nose should be long (4½in.) and wide with open nostrils. Ears set on low and lying close to the cheek.

2. The *neck* (value 5) must be long and clean, without the slightest throatiness. It should taper nicely from the shoulders to the head, and the upper outline should be slightly convex.

3. The *shoulders* (value 10) should be long, and well clothed with muscle without being heavy, especially at the points. They must be well sloped, and the true arm between the front and the elbow must be long and muscular, but free from fat or lumber

4. *Chest and back ribs* (value 10).—The chest should girth over 30in. in a 24in. hound, and the back ribs must be very deep.

5. The *back and loin* (value 10) must both be very muscular, running into each other without any contraction or "nipping" between them. The couples must be wide even to raggedness, and there should be the very slightest arch in the loin, so as to be scarcely perceptible.

6. The *hind quarters* (value 10) or propellers are

required to be very strong, and, as endurance is of even more consequence than speed, straight stifles are preferred to those much bent, as in the greyhound.

7. *Elbows* (value 5) set quite straight, and neither turned in nor out, are a *sine quâ non*. They must be well let down by means of the long true arm above mentioned.

8. *Legs and feet* (value 20).—Every master of foxhounds insists on legs as straight as a post, and as strong; size of bone at the ankles and stifles being specially regarded as all important. The feet in all cases should be round and cat-like, with well developed knuckles, and strong pads and nails are of the utmost importance.

9. The *colour and coat* (value 5) are not regarded as very important, so long as the former is a "hound" colour, and the latter is short, dense, hard, and glossy. Hound colours are black tan and white —black and white, and the various "pies" compounded of white and the colour of the hare and badger, or yellow, or tan. In some old strains the blue mottle of the southern hound is still preserved.

10. The *stern* (value 5) is gently arched, carried gaily over the back, and slightly fringed with hair below. The end should taper to a point.

11. The *symmetry* (value 5) of the foxhound is considerable, and what is called " quality " is highly regarded by all good judges.

Weight of a dog hound, from 70lb. to 80lb. ; of a bitch hound, from 60lb. to 70lb.

Such figures are, however, not required by a hound judge, who as a rule detests numerals when they are supposed to have any bearing upon the animal which he deems to be excellence itself, and far removed from any other variety of the dog known to the civilised world. Rather than on " points " and figures, he would rely on Whyte Melville, who sang so melodiously and truly of the " King of the Kennel," who stands

> " On the straightest of legs and the roundest of feet,
> With ribs like a frigate his timbers to meet,
> With a fashion and fling and a form so complete,
> That to see him dance over the flags is a treat."

In these few pages about foxhounds I have not endeavoured to lay down any law as to management and conduct of the pack, which may well be left in the able hands of the masters and huntsmen ; and, indeed, to deal fully with all appertaining thereto a whole volume rather than a few pages would be required to make the story complete. Farmers and agriculturists complain of hard times, and require all the support which can be given them. Hunting men can assist them materially in purchasing their hay and oats in the country which affords them sport; even their horses, too, in many cases. That master of hounds who purchases his chief provender from round about the kennels is the true friend of the farmer; and wheat and oats, ground together, form an excellent hound meal. When required, steep in cold water, and then place in the copper of hot water; boil to a pudding, which allow to cool, and there is the healthiest of food for the pack. Add to the mixture flesh, if it is handy, or whenever it can be procured, and you will find the cost per hound per week not more than tenpence. A well-known master of hounds recommends the above, but twice a week a little powdered sulphur is mixed with the food—his hounds never have mange, and are as sleek and glossy as can be desired. Masters, too, must not omit to pay the "poultry bills" when such are put in, for the loss to the farmer's wife of her ducks or fowls or geese is a serious matter in these days of struggling to keep the wolf from the door. Of course, one knows the heavy expenses connected with hunting a pack of hounds, and was it not stated by an old and respected master that he calculated the cost of a good run was £5 a minute? However, be that as it may, there is no doubt that every pains ought to be taken by the foxhunter, the shooter, and the farmer to act in unison, give and take a little from each other, and thus try to promote the sport, the pastime, and the work of all.

The season 1896-7 commenced in a notable way, inasmuch as three of our leading hunting establishments underwent very great changes. The *Field*, in its summary appended to its annual hunt table, says: "The decease of Lord Fitzhardinge has caused the Berkeley to become a subscription pack without a Berkeley being at the head of it, a circumstance which may not have happened before; as for the dozen or so of years during which the hounds were in the hands of a sort of company, Berkeley Castle was strongly represented in the management until a private pack was once more started, which was the second beginning of that owned by the late Lord Fitzhardinge, the subscription pack becoming the foundation of the Old Berkeley, that country being comprised in the wide area hunted by the original Berkeley Hounds in the last century. No longer, again, do we find the Duke of Beaufort's name in the list of masters, as the head of an establishment with a lengthy and interesting history. The family connection with the hunt is still maintained by the Marquis of Worcester being joint master with Mr. R. E. Wemyss; but, nevertheless, the present is a noteworthy period in the history of the Badminton Hounds, which were originally staghounds, and according to tradition only changed to fox as the result of an accident; for, had not the staghounds been allowed to run riot and hunt a fox after a blank day in search of their proper game, the transition might have been longer delayed. Thirdly, we come to the Belvoir, a famous pack, established as far back as 1730, when five noble lords, viz., John, Duke of Rutland ; George, Earl of Cardigan ; Baptist, Earl of Gainsborough ; John, Lord Gower; and Scrope, Lord Howe, met and drew up a formal agreement as to how the hunt should be carried on. All details were provided for, the sum and substance being that each of the above-named proprietors should pay a hundred and fifty pounds 'into the hands of Alderman Child,' of Temple Bar, and that more money should be paid if the hunt required it. The agreement further specified that the hounds should be nineteen in number, and not more than twenty inches high. The establishment was to consist of a steward, one huntsman, six whippers-in, and two cooks, 'to be turned off, paid, and disposed of by the majority of the party.' Twice within its long history has the Belvoir pack received outside help. On the death of the fourth Duke of Rutland, in the last century, Sir Carnaby Haggerston was at the head of a committee appointed to carry on the hunt during the minority of his son, and once more, about 1830, when the then Duke of Rutland resigned and 'became a mere subscriber,' the hounds were lent to Lord Forester and another to carry them on until the Marquis of Granby came of age, which would have been in three or four years' time; but, as a matter of fact, the late Duke of Rutland did not take to them until the year 1857, when he inherited the title. Still, the temporary masters were but warming-pans, pending the happening of a certain event; but now the severance from the family is complete, save for the subscription, which is doubtless forthcoming from the Castle. Sir Gilbert Greenall has pluckily stepped into the breach, and we may expect that he will worthily uphold the traditions of this historic hunt."

CHAPTER III.

THE STAGHOUND.

As this hound is neither more nor less than a foxhound under another name, but trained for a different purpose, I would rather he followed the latter than preceded him, though older associations and modern customs might entitle the so-called staghound, or buckhound, to the premier position.

He has been used, or, at any rate, a somewhat similar animal to him has long been used, for staghunting, and we are told by historians that, in the times of the Normans, villages were depopulated, and places for divine worship overthrown, in order that the nobles might have their parks in which to keep their deer. Woodstock, in Oxfordshire, was one of these, and, according to Stowe, the first of its kind in England. So great a hold had hunting on those whose position allowed them to enjoy the pastime, that Edward III., when at war with France, took with him his army a pack of sixty couples of staghounds; and in the reign of Elizabeth a pack was kept at Simonsbath, Somersetshire, which hunted the red deer on the moor by the Barle, just as it is hunted to-day. But it is not my province here to enter into the ancient history of each variety of dog, and, so far as the staghound is concerned, I must be contented with thus briefly drawing attention to his ancient lineage.

Although some hundred years or so ago there was every appearance of a speedy decline of stag-hunting, owing to enclosures, high fencing, and similar sport to be obtained by other means, the retrograde movement was retarded. At the present time there are eighteen packs of staghounds in England and seven in Ireland, a considerable increase on what has previously been. Owing to the working of the Ground Game Act, which, in many parts of the country, has almost exterminated hares, those who followed the latter with harriers had to give up hunting or seek a fresh quarry. The latter was mostly done, and deer, "carted" or otherwise, have thus become a common chase. The chief packs which have so changed of late are Sir John Amory's, in Devonshire; the Oxenholme, Westmorland; and Mr. Allen-Jefferys', Somersetshire. Sport with the carted deer is pretty certain, as when one hind or stag will not run as she or he ought to do, another is speedily provided,

The Staghound.

which it is hoped will take a straighter line, affording the hounds an opportunity for hunting, and, what in modern times is unfortunately considered of more importance, give horses a chance to gallop and exhibit their jumping powers at the fences, or their amiability in the lanes or on the roads.

As a loyal subject, I ought to make some mention here of Her Majesty's Staghounds or Buckhounds, kept by the State, which, kennelled at Ascot, hunt the country round about, where the overworked city man seeks to regain his failing health by a gallop over a highly cultivated country. The Royal pack of forty couples, as at present constituted, may be said to date back to 1812, when the Goodwood foxhounds were presented to the Prince Regent, as they were faster than the old-fashioned, lemon-pied Southern hounds or talbots, the original constitution of the pack.

Of the original hounds, much has been written, and in 1895 Mr J. P. Hore published his "History of the Royal Buckhounds." Without quite agreeing with all the painstaking compiler tells us as to the antiquity of the hunt, there is no doubt buck-hunting was a Royal sport even as early as the time of Edward III. In Queen Anne's time there were two packs, and when Elizabeth reigned, the hounds cost the national exchequer £164 6s. 7d. They cost more now. However, it would be out of place here to enter fully into the history of this Royal pack, and those who yearn after more knowledge of this kind can easily gain it from other sources. At the time I write, hounds are well matched and most uniform, the dogs standing about 24 inches, and the "ladies" $22\frac{1}{2}$ inches at the shoulder.

The above measurements may be taken as about the standard heights of the staghound, though the Devon and Somerset, which hunt the wild deer on Exmoor and on the Quantock Hills, are rather larger. The rough country of coombes and thick gorse necessitates as big a hound as can be obtained, so 25 to 26 inches is the standard Mr. R. A. Sanders, the present master, seeks to acquire, and he uses entirely dog hounds, drafts from various foxhound kennels. Not more than one bitch has been in this pack for a dozen years or so, and no puppies are bred by the hunt.

There is no doubt that the chase of the wild red deer is glorious sport, and the genuine lover of hunting, one who likes to admire hounds work, and the cleverness of the horse, cannot do better than run down to Dulverton in the season, and see how the Devon and Somerset hounds can go. Long stern chases are common with them, and the forty minutes bursts in the Midlands after the fox, give

The Staghound.

place to three hours here behind a more noble quarry.

The pack consists of about thirty-four couples of hounds, a certain number of which are tufters. These are mostly old hounds, whose duty it is to find the deer, work out his line, and get him separated from the remainder of the herd; the full pack is then laid on, and so the hunt goes. The number of these tufters taken out depends upon the size and nature of the covert to be drawn, four couple of them being the usual complement. They are selected from the pack on duty for the day, because of their staunchness and eagerness in drawing, but especially for their voices and aptitude for giving tongue. A mute tufter is of course worse than useless, and, as a fact, "staghounds" have a great tendency to run mute.

In autumn, say from the 12th of August to through October, the stag is hunted, and at the end of the latter month hind hunting commences and continues to April, and as many as a hundred stags and hinds have been killed in one season.

The present pack dates actually from 1827 (though antiquarians may identify it with that at Simonsbath two hundred and thirty years earlier), and with slight exception, the Devon and Somerset have ever since shown the perfection of sport.

It may be interesting to note that the "old pack," which had been bred on Exmoor, was sold to go to Germany in 1811, and what has been produced from it, with no doubt suitable crosses, is hunting there still. Although the staghunting in the West is carried out on modern lines, its ancient history is not forgotten. The houses of the country families, of the Aclands, Fortescues, Fellowes, Bassets, and many others are hung with "heads" dating from the last century; the silver buttons with the hunt device on them are handed down from generation to generation, and those worn by the late master, Mr. C. H. Basset, who resigned at the close of 1893-4, and whose grandfather hunted the hounds from 1780 to 1786, are over one hundred and twenty years old. Mr. R. A. Sanders is the present master.

In 1896, Sir John Heathcote Amery, who had hunted with great success about Tiverton, established his pack as staghounds, and without interfering with his neighbour the Devon and Somerset, who are giving him every support, will no doubt be able to afford many good runs in the future after the wild red deer.

In some other parts of the country, stags and hinds are hunted indiscriminately (the Queen's prefer haviers, cut at four years old), the former being

The Staghound.

deprived of their antlers in order that they cannot injure themselves or each other when in confinement, and both are specially fed and prepared for the chase. They are seldom hurt, either when being hunted or when taken, and the same animal will afford a run time after time.

I have always had an impression that our ordinary modern staghounds seldom go with the fire and dash other hounds do that are continually blooded, but this may be fancy or prejudice on my part. Every now and then some, perhaps well-meaning, persons, who are totally ignorant of sport, its usages and value, make uncalled for attacks upon stag hunting as usually conducted, and where the animal, at the end of the run, is saved. Their case always fails miserably, and what proof of cruelty they seek to force upon the public is unreliable and the product of a fertile imagination.

As already stated, the staghound, or buckhound, and the foxhound are identical, though the former is often enough confounded with the Scotch deerhound, a dissimilar animal in every way. The change of quarry does not appear to have made any difference in the character and disposition of the animal. The staghound is just as kindly as the foxhound, he can gallop as fast, and is said to possess as good a nose; in coat, colour, and formation they are identical—and hard, thick feet, good legs, with strong loins, are a *sine quâ non* in both.

The staghound does not undergo the operation of having his ears rounded. He can boast of having taken part in extraordinary runs, one in Essex, continuing for seventy miles before the deer was killed. But this must have been nothing to one that is said to have occurred in Scotland and Cumberland, some time in the year 1333 or 1334, when Edward Baliol, King of Scotland, went to hunt with Robert de Clifford, in his domains at Appleby and Brougham. It is said that a single hound chased a "hart of grease" (an eight year old stag) from near Penrith to Red Kirk, in Scotland, and back again, a distance that could not be less than eighty miles, even by the straightest road. The stag, in attempting to regain Whinfell Park, from whence it started, just managed to leap the wall, when it fell dead, the noble hound also falling lifeless, on the other side of the fence.

This may be true or not, possibly not. Some early writers said the dog was a greyhound that took part in this wonderful run. Others have said it was a deerhound, but it is more likely to have been an ordinary hound of the country, answering to our present staghound, than anything else. The antlers

The Staghound.

of the stag were, it is said, placed in a large oak tree in Whinfell Park, and in the course of time became engrafted there.

> Thus spoke the king: "For equal praise
> This hand this monument shall raise !
> These antlers from this oak shall spread ;
> And evermore shall here be said
> 'That Hercules killed Hart of Grease,
> And Hart of Grease killed Hercules.'"

Here they remained until 1648, when one of the branches was broken off, it was said, by certain soldiers in the Scottish Army, at that time on the "war path." Ten years later the remainder was taken down by some mischievous persons at night (Lady Ann Clifford's diary). The ancient trunk of this tree was removed from where it stood, on the high road between Penrith and Appleby, during the present century.

A pretty story is told in connection with Her Majesty's buckhound Rummager. Some years ago, Frank Goodall, the then huntsman, met with a severe accident in the hunting field, and when assistance was to be rendered as he lay insensible on the ground, Rummager was by his master's side, and for a long time would allow no one to approach him. On the story being related to Her Majesty, it was ordered that poor old Rummager should become a pensioner, have extra quarters and comfort bestowed on him, and so live out his natural life. His progeny remain in the kennels at Ascot, among the pillars of the present pack, which now has J. Comins as Royal huntsman, and the Earl of Coventry as "Master of the Royal Buckhounds." It seems rather strange that the mastership of the Royal Hounds, once hereditary, is now a "political" appointment, a Liberal holding the office when that party is in power, and *vice versa* It is said that in their early days the Brocas family held the position for 270 years, when Thomas Brocas, the thirteenth in succession, sold the appointment to the Watsons, of Rockingham Castle. The emolument connected therewith is £1500 per annum for the master, whilst the salary of the huntsman is only one-sixth of that sum.

In the above I have dealt more particularly with the Devon and Somerset Staghounds and Her Majesty's Buckhounds, they being considered the leading packs of the kind in this country. However, in Ireland we have the celebrated Ward Union, within easy distance of Dublin, the kennels being at Ashbourne, Co. Meath. These hunt three days a week. The Co. Down, South West Meath, Longford, Templemore, and the Roscommon likewise provide sport for the stag hunter in Ireland, and

The Staghound.

with the general surroundings of all these hounds no fault can be found.

In England Lord de Rothschild's may be mentioned as a strong pack, numbering about thirty couples of hounds, and they are kennelled at Ascott, near Leighton, in Bedfordshire. The Enfield Chase likewise have twenty-three and a half couples of entered hounds, and the Surrey twenty-five couples, and whose country being round about Redhill, and pretty handy for the Londoner, usually produces larger meets of riding men than some of the neighbouring farmers like.

There is a pack of twenty-five and a half couples, and a very old one, that still hunts the New Forest; and a capital centre for the visitor to work from is Lyndhurst or Brockenhurst. Captain Lovell, on his retirement in 1893, had hunted these hounds for upwards of forty years, when they were but known as the New Forest Deerhounds. It need scarcely be said here that the deerhound is a different animal altogether. Captain Lovell's last meet as master was about a record one, for a "royal" was killed after running some sixteen miles in about an hour and a half. The New Forest Hounds hunt both the wild fallow and red deer, the former annually until the first week in May. As there are comparatively few red deer in the forest, this fine beast is only hunted as occasion requires, three or four times during the season. Mr. E. F. Kelley is the present master, and he has got an excellent pack of hounds round about him.

CHAPTER IV.

THE HARRIER.

UNLESS some very considerable change takes place, it is extremely likely that the harrier will not survive very many generations, at any rate in this country. His type has not been strictly defined for years, he has varied much in height, and has lately been crossed with the foxhound to such an extent as to further endanger his extinction. Moreover, several packs of harriers have recently taken to deer and stag hunting, and thus are still further losing their identity.

Years ago much hare hunting was done on foot, and hounds were bred for this purpose, to find their own hare by questing and hunting her through all her windings and ringings, with a care that the modern foxhound-harrier, with his dash and go, would not take pains to bestow. The latter is almost as fast and keen as the true foxhound; he has, like him, to be fleet enough to get out of the way of careless riders, and give a sharp and merry burst, rather than a careful hunting run. Most hounds now kill their hare in from half an hour to an hour, and no wonder that they can do so when sometimes they have a turn with the fox, and perhaps oftener a chase with the "carted deer." The latter almost a necessity, because a mistaken and ill-judged legislation has caused hares to become very scarce in some districts, where a few years ago they were plentiful.

The harrier is quite as old a hound as any other. Caius calls him *Leverarius*, and the Book of St. Albans mentions the hare as a beast of chase in the same list as the fox, the deer, and the wild boar. Still, perhaps, as with most harriers to-day, those of Dame Berners' time would be as much at home with the timorous hare as with the cunning fox or the fleeter red deer. Some modern writers have gone so far as to say that such a thing as a true harrier, one without any dash of foxhound blood in him, is not to be found. Beckford wrote of the harrier as a cross-bred hound, and his own were bred between the large slow hunting southern hound and the beagle. They were fast enough, had all the alacrity desirable, and would hunt the coldest scent. These attributes, added to their plodding perseverance, gave them a distinctive character, which, as already hinted, has well nigh departed. Still, all the harriers of sixty or seventy years ago were not so slow and careful as Beckford's undoubtedly were, for there were complaints that in 1825, the Kirkham, Lancashire, hounds were too fast for the hares they hunted. These, however, were big hounds, and not unlike the Penistone of to-day.

There are masters of harriers whose pride is still in the purity of their strains, though maybe, at some time or other, a point or two has been stretched for the infusion of new blood to maintain the size and standard required. Not very long ago sundry letters appeared in the *Field* on the matter, resulting from certain awards at a recent dog show. In one case, Mr. Allen-Jefferys, Hythe, near Southampton, who owns a pack of black and tan harriers, which originally came from Sir Talbot Constable, with which he now hunts the deer, complained that he was beaten by half bred foxhounds. Possibly this was so, but the winners were neater all round, and smarter than the black and tans, and thus more suitable for the show ring and the bench. Owing to a scarcity of hares in his country, Mr. Jefferys' harriers have been entered to "deer," and now may be found in the table of staghounds.

I confess myself rather disappointed with Mr. Jefferys' black and tans, as they were not so good in either feet or ribs as I expected to find them. Sir Talbot Constable began to breed such hounds as these about thirty-five years ago, by crossing beagles with St. Huberts, and then breeding in and in. This being so, Mr. Jefferys may well find the puppies difficult to rear, as he says they are. He is endeavouring to perpetuate and harden the strain by crossing with a so called smooth coated Welsh harrier, black, or black and tan in colour. Mr. Jefferys claims for his hounds that they are one of the few packs of harriers without any admixture of foxhound blood, but what they lose in this respect they gain in another, for underneath them there lurks some of the bloodhound nature, and I am told they are excellent at carefully working out a cold scent, and that they take "rating" badly. However, they are interesting hounds, evidently about $18\frac{1}{2}$ inches, and I believe that they received quite their due when in the ring at Peterborough in 1891, and at Bath the following year. Not long ago I came across one of Mr. Jefferys' strain in the Oxenholme kennels, an old hound of excellent shape and form, beautiful in type, but not quite so clean in front as he had been when in his prime.

The Harrier.

The Lancashire chaps have always been very partial to harriers, and the Holcombe have for long been a noted pack. They are required big and active in the district, and although they win prizes as harriers, I consider that their height, 22 inches, should quite put them out of the category of hare hounds. The Rossendale Harriers, also 22 inches, claim to be pure harriers, but, like other Lancashire hounds, they are big ones. Mr. Sperling's 18-inch harriers, that hunt from Lamerton, near Tavistock, are more my idea of what a harrier should be. I remember, both at Peterborough and Exeter shows, seeing a few couple of lovely hounds from the Seavington Hunt, and shown by Mr. Langdon. Rosebud and Rapture especially took my fancy — a couple of "hare pie" bitches, with character enough for anything, without any lumber about them, and minus the thick, heavy bone of the foxhound. I was told the master had twenty couples at home quite as good, his hounds averaging about $19\frac{1}{2}$ inches at the shoulder.

Mr. Webber had some pretty harriers at the same Exeter show, at which hounds formed certainly the feature. I need scarcely say that harriers like the Seavington caught the judge's eye at Peterborough, though they were hardly used that year when the

Brookside beat them. The latter is one of the oldest harrier packs in the country, and it is said that it has hunted round about Rottingdean, near Brighton, for over 120 years. The present master, Mr. Steyning Beard, has a lot of hounds that it would be difficult to equal, as their success both in the field and in the ring will testify. There is in existence a painting of a pied hare that was killed on Lewes Downs by the Brookside harriers in 1771.

Sundry packs of harriers, running to not more than 18 inches, are to be found in Wales; whilst other excellent hounds in the list of the *Rural Almanac* are the Windermere harriers (late Colonel Ridehalgh's), of which Mr. Bruce Logan is the master; they hunt round about Bowness and Windermere in the Lake district. Although, comparatively speaking, small—they are about 18-inch hounds—I can scarcely call them pure harriers, though useful hounds, that have to hunt and "find" for themselves, and surmount "the dark brow of the mighty Helvellyn" often enough when the meet lies near the foot of the mountain at Wythburn. Heavy hounds would no more do for hunting the hares here than they would do for killing foxes. And with the Windermere harriers the runs are longer and actually more interesting

The Harrier.

than they usually are with bigger and, therefore, speedier hounds.

There are something over one hundred and twenty packs of hounds hunting the hare in England, less than half a score in Scotland, and about thirty in Ireland. The standards of their height vary very much indeed, from the 24-inch Sandhurst and the 23 inches of the Edenbridge and the Penistone to the 16 and 17 inches of the Aberystwith. Some are called pure harriers that have little claim to the name; others bear a variety of appellations which signify " cross-bred." It is, however, likely some greater uniformity may be reached, as a Harrier Stud Book (Waterlow and Sons) is now published, and its editor seems to be taking pains to make it reliable and useful as a work of reference.

The harrier in his purity is difficult to obtain; he should not exceed about 19 inches in height, and, as a rule, his skull is broader and thicker in proportion to the width of the muzzle than is the case with the foxhound. The harrier is often coarser in his coat than the foxhound, which may be ascribed to crossing with a rough Welsh hound, which, though rare, is still to be found in some parts of the Principality. He has not, or ought not to have, his ears rounded, and masters are not nearly so particular about their marking or colour; in fact, blue-mottled harriers, with a dash of tan in them, were often enough to be found, and considered a favourite colour until the foxhound cross was introduced. We have seen that show judges will award prizes to black and tan harriers, but foxhounds of that colour would soon be sent to the right about.

One of the most notable harrier packs is the Penistone, that are not "harriers" at all, but old Southern hounds, said to be without foxhound or other cross for two hundred years; and equally old and pure are the Edenbridge, which are called pure Old English hounds.

The Hon. C. Bampfylde had the Aldenham Piper and Valiant at Peterborough in 1891, when one of our best hound judges described the first named as about the best hound he ever saw, so straight in front, where they often fail, Belvoir tan marked and generally as "handsome as paint." This from a "foxhound man," who can, as a rule, see no hound so perfect as his own fancy, is praise indeed. Other noted packs are Mr. J. S. Gibbon's (the Boddington); the Craven, hunting from Gargrave, in Yorkshire, and from whence some hounds were sent to America last century; the Fox Bush, the old pack was destroyed on account of rabies in 1880; the Holcombe, perhaps the oldest of all; the Marquis of Anglesea's; the Taunton Vale, and Mr. Sperling's, the latter kennelled at Lamerton, in Devonshire. As already stated, few of them are without the taint of " cross."

Generally speaking, the pure harrier should have distinguishing characteristics of his own. He ought to be from 16 inches to 19 inches, and no more, not thick and cumbersome in bone, deep in chest, and not so high on the legs in proportion to his height as the foxhound; ears unrounded and set on rather low, head thicker in the skull, and tapering more towards the muzzle than is the case with the foxhound; legs and feet as good as they can be had, but it is exceptional to find the former perfectly straight in front, and so the pure hounds are at a disadvantage when competing against the "absolutely straight" foxhound cross. Stern carried gaily, loins as strong as possible, with stifles well turned and muscular. The true harrier is not such a level topped hound as the foxhound. Colour anything you like of the hound shade, although the "blue pied," with a dash of tan about the head, is handsomest; and one authority goes so far as to say that he never saw a bad hound of this colour; coat like a foxhound's, though sometimes it is longer and harsher. I have shown that some authorities admit

K

black and tan, and who shall say that they are not correct?

I should apportion the points as follows:

	Value.		Value.
Head, ears, and character	20	Stern and hind quarters	5
Neck	5	Legs and feet	15
Shoulders and chest	10	Size and symmetry	20
Back and loins	10	Coat and colour	15
	45		55

Grand Total 100.

It is not very often that classes for harriers are provided at our shows, though such are occasionally met with in addition to those alluded to elsewhere. Darlington, that lies in an excellent sporting district, in the autumn of each year holds a great exhibition of horses and dogs, has had some excellent groups of harriers, most of which were from packs hunted on foot; harriers likewise have classes provided for them at Peterborough, and at the Exeter dog show there is always a capital entry.

So far as hunting the hare on foot is concerned, the most enjoyable part, to my mind, was when the meet took place at, say, eight o'clock in the morning. The scent or line of a hare was struck. This the hounds would slowly work out, and perhaps occupy the greater part of an hour in what was called the "quest." Puss was in fact hunted fairly to her "form," or "seat," was then "see-hoed," and, after a ringing run, which all enjoyed, was killed in the open or on the road. Such hunting is seldom seen nowadays, when the meet is at 11 o'clock. The hare is roused from her "seat," and if the fast hounds, hurried on by excited horsemen, do not rush into her straight away, the run seldom lasts half an hour.

The harrier can boast of a pack of its kind whose "master" is a lady, and Mrs. Pryse-Rice shows the best of sport two days a week round about Llandovery, in South Wales. One day in December, 1896, there was an excellent meet at Pentretygwyn schoolhouse, and a hare was soon found which simply "flew," for a matter of forty-five minutes leaving horses and men far in the rear, and finally was lost to her pursuers amongst the rocks near Craigyrwyddon coverts. From the heather on Bwlch-gwyn another hare was soon afoot, and she first made her point for the open mountain, but, turning back ere she got to the fence, crossed Berthddu, Maesforch, Gorllwyn, &c., to Bronydd, and bent to the right over many farms, by Ffosywhied to Waunlwyd, where she was viewed dead beat; time one hour and twenty-five minutes. Unluckily, a fresh hare jumped up, and, it being impossible to stop them, hounds went away over Blaenglyn, Troedyrhiw, Maesbwlch, Tirygroes, and topped the open mountain for Trecastle. Turning back on the far side, they were stopped at dark on Dolfawr. Hard lines no blood after three such runs. But the gallant little pack, with their sterns up, did not seem to think so as the "master" gathered them together and proceeded on her weary trot of twelve miles back to kennel. Mrs. Rice's harriers are $15\frac{1}{2}$ inches, and have extraordinary noses, as well as being able to go a great pace. The above "day in December" is just mentioned here to show that harriers are not by any means deficient in pace, and it is extremely likely that in a hilly country, for actual hunting, they are much better than the ordinary foxhound of the shires. A couple of hours is by no means an unusual run in the mountainous districts of Wales, where, perhaps, at the present time "harriers and hare" may be seen at their best.

CHAPTER V.

THE BEAGLE.

THIS is perhaps the only variety of hound that has profited by the institution of dog shows. He has done so because he is small and affectionate, pretty and docile, and in many respects admirably suited to be a "pet dog." Unfortunately, he is so true to his instincts of hunting the rabbit, and even the hare, as to prove rather a nuisance than otherwise in country places, where his bell-like, melodious voice will be continually heard in the coverts where the little hound is bustling the game about, much to the annoyance of the head keeper and his under strappers.

The beagle, by some writers said to be the "brach" of past generations, can boast of ancient lineage. Perhaps he was one of our original British dogs, but, as an old writer very truly observes, "his origin is lost in the mists of obscurity." Whether he actually was the "brach" or "brache" is quite a matter of question, for this name was applied to any dog which hunted by scent; even the bloodhound was so called. The earliest appearance of the word appears in the Arthurian legend of Garvaine and the Green Knight (1340). " Braches bayed, therefore, and breme (loud) noise made." Markham uses it as applied to a bitch, thus : " When your bratche is near whelping," &c. Caius does likewise. Shakespeare and other writers use the word in varying senses; Jameson, in his Scottish dictionary, defining it as a hound which found and pursued game by scent. However, it does not matter much whether the " brach " was the original beagle or not, but the latter came from under his cloud about the time of good Queen Bess, who was said to be the fortunate possessor of a pack of hounds so small that they could be carried in a lady's glove. Well, either the hounds must have been far smaller than the least of our toy terriers of to-day (which is extremely unlikely), or the glove of more capacious dimensions than a " fives Dent and Aldcroft" of the present time (which is extremely improbable), or the story an exaggeration (which is perhaps true). So there is only one conclusion to be arrived at, that these so-called "singing beagles" of our virgin queen were somewhat of a myth, or that one of them, and not the whole pack, could be ensconced in " my lady's gauntlet." William III.

also kept a pack of beagles, and when, in 1695, he hunted them during a visit to Welbeck four hundred horsemen were out, a number which is not approached at the present day, when such hounds are usually followed on foot.

Approaching more modern times, George IV. had a pack of beagles of which he was so fond that one of the best portraits of himself was taken in their company, he being surrounded by his merry little pack; and most typical hounds they are, full of character, and almost better than any we know at the present day. Colonel Thornton hunted with them on Brighton Downs, and expressed himself surprised with the pace they could go, and found a good hunter more useful than a pony in following them. A good beagle is slow but sure; he dwells on a cold line until he puzzles it out, and, throwing his musically sweet voice, calls the remainder of his fellows to him and away they gallop and cry, crawling through fences or topping stone walls, on the scent of poor puss. Beagles run very keenly, but are not so savage on the line as a foxhound.

The author of "Thoughts on Hunting," having heard much of the excellence of a certain pack of beagles, sent his coachman to fetch them, in order that the diminutive hounds might be given a fair trial. The coachman was evidently not the proper person to have the charge of hounds, and, in bringing them along the road, they became terribly riotous, going for pigs, sheep, horses, cattle, birds, deer, and almost everything that moved in front of them. However, in due course the pack arrived at its destination with the loss of only one hound; and, on being asked what he thought of them, the coachman replied that they were the "best hounds he ever saw, for they would hunt everything." At the close of last century Colonel Hardy had a pack of beagles which were taken to the meet and to the kennels again, when possible, in a couple of hampers strapped across the back of a pony. It is said that these hounds, kennelled in a barn prior to hunting next day, were stolen therefrom; hampers, horse, and all disappearing, nor was their whereabouts ever discovered.

"Stonehenge," in "Dogs of the British Isles," gives an interesting account of the late Mr. Crane's rabbit beagles, a Dorsetshire pack, which all round has certainly never been excelled for excellence in the field, and beauty on the show bench. "Idstone," the writer of that article, says:—

" He has seen them on a cold, bad scenting day work up a rabbit and run him in the most extraordinary manner, and although the nature of the ground compelled the pack to run almost in Indian

The Beagle.

file, and thus to carry a very narrow line of scent, if they threw it up it was but for a moment. Mr. Crane's standard is 9in., and every little hound is absolutely perfect. I saw but one hound at all differing from his companions, a little black-tanned one. This one on the flags we should have drafted, but when we saw him in his work we quite forgave him for being of a conspicuous colour. Giant was perhaps the very best of the pack, a black-white-and-tanned dog hound, always at work, and never wrong. He had a capital tongue, and plenty of it. A bitch, Lily, had the most beautiful points. She is nearly all white, as her name implies. Damper, Dutchman, Tyrant, are also all of them beautiful models. The measurement of Damper was: Height, 9in.; round the chest, 16in.; across the ears, 12in.; extreme length, 2ft. 4in.; eye to nose, $2\frac{1}{8}$in. Mr. Crane's standard is kept up with great difficulty. He has reduced the beagle to a minimum. Many of the mothers do not rear their offspring, and distemper carries them off in troops. Single specimens may occasionally be found excessively dwarfed and proportionately deformed. These hounds would perhaps be wanting in nose or intelligence if they could be produced in sufficient force to form a pack; but Mr. Crane's are all models of symmetry and power, and are as accomplished and as steady as Lord Portsmouth's hounds. The Southover beagles are as small as it is possible to breed them (in sufficient numbers to form a pack) without losing symmetry, nose, intelligence, and strength."

The above was written more than forty years ago, and Mr. Crane died in 1894. He kept his favourite little hounds right up to the time he died, and, so far as can be made out, was one of the very few men of late years who had anything like a substantial pack of hounds which did not go over, say, 10 inches in height. He had produced his in conjunction with Mr R. Snow, Chudleigh, and in the end both owners must have bred a little too much in and in. During a correspondence with Mr. Crane, some two years or so before his decease, he told me he had latterly lost a great many hounds from distemper and other causes, and towards the end his inimitable and diminutive pack had dwindled away, until not more than three or four couples were left, and those of no great merit. Seven couples of old and young hounds died almost at the same time, so it can easily be seen their replacement was impossible.

Had Mr. Crane lived a few years longer, perhaps he would have been able to obtain some new blood, for just now our little rabbit beagle, pocket beagle, dwarf beagle, or whatever you like to call him—and name him anything but a toy—has quite an increasing number of admirers. At the most recent show of the Kennel Club, held in October, 1896, there was the best entry of beagles brought together of late, still, at some of the Sussex shows held a few years back we have seen capital gatherings. Now the extra collection had been attracted at the instance of the Beagle Club, who guaranteed a certain proportion of the prizes. The tiny hounds, such as were classed under 10 inches, shown by Mrs. Chesshyre, of Walford, and by Mr. W. R. Crofton, of Totton, Hampshire, were extremely dainty creatures, well made, full of muscle as a rule, and hardy enough to kill a rabbit or to beat the coverts, for which most of them are used. Such have neither pace nor strength to run down a hare, but are merry hunters; and so long as by inter-breeding they are not allowed to degenerate into toys, with crooked legs, huge round heads, weak faces, and spindle shanks, our really old-fashioned and charming little "royal beagle" may continue to have an increased number of admirers.

At one of the Kennel Club shows, held over twenty years ago at Alexandra Park, Muswell Hill, Mr. G. H. Nutt showed a lovely pack, and treated his many friends with a taste of their quality. The late Mr. E. Sandall ran a trail, and after due law the little hounds were uncoupled. They soon made out the line, and merrily throwing their voices, gave us a pretty bit of hound-work through the shrubberies. Up to within two or three years ago Mr. Nutt kept beagles near Pulborough, both wire haired and smooth, but these were larger than those he had at the London show named. He was master of as neat a little pack as man need desire, which he mostly used to beat the coverts for rabbits and pheasants, instead of employing human labour, which I always considered a little more dangerous for the dog than it would have been for the man.

Greater attention appears to have been given to the beagle in the South of England than elsewhere, and the county of Sussex has usually been noted for them. Indeed, the handsome blue-mottled specimens were at one time known as Sussex beagles; and I fancy that from this county first sprang the variety with a wire-haired coat, not unlike a miniature otter hound or Welsh hound in appearance. Mr. H. P. Cambridge, of Bloxworth, is alluded to by "Stonehenge" as having a pack of 13-inch beagles in which there were some rough hounds. One of the best of these, black, tan, and white in colour, originally came from near Cranbourne. About thirty years ago I saw a peculiar little beagle, some

The Beagle.

12 inches in height, with extraordinarily long ears, characteristic face, but rather long in the body. Merry was wire-haired and sandy in colour, not unlike a pale-coloured Irish terrier. She was in the North of England, but where she came from I could never make out. Her first public appearance was on the bench, where she was shown by her owner, a sporting dealer in oilcake, who had been a great wrestler in his day. Mr. W. Lort, the judge, was so taken with the little hound that he gave her first prize in the "variety class." She had a lovely voice—a thorough hound, but quite unlike any beagle I ever saw before or since.

Recently, a number of excellent black and tan beagles have been introduced, some of them so perfect in their way as to beat others of the more orthodox colour. The old bitch Musicwood, bred by the late Lord Wentworth, appears to have been the progenitor of many of these black and tans; she was at one time the property of Mr. E. J. Cackett, who then resided near Brentwood. They are mostly about 14 inches in height, and the best specimens of the strain are undoubtedly Rasselas and Forester, which were placed first and second in an ordinary class at our last great show. Mr. Joachim has been extremely successful with the one, and Mr. Lord not much less so with the other. Musicwood has, indeed, been a useful matron, for at the show in question she was dam of a first and second prize winner in larger sized dogs, great dam of first and dam of second and third in bitches, grandam of the first prize winners in rabbit beagle dogs and in bitches, and grandam of both the dog and bitch which won the championships. Her stock are not all black and tan, some being ordinary hound marked and blue-mottled; but almost all her progeny have turned out well. These black and tan beagles are no doubt interesting, but I consider them a bad colour; they are difficult to see in the distance, and are not nearly so pretty as the "mottled" or "spotted beauties" which are much the commoner of the two. Perhaps these black and tans have been placed over others on account of their undue length of ear, which, folding bloodhound-like, should certainly not be taken as a beagle characteristic.

Amongst the best of rabbit beagles some dozen years or so ago was the blue-mottled "Blue Belle," shown by Mrs. Reginald Mayhew, and afterwards in America. Here was about as perfect a little creature as could be imagined, and the most hypercritical could only say she was a little weak in face. She had such character, the best of legs and feet, so difficult to obtain in perfection on either beagle or

The Beagle.

harrier, a perfect body, loins, back, stern, and ears to correspond, and she was as merry as a grig and when on the line of hare or rabbit as melodious as a peal of wedding bells. Blue Belle was purchased at one of the Sussex exhibitions when a puppy for about thirty shillings.

Since that time several lovely little hounds have been introduced, Mr. Crofton's Opera and Prima Donna, barely 10 inches in height, being, no doubt, the choicest of the smaller ones. Of the larger, Mr. Lord's Robin Hood and Lignum have never been excelled, and Mr. Joachim's Reader, Lonely, Lonely II., and Piccolo are as handsome a two couple as man need desire. At Brighton one annually sees a handy lot of beagles, which are used for work on the Downs, the master of them (Mr. F. Daniel) being ever foremost in advocating their interests.

Most of these smaller beagles are used for rabbit hunting and for working the coverts, which duties they perform most admirably. Mr. Lord has a very ingenious way to get a maximum amount of work out of his pets. Residing not far from large, uncultivated tracks of moorland, about three-quarters of an hour before unkennelling his hounds he sends out a man with a drag, who lays it for three or four miles, and then liberates a rabbit, the latter usually adding another mile to the hunt. His meets last season were every Saturday at ten o'clock from November to April. He also shoots rabbits over them. Mr. Lord's beagles are from 11 inches to 12 inches in height.

Mr. Crofton, who has kept beagles for more than twenty-five years, likewise uses his for rabbit hunting, rabbit shooting, and an occasional drag hunt. He prefers them 10 inches, or as much under as he can get them. His earliest hound was picked up in Winchester, an almost perfect little fellow, which belonged to a builder there; there was no pedigree with Pilot, but his blood must have been of the purest, as when mated with a bitch obtained from a gamekeeper not far from Stockbridge, excellent puppies resulted. Later, another bitch was added to these kennels from Sussex, but, owing to various circumstances, Mr. Crofton was never able to attain to the dignity of the mastership of a full pack. Still, he has always had a few couples of hounds not exceeding 10 inches, and his smallest were a couple which did not exceed 8 inches. These were excellent workers, and lovely little pets. One was presented to a lady who resided in London, and the way it contrived to find material to hunt in Kensington Gardens was extremely funny. It went away on the line, throwing its voice merrily, much to the amusement of everyone. Mr. Crofton doubts if he ever possessed a more perfect beagle than this little favourite called Tiny.

As to breeding beagles, Mr. Crofton says that he is in favour of breeding in and in to a considerable extent, but when he finds that the puppies are deteriorating in any point, he buys a young bitch whose pedigree he knows to be good, and particularly strong, even to exaggeration, in certain points where the others fail. This is better than using a strange dog hound. His beagles, with slight exceptions, are kept in kennels, and after a day amongst the rabbits care is taken that they are thoroughly dried before being fastened up for the night. By judicious treatment Mr. Crofton finds his little favourites to be quite hardy, well able to do severe work, and are not more liable than other dogs to disease. Moreover, he considers his smallest hounds the best workers, and the most intelligent and pleasant as companions. These rabbit beagles weigh pretty heavily for their size, owing no doubt to their thickness of bone and strong backs; such as are about twelve inches run from 13lb. or 14lb. to nearly 17lb. each; whilst the eight and ten inch go up to 9lb. or 10lb. in weight.

Perhaps there is a fashionable future for these

miniature hounds, especially as the Beagle Club is encouraging them. Previously they were heavily handicapped in the show ring by having to compete against larger hounds, and here, as in coursing and horseracing, "a good big 'un can always beat a good little 'un." Still, there is a quaintness and a character about these rabbit beagles which I always greatly admired, and their merry movements and silvery cry after their game delighted me much. It does not matter much what colour the beagle is; many prefer the blue mottles, but any hound colour will do—even black and tan.

During the past few years the wire coated beagle has not been much in evidence, and few seem to care for them now that Mr G. H. Nutt has given over his pack. It has been said most of these "wire-hairs" contained a terrier cross, which showed itself in the production of shy puppies distinctly deficient in voice. Mr. Gwynne, of Folkington, Sussex, however, owns a nice little pack of wire coated hounds which are entirely free from any suspicion of terrier strain. Some fifteen or sixteen years ago Mr. Gwynne obtained two and a half couples which he was told had been produced with wire coats through a remote cross with the otter hound. Long before that time a Sussex farmer kept a few couples of the wire haired beagles at Chiddingly;

they stood about fourteen inches, and bore a reputation of "always being able to kill their hare, however bad a scenting day it was." Mr. Gwynne keeps them chiefly for rabbit shooting, and they work wonderfully well. The kennels contain some seven or eight couples (not including puppies), and the endeavour is to keep them to about thirteen inches in height, but some are an inch less, others an inch or so over the standard. Since Mr. Gwynne has devoted attention to them, he has been compelled to use a smooth beagle as an out-cross.

In 1892, a stud book of packs of beagles was published by Waterlow's, it forming part of the one for harriers already alluded to. The first volume contained the names of a dozen packs only (there were over double that number in existence), which are supposed to be a foundation stock, but I am afraid that some of the entries are not so pure as many of our show hounds, which were not included; nor were Mr Crane's, Mr Nutt's, and Mr Ryan's, the latter the Kerry beagles, alluded to later on. The volume has been continued yearly, but with no improvement, so far as the hounds specified are concerned.

It is common knowledge that masters of hounds abominate dog shows; still when the very best of a variety are to be found oftener on the bench than in the field, animosity against exhibitions must be sunk. Most of the packs entered in the Stud Books, consist of big, rather large hounds, many from thirteen to sixteen inches, and the oldest pack is the Royal Rock, hunting from near Birkenhead, Cheshire, established in 1845 by Colonel Anstruther Thompson, who brought them out of Essex. The Bronnwyd beagles, Sir Marteine Lloyd's, with the kennels at Llandyssil, South Wales, in his family since 1846, have been carefully bred from true strains. The Cheshire Beagle Hunt Club have some hounds good both in appearance and work, which on more than one occasion have won leading honours at Peterborough. Christ Church, Oxford, has beagles of its own, originally established in 1874, but the pack experienced vicissitudes, especially in 1886, when, dumb madness breaking out, the entire kennel were destroyed. The then Master, Mr. F. B. Craven, soon obtained twelve couples of merry little hounds, and the establishment is now as strong as ever. Near London, at Surbiton, Colonel Turner and Mr J. Fisher are joint masters of the hounds which Mr. R. W. Cobb got together in 1882, and the Stud Book (1895) includes the Cursis Stream Beagles, with kennels at Chapelizod, near Dublin, Mr. J. Godley being master. The Peover, Cheshire, Mr. R. L. Crank-

The Beagle.

shaw master, is also an important pack. According to the hunt tables in the *Rural Almanac*, there are about forty packs of beagles hunting in various parts of the country, some of which no doubt have more than a dash of harrier blood in their veins.

In appearance the beagle is a diminutive harrier, with equally long and pendulous ears, not so level in back as a foxhound, but in other particulars much like him. However, the best beagle colour is certainly the "blue mottled," already mentioned, but in addition the ordinary hound markings are good, and black and tans, not of the Kerry size, are repeatedly met with, and are evidently admissible. The smooth coated hounds are usually understood to be most desirable, but the rough, or wire haired variety is admired by many persons, and in all respects is equally as good as the other. In hunting, the beagle is a merry, keen, hard worker, he can make casts for himself, and possesses a peculiarly bright, clear, and silvery voice. The smaller, or rabbit beagles, are especially sweet in their cry, and no doubt on this account obtained the name of "singing beagles," by which title they were known hundreds of years ago. In height there is much variety, those used for rabbits varying from nine inches, the standard of the late Mr. Crane's, at Southover, up to, say, twelve inches.

Others vary from twelve to sixteen inches, but when we reach the latter height, there is a near approach to the harrier, and so to the foxhound; the cross with the latter having been made with the idea of improving the legs and feet of the smaller hound, a change of blood that naturally has a tendency to do away with type.

The following scale of points and description of the beagle has recently been issued by the club which looks after its interests :

Head of fair length, powerful without being coarse, skull domed moderately wide with an indication of peak, stop well defined, muzzle not snipey, and lips well flewed.

Nose black, broad, and nostrils well expanded.

Eyes brown, dark hazel or hazel, not deep set or bulgy, and with a mild expression.

Ears long, set on low, fine in texture, and hanging in a graceful fold close to the cheek.

Neck moderately long, slightly arched, and throat showing some dewlap.

Shoulders clean and slightly sloping.

Body short between the couplings, well let down in chest, ribs fairly well sprung and well ribbed up, with powerful and not tucked up loins.

Hind quarters very muscular about the thighs, stifles and hocks well bent, and hocks well let down.

The Beagle.

Fore legs quite straight, well under the dog, of good substance, and round in bone.

Feet round, well knuckled up, and strongly padded.

Stern of moderate length, set on high, thick, and carried gaily, but not curled over the back.

Colour, any recognised hound colour.

Coat.—Smooth variety: smooth, very dense, and not too fine or short. Rough variety: very dense and wiry.

Height, not exceeding sixteen inches.

General Appearance.—A compactly built hound, without coarseness, conveying the impression of great stamina and vivacity.

Classification.—It is recommended that beagles should be divided at shows into rough and smooth, with classes for " Beagles not exceeding sixteen inches and over twelve inches," and " Beagles not exceeding twelve inches"

	Value.		Value.
Head	20	Hind quarters	10
Ears	10	Legs and feet	20
Eyes and expression	10	Stern	5
Body	15	Coat	10
	55		45

Grand Total 100.

Pocket beagles must not exceed ten inches in

height. Although ordinary beagles in miniature, no point, however good in itself, shall be encouraged if it tends to give a coarse appearance to such minute specimens of the breed. They shall be compact and symmetrical throughout, of true beagle type, and show great quality and breeding.

Disqualifying Point.—Any kind of mutilation. (It is permissible to remove the dew claws.)

The real and proper work of the beagle is to hunt hares and even rabbits, and such charming little hounds as some of those already alluded to, do this work wonderfully well. Any man of ordinary pedestrian powers can follow them from start to finish, for a rabbit does not as a rule live long before hounds—and, as all know, will go to ground at the earliest opportunity. The hare, too, fails to go away at such a break neck pace when the slower beagle is plodding after her, as she succeeds in doing when bullied and flustered by the dashing harrier with a lot of foxhound blood in him.

From the earliest times there have been at least three varieties of the beagle, ordinary smooth coated, rough or wire haired, and others black and tan in colour. Richardson, in 1851, writes of a Kerry beagle, which, he says, is "a fine, tall, dashing hound, averaging twenty-six inches in height, and occasionally, individual dogs attain to twenty-eight

inches. He has deep chops, broad, pendulous ears, and when highly bred is hardly to be distinguished from an indifferent bloodhound." The same author further says they are used to hunt the deer, and that there are two packs in the neighbourhood of Killarney.

I have made enquiries in various parts of Ireland, as to the survival of the Kerry beagle and his present whereabouts. One of the packs alluded to by Richardson—that of Mr. Herbert, at Muckross—was discontinued as long ago as 1847. These hounds were twenty-six inches in height, most of them black and tan in colour, some of them all tan. The other pack alluded to by the same authority, that of Mr. John O'Connell, at Grenagh, Killarney, was dispersed at the same time, which was during the distressful period of the great famine, when many of the Irish gentry, almost ruined, were compelled, under the Encumbered Estates Act, to sell their family domains at an enormous sacrifice. I could name more than one instance where a valuable estate was sold for five years purchase! The late Mr. O'Connell's hounds, were likewise black and tan. A few couples of these hounds were taken by Mr. Maurice O'Connell's nephew to Mr. John O'Connell, who kept them at Lake View, increasing his pack to about twenty couples. In 1868 he, however, handed them over to Mr. Clement Ryan, of Emly, co. Tipperary, who now preserves the only pack of Kerry beagles (the Scarteen) in the kingdom—not many years ago they were the most popular hounds in the south of Ireland.

At Darrinane a pack was kept for many generations; the late Mr. Buller, of Waterville, and Mr. Chute, of Chute Hall, all in County Kerry, had small lots of hounds. I have had kindly forwarded to me a description of this hound as he ought to be, and it was compiled by Mr. Macnamara, of Killarney, who has made a special study of the variety.

"*Head.*—Moderately long broad skull, oval from eyes to poll, about same length from nasal indenture between eyes to point of nose—should slope or slightly arch from eyes to point of nose. Forehead low, eye-brows strong and raised somewhat, cheeks not full. Eyes large, bright, and intelligent, varying in colour from bright yellow to deep buff, and deeper brownish yellow. Muzzle long, slightly arched round, and full under. Nose fine in texture, not square, but slightly tapering. Nostrils large. Upper lips hanging, and fuller towards the corner of the mouth. Teeth level, of elegant form, and strong.

"*Ears.*—Large, pendulous, falling below the neck, and set on low on the side of the head.

"*Body*. — Muscular, fairly thickset, moderate length, strong, well set on legs.

"*Neck*.—Slightly arched, thick, nearly level with the back of the skull at the point of joining. Skin full in front, and dewlap developed.

"*Chest*.—Deep, not broad underneath. Shoulders strong, and broad across the back, which is moderate in length, and strong.

"*Loins*.—Broad and muscular, and slightly arched. Thighs thick and slightly curved.

"*Tail*.—Long and evenly furnished with hair, thickest at the root, and carried curved upwards from the loins.

"*Legs*.—With plenty of bone and muscle, short, and strong; feet round and close.

"*Coat*.—Hard, close, and smooth.

"*Colour*.—Black and tan ; blue mottled and tan ; black, tan, and white ; tan and white.

"*Height*.—22 inches, more or less, which should depend upon the depth of the body."

I have dwelt thus long on this hound because, so far as I am aware, its description has not hitherto been published, and because there is a likelihood of this fine old variety becoming as extinct as the dodo, and, perhaps, it is in danger of being forgotten altogether.

Mr. Ryan writes me that his hounds average about

twenty-four inches, are smooth coated, black and tan, with " very long ears, and hanging jowls, but have no strain of the bloodhound in them. They are remarkable for their tongue, which is rich and wonderfully sweet. Their noses are very keen, and in work they are true and persevering. Not so fast as the foxhound, they possess a considerable turn of speed, are docile, and take to hunting at once."

These beagles at Emly were formerly restricted to hare hunting, but with the increasing scarcity of that quarry the master has had to fall back upon deer, and he and their followers have been very much pleased with the sport they afford with the hare until November, and with the deer for the remainder of the season. Mr. Macnamara further says that their cry in the chase is full, sonorous, and musical; when hunting in full cry the head is thrown upwards frequently; on trail their note is of prolonged sweetness.

Allusion has been made to the Stud Book, which, published by the Association of Masters of Harriers and Beagles, has now reached its sixth volume. It is carefully edited by Mr. L. E. Rickards, and will no doubt be useful in preserving the identity of both these varieties of the hound.

CHAPTER VI.

THE OTTER HOUND.

THERE is no finer type of the canine race in this country than the otter hound. His hardy, characteristic expression, shaggy coat, and rough wear and tear appearance, have always reminded me of that ancient British warrior so often depicted in our boyish story books, but who, perhaps, with his coat of skins, his shield, and hirsute face, was the invention of the artist rather than the actual inhabitant of our island.

It has been said that the otter hound is a cross between the Welsh harrier, the southern hound, and the terrier. Perhaps he may be so, but more likely not, for a good well-grown specimen has more coat than any ordinary terrier or the rough Welsh hound, and he is bigger than either. My own opinion is that he has been crossed with the bloodhound at some not very remote date. The black and tan colour often appears in some strains, and his voice in many cases resembles the full, luscious tones of the bloodhound more than the keener ring of the foxhound. Prior to the outbreak of the Franco-German war, Count de Canteleu sent a number of French griffons to Scotland, where it is said that they were dispersed throughout the country. However, I have not been able to trace their blood in any of our modern hounds. Still, these French hounds would no doubt have been very useful for that purpose. Some twenty-five years or so ago, Mr. J. C. Carrick, of Carlisle, was desirous of getting a fresh cross into his pack, and, with that intention, obtained a hound—a southern hound it was called—from the Western States of America. No pedigree could be obtained, but it was a particularly handsome animal, and more like the picture of the southern hound in Youatt's book on the dog than anything I ever saw. Mr. Carrick was afraid of the fresh blood, so the Virginian importation did good duty on the show bench in the variety classes instead of impurifying a pedigree which was quite as free from taint as that of any other variety of the dog.

I forget who recommended a cross between a bulldog, an Irish water spaniel, and a mastiff, as the most likely way to produce otter hounds. Certainly an ingenious idea, and worthy of the writer, who thus easily got out of a difficulty which more practical and learned men than he had failed to solve. We have the otter hound, let that suffice, and let his valued strain be perpetuated, and the popular masters of our packs long continue to give the best of all sport to those somewhat impecunious individuals who are not provided with the means to keep a hunter or two to gallop after foxhounds. Forty or fifty years ago otter hunting appeared to be on the wane. Perhaps the rising generation of sportsmen of that era became discontented with the nets and spears that were commonly used to facilitate the kill. These cruel appliances are now abolished, and the only place fit to contain them is the lumber room or the museum of some country town. Hounds are so bred that they can, with a minimum amount of assistance, kill their otter unaided, and specially excel in their work during the early part of the hunt, if they are but let alone.

Throw off on the river's brink, and hounds will soon hit the line of an otter, if one has been about any time within three or four hours before, or maybe they will speak to scent even older than that. The olfactory organs possessed by the otter hound have, to me, always seemed something extraordinary. The cold, damp stones by the water's edge, or a bunch or clump of grass adjoining, are not the places where scent would lie well. Still, there is the fact : a hound will swim off to a rock in mid-stream, put his nose to the ground, sniff about a little, and, if the otter has been at that spot even for only half a minute, that hound will throw up his head and, in a solo so sweet to the ears of a hunter, let all know that he is on the line.

And it was " Ragman " who never told a lie—can I call him a canine George Washington, without disparagement to America's great president? I have seen foxhounds well entered to the otter, but the rough hounds were always first to own a stale drag. The latter are so much more staid and steady when past their puppyhood; know their work so well, appear to enjoy it too, and take to hunting their favoured game at quite an early age.

It is stated of the Rev. John Russell, the great Devonshire sportsman, that, desirous of having a pack of hounds to hunt the otter, he endeavoured to make one. He said he followed the rivers for two seasons, during which he walked upwards of three thousand miles, and never found an otter, although he says " he must have passed scores, and he might as well have searched for a moose deer." No doubt the popular clergyman's foxhounds had been entered to fox. Now, with even a lot of otter hound puppies quite unentered, he would not have had such long and fruitless journeys; they would soon have hunted something, and if now and then they had run riot on a water rat, a moor hen, or a rabbit, they would have struck the scent of an otter before very long— *i.e.*, if such game were plentiful in the district.

My early experience of otter hunting was much sooner consummated than that of the Devonshire sportsman. We had an otter hound puppy, quite unentered, an old bitch, dam to the puppy, and a few terriers. The second time out we struck a strong scent by the edge of a lovely stream in our north country. Old Rally, who, later on, very often failed to speak, even on a strong scent, now gave tongue freely; her young son put his nose to the ground, threw up his head, and yelled every now and then, and quite as often fell head over heels into the water; the terriers yelped and barked, and evidently thought they were in for a big rat battue.

The young hound settled down and swam across the pool. Higher, Rally marked under a tree root. An angler hard by prodded his landing-net handle down into the ground; all of us jumped upon the surface, and quietly there dived out a huge otter! And he made his way down stream. Then we had him in a long pool, about twenty yards wide, nowhere more than five feet deep, no strong hovers on either side the bank; but below us was dangerous ground. So a shallow was guarded by two of us, with our breeches rolled up and long sticks in our hands.

Well, we hunted our otter up and down that pool for two hours. He was given no rest; he came quietly to a corner where the water was shallow; Rally and her big puppy were there. They saw the round, brown head and bead-like eyes, and furiously rushed on to their game. What a row! What a fight! The terriers were there; all of us were there. Torn jackets and torn coats. It was a wonder that during the *melée* our otter did not escape and we ourselves be the bitten ones. How it all came about none of us well knew, but a quarter of an hour later, three lads, a man, and a fisherman, were sitting in a green meadow, where wild hyacinths made the hedgerows blue and the clover was imparting fragrance to the air. They were sitting there with their hounds and their terriers, and whilst the scratch pack rolled and dried themselves amongst the earlier summer flowers, we were gazing in astonishment at an otter weighing $25\frac{1}{2}$lb.—one that we had killed ourselves with the aid of our two hounds and terriers. We had walked three miles to perform this feat, and, need I say, that in less than two years from that time that locality had as good a pack of otter hounds as man need desire. Our Mentor of the day was our huntsman.

Notwithstanding this experience of my own, almost all old hunters say that many years careful work are required to perfect a pack of otter hounds. Squire Lomax, of Clitheroe, over a quarter of a century ago, had the misfortune to lose his entire pack through an attack of dumb madness. Now his were perhaps the most accomplished lot of otter hounds any man ever possessed. Each hound was perfect in itself, and the pack might have found and killed an otter without the slightest assistance from their esteemed master, who had taken years to bring them to their state of perfection. " You will soon get another pack together, Mr. Lomax," said a friend. " No," was the reply, " my old hounds took me the best part of a lifetime to obtain, and should I recommence again, I should be an old man and past hunting, before I got another lot to my liking." Mr. Lomax for years hunted the Ribble, Lune, and other rivers in the north.

Mr. Gallon, of Bishop Auckland, who met his death whilst otter hunting in Scotland, was another great authority on this hound, and his opinion was pretty much the same as that of Mr. Lomax. But good sport can be had without having hounds quite so perfect as those mentioned.

I am, however, getting a little in advance of my text, and something must be said of the earlier days of the otter hound. King John is said to have had a pack, of which he was very fond. Although thus early otter hunting was considered royal sport, the otter was only placed in the third class of the beasts of the chase, ranking with the badger and the wild cat—even the timid hare and the hard-biting marten taking precedence. However, that he was highly valued, even in those days, for the amusement afforded, may be inferred from the fact that Edward II. (time 1307), had, as part of his household, a huntsman and subordinates to look after his otter hounds. Sometimes the King's otter hunter resided in the hall, and was served there; on other occasions he had his own residence, and lived as he liked. Anyhow, he had "twelve otter dogges" in his care, and in addition a couple of greyhounds. Then there were "two boys" to look after the hounds and feed them. The master of the otter hounds was, as the times went, fairly well rewarded for his duties, he receiving in addition to "a robe in cloth yearly, or a mark in money" —the latter 13s. 4d.—and an extra allowance of four shillings and eightpence for shoes, twopence per day wages. Each of the so-called "boys" was remunerated at the rate of three halfpence per day. The latter did not appear to have any perquisites (tips are a more modern institution), but they would doubtless reside in the house or at the kennels.

It would have been interesting to know as a certainty the class of hounds the above were, but there is little doubt they were hard in coat and rough in hair, much as they are at the present day. Some time later the otter hound appeared to become less fashionable. He was kept by the "tinkers," and similar class of roving individuals, on the northern borders. There were a few in Wales. Early in the present century they were not uncommon in the south of Scotland, in Devonshire and the west, and in the north of England. Since, the otter hound has become a greater favourite, and at the present time, during the season, which may be said to last from the middle of April to the end of September, some eighteen to twenty well regulated packs hunt the otter in various parts of the kingdom.

In a few cases, usually in Devonshire, foxhounds are almost entirely used; elsewhere the packs are composed of the rough-haired otter hound, with occasionally a couple or so of foxhounds to assist them. Still, each variety of the hound should stick to that game for which nature intended him, the foxhound to the fox, the harrier to the hare, the otter hound to the otter. The latter is mostly followed on foot, and the foxhound is too quick and fast, though many like him because of his dash. In the staidness and care of the otter hound lie his character, and he will give better sport in most cases at his own game than any other hound.

Some of the most noted packs of the present day are those of the Hawkstone, which originally belonged to the late Hon. Geoffrey Hill, who died in 1891. They ultimately passed into the hands of Mr. R. Carnaby Forster, who hunted them until 1895, when Mr. H. P. Wardell took the mastership, and who continues to show excellent sport. Mr. Hill, who hunted from Maesllwch Castle, in Radnorshire, had the pack from his brother, Lord Hill, in 1869, and from that time to the day of his death had improved it immensely. There were twenty-five couples in the kennels, all good-looking, handsome, rough hounds, perhaps not so perfect in this work as those of Mr. Lomax, but in "sortiness" they have never been equalled. They were well cared for; the members of the hunt had a handsome costume, and hounds were taken to and fro in a van made for the purpose. From 1870 to 1890 these hounds killed 704 otters, no fewer than sixty-two being accounted for in one season, the best on record that of 1881. In 1893 they killed forty-one otters in forty-eight hunting days, but if a pack kills from a dozen to two dozen otters during the four or five months they hunt, a bad record is not made, for sometimes when the waters are in flood, or the hay crop remains uncut, hounds may not be out for a week, or even a longer interval may intervene between one meet and another.

The Carlisle hounds are another noted lot, and, with a slight interval, during which Mr. James Steel was the master, that position was occupied by Mr. J. C. Carrick for over a quarter of a century, viz , until 1894, when Mr. G. A. Mounsey Heysham became master, and now, in 1897, he has the assistance of Mr. Carrick as secretary. For some time the Carlisle hounds were as invincible on the showbench as by the river. Then "the Kendal" sprang up in the sister county, and, with the late Mr. Wilson, of Dallam Tower, as master, Troughton as huntsman, and having extraordinary success in breeding young hounds, they won all before them in the ring. Afterwards the late Mr. W. Tattersall took these hounds in hand, hunting them until 1891, when they were sold as stated below. However, Sir Henry Bromley, who in 1895 came into the Dallam Tower estates, resuscitated the Kendal pack, and is hunting them at the present time, there being about twenty couples of hounds in the kennels.

The Kendal Ragman was particularly successful at stud—no one ever had a better hound at work, and he lasted eight seasons. He was a black and tan, rather short in coat to be quite right, but what there was had an extraordinary texture, so hard and close and crisp that I have seen the water standing in drops thereon, quite unable to penetrate the dense covering. This hound it was I saw take the head of an otter right in its jaws as the game came up for a breather close to the bank upon which Ragman was standing. The otter was very nearly finished outright; it would have quite killed any other animal, for the fangs of the hound had gone deeply through the bone of the skull, perhaps just missing what might have been a vital part. These Kendal hounds were sold for something like £200 to Mr. Carnaby Forster, of Tarporley, Cheshire, at the commencement of 1891, who incorporated them with the Hawkstone already alluded to. This was, perhaps, the cheapest pack of hounds ever sold; there were about twelve couples, with some terriers, and I am pretty certain that, placed publicly in the market, £1000 would have been obtained for the lot.

Another old master of otter hounds is Mr. John Benson, of Cockermouth; but half a dozen years ago his hounds were discontinued, and in their place came a subscription pack, of which Mr. Harry Clift, who has served a very long apprenticeship to the

The Otter Hound.

sport, was at the head. But more changes were brewing here, and at the present time Mr. H. P. Senhouse is master, and Mr. J. H. Jefferson is working and hunting secretary. Mr. F. Collier now hunts his late uncle's hounds, which are perhaps better known as the Culmstock. Mr. W. Collier, down Devonshire way, hunted the otter for over fifty years, and Mr. Cheriton in the west likewise, but both appear to have preferred the dash and go of the foxhound to the sedateness and care of the pure variety. Mr. W. C. Yates has had some good hounds in his time. I once saw the latter—Mr. T. Wilkinson, of Neasham Abbey, hunting the pack during an off season, when he had not one of his own—kill three otters in one day, in Lancashire. Mr. Yates latterly hunted in Ireland, but in 1896 he sold the whole of his pack to Sir Henry Bromley. The Squire of Neasham, after an idle season or two, again got together his favourite hounds, and is still hunting in the neighbourhood of Durham, and goes into Northumberland occasionally. The latter county once had a pack of its own, the property of Major Brown. In Scotland, Captain Clarke Kennedy, some years ago, kept otter hounds; so did Dr. Grant, of Knockgray; and the Duke of Athol and others, nor can the west country hounds of Mr. Trelawny's be omitted.

Of more recently established packs, there are the Dumfriesshire, with a popular master in Mr. J. Bell-Irving, and an equally popular huntsman in Mr. W. Davidson; Mr. Edmund Buckley's (Wales); The Rug, the Hon. C. H. Wynne, master; The Pembroke and Carmarthen, Mr John Evans, master; and the Bucks, Mr. W. F. E. Uthwatt, master; may be specially mentioned. There are also other otter hounds hunting in Devonshire, Somersetshire, Hampshire, Yorkshire, Carmarthenshire, Merionethshire, Brecknockshire, in county Wexford, and near Dublin. Captain Dawson (Otley, Yorkshire) kept a pack of otter hounds for some years, but sold them to Sir Henry Bromley, in 1894, because of the scarcity of otters in his locality. Then Sir Cecil Legard had a pack in Yorkshire, which he gave up about the same time for a similar reason, and his hounds went to Mr. Assheton Smith, of Vaynol Park, who only kept them a couple of seasons, when they were sold to Mr. John Evans, master of the Pembroke and Carmarthen Otter Hounds.

The dog otter hound should stand about 25 inches at shoulder, the bitch about 23 inches. The best and most favourite colours are the blue and white, though not so much mottled as the beagle, and a hard looking pepper and salt colour. Yellow and fawn, and yellow or fawn and white hounds are likewise good old colours, and, as I have said, black and tan is not amiss, with, maybe, white on the breast and feet; but black tan and white in patches is not nice on an otter hound, however gaudy it may be on others of the race. I have also seen one or two almost white hounds, but never one of the latter with the correct coat, which should be hard and crisp and close, as water and weather resisting as possible, and not too long. Often the long coats incline to an indication of silkiness in texture, which, however, is preferable to a soft, woolly jacket. In build an otter hound should be like a foxhound, strong, level, and well put together, stern carried gaily, feet close and particularly hard, and this is even more desirable than in a foxhound, as being one minute in the water and another on the hard rocks and stones tries the pads very much. A big foot is likely to increase the pace in swimming. The head must be long, jaws strong and powerful, eyes giving a certain sedate and intellectual appearance; they sometimes show the haw, which is no defect. Ears long and pendulous, close set, in order that the water may be kept from penetrating into some of the delicate internal parts. However, what an otter hound ought to be the illustration preceding this article will best inform the reader searching after information. A nice weight for a dog hound is from 60lb., to 75lb., and for a bitch about 10lb. less.

POINTS.

Value.		Value.
Coat 20	Head and ears 20
Legs and feet............ 20	Back and loins 10
Hind quarters and stern 10	Shoulders 5
Neck and chest 10	Symmetry and colour 5
60	40

Grand Total **100.**

CHAPTER VII.

WELSH HOUNDS.

MANY writers have more or less casually alluded to Welsh hounds, but their information does not go beyond telling us that they resemble foxhounds in all but coat, which in the Welsh variety ought to be wiry haired and not quite smooth. And as a fact we know so little, or absolutely nothing, about the origin of the ordinary English foxhound, that it is no wonder we are equally lacking in information concerning the Welsh hounds, whose praises have so often been sung. What the hounds were like which are included in the rules and regulations of Howell the Good, there are no means of knowing; nor, as far as one can discover, is there any book or magazine article which attempts to sketch, even in the merest outline, the history of the Welsh hounds; whilst, equally noteworthy and somewhat odd, no drawing or illustrations of them have hitherto appeared in any book about dogs.

In the hunting treatise of Edmond de Langley,

Duke of York, fourth son of Edward III., mention is made of Kennitis. Now, a rough Welsh rug or cloth was, says Jesse, called a Kennet, and he thinks these Kennitis might have been the Welsh harriers sent by the Prince of Wales to Count d'Evreux.

The earliest Welsh hounds known appear to have been kept at Margam, and were the property of Sir Thomas Mansel, who, records tell, gave them to Mr. Jenkins, of Gelly, and these were more or less rough or wiry-haired. A correspondent, a famous Welsh fox hunter, informs me that these old Gelly hounds were for the most part black and tan in colour, varying in height from 17 to 21 inches; excelling in legs and feet. Their heads and ears more inclined to the bloodhound type, than do those of the modern strains, having considerable peak, and ears hanging well down and pendulous. Their necks, backs, and loins were good. Their voices were exceptionally fine, one old sportsman likening the music of the Gelly pack when in full cry to the tones of an old church organ. It must not be forgotten, these far-reaching notes were of great importance in hunting this rough and in those days sparsely populated country. The present squire of Gelly still retains some few of the old strain.

There are many packs of hounds in Wales which

Welsh Hounds.

are actually only Welsh in name, and much confusion has been caused by the inference conveyed by many writers that all foxhounds and harriers in the Principality are of the old wiry-haired or hard-coated strain. Such is far from being the case, and it is doubtful whether even the hounds of Squire Talbot, which, to the glory of the pure Welsh hounds, are credited with an extraordinary run from Margam to Llanelly, were quite free from " foreign " strain.

Not very long ago a hunting correspondent of the *Field* was astonished to find a so-called pack of Welsh hounds the common foxhounds of the shires and elsewhere; and so recently as last year the writer went over to Aldridge's to see a pack of Welsh hounds which had been sent up, from the neighbourhood of Aberystwith, for sale. These, too, were English foxhounds, many of them of fashionable blood, and none of them had an atom of "wire-haired" coat to denote that they were originally descended from the native hound of the Principality. This was Mr. Vaughan Davies' pack.

At the time the Gelly hounds were in their prime, there was another noted Welsh pack kept by the late Squire Jenkins, Lanharran (uncle of the present squire), but they differed greatly from the "Gelly" in colour, for they were mostly white—lemon and white sometimes turning to darker colours, such as red and a grizzled black and tan, but white predominating —being the favourite colour of the Squire. Here they had smooth as well as rough hounds, and particular attention was paid to their music. I have heard it stated by old hunters who knew these hounds well, that of all the packs they had ever hunted with, they never saw or heard one that excelled the Lanharran. After the death of Mr. Jenkins, they were handed over to the late Mr. W. Morgan, Tremains, who carried them on until his death. They were later on removed to Braich-y-Cymmer, in the Ogmore Valley, where, after a few years, they found their way back again to Llanharron. From thence Col. Blandy Jenkins drafted them to different packs now hunting in Glamorganshire—principally to the Ystrad. There was another pack of Welsh hounds, viz., the "Croescade," kept by one of the best sportsmen and finest judges of Welsh hounds that Wales ever possessed —the late Mr. William Perkins, of Croes-cade. These were similar hounds to the Lanharran, both in make and shape, but their voices were not so fine. I believe in the present day a good deal of this blood found its way into the kennels of Lord Tredegar and the Llangibby.

I should rather fancy that the pack of hounds

which contains the greatest amount of " pure Welsh blood " is that of the Ynysfor, hunting round about Penrhyn Deudraeth, Merionethshire, and of which Mr. John Jones is the master. This is a smallish pack of thirteen couples, which hunts pretty much all the year round, after the season for fox being over, otter hunting being successfully followed. The country is perhaps as rough as any in the United Kingdom, and Mr. Jones finds the Welsh wire haired hounds, of which about half his pack is constituted, the best animals for his purpose. They have been in his family for three generations, which extend in this case over one hundred years. The father of the present master bred from the hounds of old Mr. Rumsey Williams, of Penrhos, who kept a pack, mostly of Welsh blood, near Carnarvon at the beginning of the century, and in a great measure the present Ynysfor hounds are largely descended from them. Fresh blood has from time to time been obtained from various districts in South Wales, where the rough haired hound is generally believed to have been originally produced, or, at any rate, two or three generations back, it was more easily to be found there than elsewhere.

More recently, Mr. Jones secured new crosses from the kennels of the late Colonel Pryse, of Peittyll, near Aberystwith, and from other hunts in the southern portions of the Principality; whilst in a few cases he has crossed with well-bred English foxhounds. The hard, wiry coats, however, remain in most instances, as well as the peculiar character and excellences common to the Welsh harrier. As is the custom with most hounds which hunt a rough country, the meets are in early morning, and foxes are found by hounds questing and hunting the drag until their game is put away, then the run is generally over terribly rough country, in which, of course, hounds are at times left very much to themselves. For this purpose nothing can excel the Welsh "wire hairs," even if they have a remote bar sinister on their escutcheon. These Ynysfor hounds are from 20 inches (bitches) to 22 inches (dogs) in height, and vary in colour, some being black and tan, others wholly tan, whilst the remainder are the ordinary hound colours.

Of course, what has been written here, and appears later on in the chapter, more or less indicates that the really pure Welsh hounds, absolutely without any intermingling of foxhound or harrier blood, are most difficult to obtain, but that such are still highly valued in some quarters may, I think, be taken for granted.

There are other packs containing more or less Welsh blood still existing in the Lanwonno, Ystrad,

Tyn y Cymmer, Treharris, Merthyr Old Court, and the Pentyrch; the latter are black and tans, and it is said they originally came from the Gelly. When living in Glamorganshire the present master of the Pembroke and Carmarthen Otter Hounds hunted them for both fox and hare. The last named pack possess two wonderful Welsh hounds of the Lanharran strain, Langer, and Gaylass. They are lemon and white in colour, and have hard coats, good voices, and no day is too long for them. They were originally purchased from the Llangibby Otter Hounds.

At the present time there is a certain demand for these Welsh wire-haired, hard-coated hounds; for, however opinions may differ as to their qualifications when placed alongside the modern foxhound, there do not appear to be two opinions as to their suitability for otter hunting. Masters of hounds fortunate enough to possess a couple or so, speak of them most eulogistically, especially so far as their hard, crisp, water-resisting coats are concerned; arguing that a coat of this character is more readily dried than the rougher one of the true otter hound; moreover, it is not so much in the way when swimming, and their constitutions are good. I do not think there is anywhere in the Principality or elsewhere an entire pack of the pure Welsh hound, either of harrier or of foxhound stamp (for there are two varieties), with the wire-haired, crisp coat. The colours are various, a few being black and tan, whilst ordinary hound markings, and such as are of a dark grizzled red and white, appear to be most in favour.

In going through the annual hunt table published in the *Field* on Oct. 17, 1896, I found there were some twenty-four packs of hounds kennelled in Wales, but only one is alluded to as Welsh, and this is the Merthyr Old Court pack, which are Welsh harriers, but their height is not given. They hunt from near Merthyr Tydvil. There are Welsh hounds in the Llangibby and also in the Pembrokeshire and Carmarthen. As already said, masters of otter hounds value the strain or variety highly. Mr. T. P. Lewes, who hunts from Ffosrhydgaled, Llanfarian, near Aberystwith, has a few couples of pure bred wire-haired Welsh foxhounds; and in the Ynysfor, whose kennels are at Ynysfor, Merionethshire, the variety may be found as already alluded to. Mr. J. H. Jefferson, Cockermouth, secretary of the West Cumberland Hunt, tells me that they have one or two Welsh hounds, which are valued highly, and they would breed more of them were they able to find suitable material.

The Hon. H. C. Wynn, at Rûg, near Corwen,

Welsh Hounds.

and Mr. E. Buckley, at Newtown, Montgomeryshire, both appreciate this variety, and to these two gentlemen I am very much indebted for being able to produce the illustration which precedes this chapter. Here are two types of the Welsh hound, the one the Hon. H. C. Wynn's bitch Lively, an unmistakable harrier; the other Mr. Buckley's Landmark, quite the foxhound in character. The latter is undoubtedly one of the finest hounds I ever saw, straight in front, with beautiful shoulders, lovely neck, perfect feet, and as sound now as when in his prime, although he must be six years old, and has done a big share of hard work during his time. With loins and hind quarters equally perfect, he is as level and as symmetrically made as any dog I ever saw. In colour he is red-grizzle and white, and his coat is hard, crisp, and as thoroughly water and weather resisting as that found on any hound; his height is $24\frac{1}{2}$ inches at the shoulder, and he scales 84lb. when in nice working condition. It will be seen that his ears are rounded. He, with a similar hound, came from Mr. Reginald Herbert, master of the Monmouthshire; they had no pedigree, but were said to be pure Welsh foxhounds—a description which is, doubtless, thoroughly correct. Lively is much the same colour as Landmark, but perhaps the grizzle red is rather more tawny than that of the dog; she measures 20 inches in height at the shoulders, is 54lb. in weight, and is likewise an old hound without pedigree. Mr. Wynn bought her with a similar hound in Ireland, whither she had been sent from Glamorganshire; her kennel companion was killed in the kennels at Rûg. Lively is an excellent hound in work, and as a brood bitch has proved most successful. Unfortunately, she has always been mated with a smooth-coated English harrier, the puppies being very often all wire coated, some of them possessing more coat than their dam, who is a pretty bitch, with considerable character about her.

These hounds are excellent types of their family, and Mr. Wardle's drawing conveys better than words can, what an old-fashioned, wire-haired, Welsh hound is like. Mr. Buckley says he finds his couple or so "useful for otter hunting, as they take the water well, and do not seem to feel the cold so much as otter hounds, because their coats dry sooner than the longer ones of the latter when coming out of the water. They show extreme delicacy of nose in picking up and working out a cold drag; but their voices are very poor and their note quite commonplace as compared with the melodious otter hound."

The Hon. H. C. Wynn speaks in similarly eulogistic terms of the Welsh breed, and of his good bitch Lively in particular. She has produced him the very best hounds he has in his pack—a workmanlike lot, who can hunt hare and fox and otter, as occasion requires, and do this three or four days a week and turn out fresh and frisky at the end. One of the stud hounds in the pack is Curfew, a son of Lively's, who, although sired by an English hound, has as much, or more, coat than his dam. He is a fine fellow, about 21 inches in height, and can drive hare or otter as well as any hound. Of the Welsh hounds, Mr. Wynn says "they excel in working without assistance, and are seldom at a loss, even when the huntsman is not with them, when they overrun the line. When such is the case, they will spread out like a fan, individually try here, there, and everywhere, with the inevitable result that some hound or another hits the missing line, speaks to it, and other hounds, galloping up, do likewise. Then they are away as brisk as ever; there is no sitting down and waiting about for assistance." As a matter of fairness, I must state that all owners of Welsh hounds do not speak in a similar strain. A well known master, who owns a few couples, says that where "there is one good hound there are fifty bad ones—noisy, riotous, ugly, ill-conditioned brutes," and this he ascribes to in-breeding. Most of the finest hounds have, he says, degenerated in the matter of bone and substance, and after three seasons' work they are inclined to hang on the line of a fox and become noisy. The latter fault he finds not only with the pure Welsh hound, but with the foxhound cross.

Some time ago a hunting correspondent in the *Field* took exception to some Welsh or half bred Welsh hounds he saw, accusing them of "babbling" and other heinous offences. They were not, however, long without having their cause thoroughly championed by those who knew a great deal more about hounds than did the fault finding writer in the first instance. I do not think I can do better than reproduce the letters of, at any rate, the two writers who first came to the rescue of the strangely vilified hounds.

"Linehunter" wrote: " I venture to think that your correspondent is not in possession of sufficient data regarding the Welsh foxhound to warrant the conclusion he appears, judging from his letter, to have arrived at. He speaks of the Welsh hound as being so 'shy' as to require to be 'coaxed over a road if horses are standing in it.' He also describes him as being so free with his tongue as to throw it continually 'when casting for the line.' Further he asserts that he will not 'stand the whip.'

" With regard to shyness, it is quite possible to find some trencher-fed packs, many of whose members would trot off home if they had a severe cut with a thong, the reason really being that such packs have next to no kennel discipline; and, when collected together for a day's sport, extremely resent chastisement for hare or rabbit hunting, and accordingly go home to Molly the milkmaid, or whoever has been the best friend of their infancy, for comfort to their wounded feelings. I have occasionally seen a hound go home in this way, but very seldom. In all my experience of Welsh and Welsh crossed hounds, I have never seen such an occurrence as 'coaxing hounds across a road' because they were in abject fear of horses standing in it. Occasionally a puppy or two may not relish a crowd of horses, but, 'given a decent scent,' as the venerable master of the Llangibby observed to me, 'they would go through a regiment of soldiers.'

"Such shyness as I have noticed in Welsh or crossed Welsh hounds has been due rather to defect of discipline than to defect of character. If a hound be kept at a farm and only brought to kennel for hunting he will not stand the amount of whip and rating that a kennelled hound will readily endure. The master of the Llangibby, Mr. John Lawrence, whose unrivalled experience of Welsh hounds entitles his opinion to the greatest consideration, assures me that he considers the charge of shyness as against the Welsh hounds devoid of all foundation.

"There is a point in their character that I must not fail to notice, and that is their curious and sturdy independence. Doubtless many hound men would dislike this trait extremely. We do not. We cherish it as most precious, a quality second to none in the animal's composition. Without it we should not kill half the wild stout foxes that we do. I do not know that I can explain this quality better than in the words of a gentleman who saw the Llangibby account for a fox in a difficult country, and said, 'Lawrence, your hounds don't hunt like hounds, but just as if they were wild dogs.' This conveys my meaning. They hunt as a wild animal pursues his prey, to kill and have its blood, paying as much attention to the game they have in hand and as little to their huntsman as they conveniently can. At a check, when an unjumpable ravine or a dingle that must be circumvented intervenes between them and their huntsman, you do not see them standing still shaking their sterns, and looking wistfully for their human friends to come and tell them where to try. No; they spread here and there, all over the place, busy as spaniels, crossing and traversing, till presently one hits it off, and away they go to cry. This very independent nature of theirs makes them a trifle more headstrong in their work than some men might like. For instance, you have to stop them about six times before you can get them off a fox's line, and they will break away and rush at a covert through all the whips that ever rode and holloaed. But did not Whyte Melville write of his typical hound that

> Rating and whipcord he treated with scorn?

Independent, wilful, determined they are, and not the sort to be 'tufters' staghunting, and stand still politely at the crack of a thong. Shy they are not. If shyness were one of their weak points, would they stand the crowds out otter hunting, or would those two bitches by Llangibby Danger and Sultan, to borrow 'Brooksby's' words, 'in fair weather and foul, on a cold scent or a hot one,' have gone to the front with the Pytchley? No, they would have come home post haste to Wales to recount how those terrible 'fields' of the shires rode over their sensitive sterns.

" And now as to their babbling when casting for a line. I think I speak correctly when I say that this fault is rare. I have often seen Welsh hounds mad to begin work, hardly restrained by the whips, throwing their tongues all the way from the meet to the first draw. Allowed to go, I have often seen them rush with a crash of music, at the fence of the covert. Once inside, silence reigns until one of them crosses the drag. Let us have a clear understanding as to the difference between speaking on a drag and babbling. The Llangibby master desires me to say that any hound that threw his tongue while casting for a line would cease to be a member of his establishment, for that, in his opinion no fault could be worse. Speaking to a drag is an entirely different thing. This the Welsh hounds do, and, in fact, often hunt the drag of a fox for a considerable distance, with abundance of music, up to where he is lying.

" The practice in vogue years ago was to draw a mountain side or other likely ground very early in the morning, and allow hounds to follow the steps a fox had taken in the night until he was unkennelled. I have heard old sportsmen say that this drag work was the prettiest part of the day's hunting.

" Nowadays, when hounds meet at ten or eleven o'clock, and when foxes are far more abundant than they used to be, the drag-hunting system is not often tried. Nevertheless, it has been quite common in recent years, and fairly late in the morning, to hear such hounds as old Llangibby Wiseman and Mr. Blandy Jenkins's Charmer, or the present Llangibby Danger, speaking to the line of a last night's fox, and their bell-toned comrades joining in one after another, until a crash of voices, hoarse and

Welsh Hounds. 189

heavy, long-drawn and deep, shorter and higher pitched, where English ancestry comes in to modify, proclaims that an old traveller is on foot to try conclusions with the relentless foes, 'the yell of whose war cry is borne on the breeze.'

" But let all houndmen interested in my favourites take notice that they are a dying race, as every year passes fewer in number, more and more crossed with English strains. Soon they will be 'improved off the face of earth,' unless more lovers of such antiquities are found. The policy of crossing with English blood has been admirable up to a certain point; but the difficulty now is to find a real Welsh hound to maintain the balance of qualities. They are nearly all half, quarter, and eighth bred. Nevertheless, there is sufficient of the old-fashioned blood in some South Wales kennels to preserve the old reds and grizzles well into the next century, if someone would stick to breeding them without further admixture of English blood."

Another correspondent, signing himself "Welshman," wrote : " I am quite ready to admit that some people may have noticed peculiarities in the Welsh hound, such as 'speaking to a drag,' which must have astonished them considerably. In days gone by, when hounds were kept in Wales (as they are now in some of the more mountainous and unrideable parts) for the sake of destroying foxes, and foxes were scarce and very hard to find, this power of 'owning to the drag' of a fox was most essential, and I have not the slightest doubt that it was one of the most valued and chief characteristics of the old Welsh foxhound. Now things are changed, and there are very few packs in Wales where the Welsh hound has not been crossed with the English, and consequently their 'cry' has considerably diminished (in fact, it must have been with one of the few remaining pure, or nearly pure, Welsh packs that Lord Willoughby, who had written to the *Field* on the subject, can have noticed hounds speaking to a drag), and I think that so far as 'speaking to a drag,' or 'throwing their tongue when being cast' (this must be wrong at any time), is concerned, the loss is a step gained in the right direction; but here I must stop and claim, for the cross-bred Welsh hound, hunting powers superior to the best bred hounds in England.

"With regard to their showing symptoms of 'shyness,' I do not think it is a general trait in their character, but they would be likely to appear so, unless entered amongst large fields of horsemen, but this would apply to all hounds equally. Your correspondent does not state what other 'disadvantages' they may have, but goes on to say that 'the Warwickshire hounds when drafted into Wales develop all, or many, of the good qualities of steadiness and staunchness of the Welsh hound.' This is a sweeping assertion, and, if true, would (unless he claims for the Warwickshire hounds exceptional hunting qualities denied to other English packs) have caused the Welsh foxhound to have become extinct long ago, as there can be no doubt that, in other respects than hunting qualities, the English hound holds the field. As a matter of fact, I have heard from those who ought to be able to give a practical opinion (*i.e.*, those who have entered the two sorts side by side in the same entry) that the only advantages the English hound has over the Welsh are looks and stoutness, and perhaps some would add steadiness from riot during their first season.

"There can be no doubt that the English hounds have for generations been fairly tried in many Welsh packs, and, with the exception of the above named qualities, they have been found wanting; whilst, on the other hand, I have never heard an instance where the cross-bred hound (for I do not believe in the pure-bred Welsh hound in any country except where riding to hounds is impossible) has been fairly tried and found wanting in England. If the English huntsmen are certain that the hunting qualities of their hounds cannot be benefited by the cross, their reluctance to try it is intelligible, for most assuredly the Welsh blood will not improve the appearance of their packs; but can they be thus sure without a fair trial ? I think not."

About the same time, " Cymru Bach," who also thoroughly understood what he was writing about, said : " As a Welshman who has hunted Welsh hounds all the year round for some fifteen years, the epitaph on the tomb of my father's old huntsman, containing the following doggerel, defines the various sports :—

> Here lies old Rice, a huntsman nice.
> Who cares for neither fox, hare, or otter :
> His hounds he'd feed whene'er they'd need.
> With horseflesh from the slaughter.

And he hunted all in their turn, with an occasional moonlight diversion after a badger. . . . Were I still hunting in Wales I would have none other than Welsh hounds, considering them to be more suitable to the country than the English, which, from high breeding, high feeding, or continual lifting to get out of the way of the modern steeplechaser, have not such good noses as the Welsh hounds. In England I should be very glad to see a judicious cross to help to remedy this serious defect; but this will never be as long as

Welsh Hounds. 193

there are hound shows, and hard riders on blood horses; you cannot cross a Welsh hound (rough) with an English hound (smooth) to make a picture. The Welsh hound is a more determined worker, which remark will also apply to hounds in the mountainous countries of the north of England, such as Cumberland; both parts of the country claiming that they can hunt a fox until darkness, when a peg has been put in the ground where they have been called off, and the hounds taken to the spot early next morning again to continue the run. I am writing of some thirty years ago, when daybreak was the time for the meet, which is not the case in these indulgent days. The Welsh hound is especially a good hunter along a road, over a plough, and even on heavy snow. I have had some really good hare hunting on the mountains. The Welsh hound has plenty of music, which is very cheery, and essential in hilly and woodland countries, and without which the hounds would often be lost for the remainder of the day. The Welsh hound may be more shy, when brought into England, than the English hound, which might be accounted for thus : In Wales the fields are small, counted by their tens, while in England they are counted by their scores. At home I do not consider it has this fault. The Welsh hound is not so fast as the English hound,

O

because, if with all its music, speed were added in such a country, the fields would never see or hear any more of the pack until it had found its way back to the kennels during the following week probably.

"I cannot agree that the Welsh hound takes more whip, that is in cases where discipline is taught in the kennels, on the *suaviter in modo et fortiter in re* principle. As an all-round worker the Welsh hound is certainly bad to beat. All my lot, principally wire-haired, were very good on an otter, and after Christmas, with the assistance of a few old foxhounds as finders, were very steady on our mountain foxes; and many a badger have they accounted for on our moonlight excursions. Hares were supposed to be their legitimate game, and we could kill plenty, with often a straight-necked one going over the hills and far away, as if a fox were in front of hounds. At this sport I never lifted them, giving wily puss every chance for her life. I remember on one occasion suddenly losing our hare on an open hill, and trying round and round to put her up again; she had doubled back, and at last catching sight of her squatting in a deep wheel rut nearly covered over with water; hounds must have walked over her several times. I took them to the spot over and over again, before they got her up of her own accord; needless to say she ran only a very short distance, being stiff and chilled, before they were rewarded with their well-earned whoo-whoop and a taste of blood. I consider the Welsh hound the best for Wales, the English hound for England; the styles of hunting, owing to the natural as well as the other requirements of the two countries, more especially in the present day, being so vastly different.

"During the past fifty years English hounds (smooth coated) have been extensively used in Wales, and, such being the case, the cross that is now being 'tried so successfully' should not be called a cross with the Welsh hound, but rather with the hound from Wales, virtually an English hound, which has undoubtedly increased its scenting qualities from such cross, the colder hunting country and the lesser amount of lifting. I think there are very few cases where English masters of hounds have crossed with the original rough Welsh hound— in fact, there are very few in the Welsh packs. In the Radnorshire and West Herefordshire, which Col. Robert Price, a late master, had hunted for more than five-and-twenty years, there were several of the old wire-haired Welsh hounds, which he always valued at their weight in gold; but he was compelled to go with the times, and get a strain of English blood for his flying Herefordshire country, where horses and men are faster than those over the Welsh hills, and where hounds must be got out of their way."

Mr. P. J. Savile Foljambe wrote that in 1871 he purchased, at Lord Wemyss's sale, three unentered bitches, by Lord Queensberry's Talisman, a hound with a good deal of Welsh blood in his veins. Two of these bitches were most determined hard runners, with plenty of tongue, but not too much of it. The third had the best nose over dry or rough fallows of anything in the kennel. She was, he believed, the best all-round foxhound he ever had, and a capital fox finder. Three or four of the litter, which Mr. Foljambe did not take, were of the colour of bloodhounds.

I think that a capital case in favour of the Welsh hound has been made out, and one has yet to find where the cross, when properly done, has not been found useful in its introduction with the modern foxhound. To hunt the otter, the Welsh hound, in the state as pure as it can be obtained now, is said to be harder than the ordinary otter hound, and his close, hard coat sooner dries than the longer and often softer one of the hound so common in the north of England. There appears to be two types of the Welsh hound nowadays, whatever was the case

Welsh Hounds.

formerly, and there is quite as much difference between Landmark and Lively—portraits of which head this article—as there is between a foxhound of 24 inches and a harrier of 18 inches. The description of them, as given on another page, is that of the Welsh hound as he ought to be, and this chapter cannot better be concluded than in the words of an English M.F.H., who, with considerable experience of the Welsh cross, wrote : " It is probably needless to say that, if a master of hounds wants to show at Peterborough, or is very particular about the looks of his pack, he must have nothing to do with the Welsh cross. I do not know anything about pure Welsh hounds, but this makes the third season in which I have hunted some hounds with a Welsh cross in them. The two disadvantages of the cross seem to me to be appearance and the difficulty of breaking these hounds from riot. They require a great deal more whip than English hounds, and it takes far more trouble to get them steady. The advantages appear to be these: They enter quicker than English hounds; they hunt better by themselves, and persevere more when their huntsman cannot get to them; they have more tongue, and, I am inclined to think, rather better noses. I have never had one of these hounds which babbled, or threw its tongue when going into covert, and I have never seen any sign of their being afraid of coming through horses."

Allusion has been made to the special faculty the Welsh hound is said to possess in hunting the drag or "quest," *i.e.*, in striking the scent of a fox where he has been on the prowl over night or early morning, and slowly and carefully making it out until he is unkennelled. This hunting the " quest " is not entirely confined to Welsh hounds and to Wales; for it is still the custom with such packs as the Ulleswater, the Coniston, the Eskdale (Cumberland), and perhaps of some others which meet in the North of England. In my early days most north country harriers adopted a similar method, and, meeting at eight o'clock in the morning, there was always some pretty questing and hunting the " drag " before puss was " see-hoed " away from her form in the stubble or in the hedge bottom. In such cases there is no danger of hounds being ridden over, and it is a custom which must certainly improve the scenting capabilities of hounds. I fancy it is in the latter particular that our wiry-haired Welshman has been oftenest found useful when mated with the foxhound, which, however perfect he is said to be, can, like anything else in this world of ours, be improved and made even " more perfect."

CHAPTER VIII.

THE DEERHOUND.

FAILING any further information on the subject than we at present possess, it will always be a moot point whether the hounds used for Queen Elizabeth's delectation at Cowdray Park, in 1595, that "pulled down sixteen bucks in a laund," were ordinary greyhounds or Scottish deerhounds. The latter were likely enough to be fashionable animals at the close of the sixteenth century, for they had already been described by Hector Boece, in his History of Scotland, printed in France 1526-7, which by royal command was translated into English in 1531. Thirty years later, Gesner, in his "General History of Quadrupeds," gives an illustration of three "Scottish dogs," one of them answering to our modern deerhound in general appearance. The drawing for this was supplied by Henry St. Clair, Dean of Glasgow at that time, whose family kept the breed for very many years, an interesting story in connection therewith being told on another page.

Good Queen Bess was fond of her dogs and the sport they showed, and there is nothing unreasonable in supposing that those provided for the purpose above-mentioned in Cowdray Park were in reality deerhounds. However, whether my supposition be correct or otherwise, there is no gainsaying the fact that this mention in the Scottish history is the earliest to be met with where the deerhound is actually alluded to.

That he was highly valued by the clans or chieftains of his native country may be judged from the following pretty story told by Boece. On one occasion many of the Pictish nobility repaired to Craithlint, to meet the King of Scots to hunt and make merry with him, where they found the Scottish dogs far excelled their own in "fairness, swiftness, and hardness, and also in long standing up and holding out." The Scottish lords gave their guests both dogs and bitches of their best strains; but they, not contented, stole one, belonging to the king, from his keeper; and this the most esteemed hound in the lot. The master of the leash being informed of the robbery, pursuit was taken after the thievish Picts, who, being overtaken, refused to give up the royal favourite, and in the end slew the master of the leash with their spears. Then the Scots mustered a stronger force, including those who had been engaged in hunting, and they fell upon the Picts. A terrible struggle took place, one hundred of the Picts were slain and "threescore gentlemen" on the other side, besides a great number of commoners. The latter, poor fellows, not being deemed worthy of numeration in those bloodthirsty times, and, so long as the hound was recovered, little thought would be given to the dead "commoners" who fought for its possession. Moreover, it was stated few of the combatants knew what they had been fighting about.

Another interesting story is that relating to the family of St. Clair. King Robert Bruce, in following the chase upon the Pentland Hills, had often started a "white faunch deer," which always escaped from his hounds. He asked his nobles if any of them possessed dogs that they thought might prove more successful. Naturally, there was no one there so bold as to affirm his hounds better than those of the sovereign, until Sir William St. Clair came forward. He would wager his head that his two favourite hounds, "Help" and "Hold," would kill the deer before she could cross the March burn. Bruce, evidently of a sporting turn, at once wagered the Forest of Pentland Moor, to the head of the bold Sir William, against the accomplishment of the feat. The deer was roused by the slow, or drag hounds, and St. Clair, in a suitable place, uncoupled his favourites in sight of the flying hind. St. Clair followed on horseback, and as the deer reached the middle of the brook, he in despair, believing his wager already lost, and his life as good as gone, leaped from his horse. At this critical moment, "Hold" stopped her quarry in the brook, and "Help" coming up, the deer was turned, and in the end killed within the stipulated boundary. The king, not far behind, was soon on the scene, and, embracing his subject, "bestowed on him the lands of Kirton, Logan House, Earncraig, &c., in free forestrie." Scrope says the tomb of this Sir William St. Clair, on which he appears sculptured in armour, with a greyhound (deerhound) at his feet, is still to be seen in Rosslyn Chapel.

A common but erroneous idea has prevailed, that the Irish wolfhound and the Scottish deerhound were identical, and, indeed, that the latter was merely an ordinary greyhound, with a rough, hard coat, produced by beneficent Nature to protect a delicate dog against the rigours of a northern climate.

About the end of the sixteenth century (1591), we are told that the Earl of Mar had large numbers of deerhounds, but at the same period the Duke of Buckingham had great difficulty in obtaining Irish wolf dogs, a few couples of which he wished to present to "divers princes and other nobles." So the Irish dog was even then becoming extinct, but the Scottish one survives to the present day, and is now more popular and numerous than at any previous period of his existence. Still, judging from what Pennant, writing in 1769, says, the deerhound must, about his time, have been rare in certain districts, for he says, " he saw at Gordon Castle a true Highland greyhound, which has become very scarce. It was of large size, strong, deep chested, and covered with very long and rough hair. This kind was in great vogue in former days, and used in vast numbers at the magnificent stag chases by powerful chieftains." Even the Kings of Scotland were wont to command those of their subjects who had good hounds to bring them together in order that they should have a suitable hunt, and their commands were freely responded to by the presence of the Earls of Argyle, Huntly, Athol, and others.

Towards the close of the past century and early in the present one the deerhound was by no means so uncommon in various parts of Scotland as some have inferred. A good many were scattered up and down in various holdings, especially in the western portions of the Highlands, extending to the Hebrides. The smaller farmers kept one or two, and so did many of the shepherds, who were never loth to chase and kill a deer, and when a stag, or even hind, was not to be had, the deerhound was trained to hunt and kill foxes and otters, and other small game or vermin. After the rebellion of 1745, a good deal of uneasiness and unpleasantness remained, and the animosity caused thereby was a long time in being allayed. In many instances the Highland residences were neglected, their owners going to reside on the Continent or elsewhere. Their hounds were, therefore, spread abroad in out-of-the-way places, and thus perhaps came the impression conveyed by Pennant of their scarcity. Mr. George Cupples ("Scotch Deerhounds and their Masters") tells us the lowlier families used these hounds in competing against each other, and matches between certain celebrated hounds in adjoining districts were frequent. No doubt the deerhound, under such surroundings, would improve, especially as he was, to a certain extent, more of a companion than when kept in a large kennel.

In Johnson's tour to the Hebrides in 1773, Boswell makes several allusions to the dogs and hounds. He says: "In the Isle of Sky is a race of brindled greyhounds larger and stronger than those with which we course hares, and these are the only dogs used by them (the islanders) for the chase. . . . The deer are not driven with horns and hounds.

The Deerhound.

A sportsman with a gun in his hand watches the animal, and when he has wounded him traces him by the blood." The same quaint volume says that on one occasion the young laird of Coll "was sporting in the mountains of Sky, and when weary with following his game repaired to Talisker. At night he missed one of his dogs, and when he went to seek for him in the morning found two eagles feeding on his carcase." Scottish hounds were by no means uncommon then in the Hebrides and on the western coast, where considerable pains were taken to preserve the strain in its purity and strength, and no doubt, in a great measure, we are indebted to these smaller farmers for preserving a fine variety of the canine race when it was within quite an easy distance of almost entire extinction. It is possible that, had the Irish wolfhound been favoured in a similar manner, and obtained equally warm admirers, there would have been no occasion for the resuscitation of the breed by the introduction of the deerhound and German boarhound cross.

One or two authors have assumed that the modern deerhound is a cross between the foxhound and the greyhound, or between the bloodhound and the greyhound, but this I consider quite incorrect, nor in my researches have I been able to come across anything likely to sustain such a statement. If the deerhound is to be found in greater numbers now than previously, it is only because more attention is paid to his breeding, and because the many strains that a hundred years and more ago were in the out of the way places of the Highlands have, by better communication, been brought within the radius of canine admirers. Scrope, in his "Deer Stalking," published in 1838, has naturally much to write about the deerhound. He it is recommends the foxhound and greyhound cross, and says that the celebrated sportsman Glengarry crossed occasionally with bloodhounds, still Macneill of Colonsay, who wrote the article in "Days of Deerstalking," that deals mostly with those hounds, confesses that there were still pure deerhounds to be found when he states them to be very scarce at the time he wrote. Maybe they were scarce, but not sufficiently so as to induce people to attempt to reproduce them by such an unhallowed alliance, and perhaps, as stated above, they were not quite so scarce as he imagined. In addition to the hounds kept by the farmers and shepherds, Lord Seaforth had a large kennel, and the strains of the MacDonnels of Invergary House, of Cluny Macpherson, of Colonel Mitchell Strathmaspie, of the Lochiels in Lochaber, one of whose hounds was said to have killed the last wolf in Scotland; of the Dukes of Gordon, of the

The Deerhound.

McKenzies, Macraes, and Macleods, were all of considerable reputation. The pedigrees were carefully guarded, and it is said that Dr. Ross, parish priest at Kilmonivaig, was prouder of the blood of some of his hounds, which were said to be of a pure and rare strain originally possessed by the Duke of Gordon, than he was of his own ancestry, traceable to the Earls of Ross.

A favourite sporting author from my earliest boyhood days has been Charles St. John, who, in his " Highland Sports," writes so charmingly and naturally of all he saw and shot and caught during his excursions. He wrote but eight years after Scrope, still he says that the breed of deerhounds which " had nearly become extinct, or, at any rate, was very rare a few years ago, has now become comparatively plentiful in all the Highland districts, owing to the increased extent of the preserved forests and the trouble taken by different proprietors and masters of mountain shootings, who have collected and bred this noble race of dogs regardless of expense and difficulty." Not a word about Macneill's crosses or of those of Glengarry; and I am happy in the belief that our present race of deerhounds does not contain the slightest taint of bloodhound or foxhound blood. If it did, surely the black and tan colour and the greyhound markings would continually be appearing.

I have yet to see a black and tan deerhound, or one similar to a foxhound in hue.

What a striking and life-like picture St. John draws of Malcolm: "as fine a looking lad, of thirty-five, as ever stepped on heather," and of his two hounds, Bran and Oscar, whose descriptions tally with what I shall later on give to be those of a deerhound. There was no bloodhound or foxhound stain in Bran and Oscar, and well might such handsome, useful, faithful creatures, or similar ones, be worth the £50 a-piece they would have brought even forty-five years ago.

Since St. John wrote, many deer forests have been broken up into smaller holdings, and to this, perhaps, may be attributed the fact that "coursing deer" is not followed so much as in his time. There are still a few forests in which a deerhound may be taken out to assist at the termination of a stalk; but as the red deer is now mostly killed in "drives," a sort of battue in which the shooter can sit at ease until the deer come along, to be shot in a somewhat ignominious manner, the deerhound as such is little used. A stalker will find one useful at times, but even he is supplied with such a perfect rifle, so admirably sighted, and he is such a good shot that the stag seldom requires more than the hard bullet to kill him almost dead upon the spot.

The Deerhound.

Some few years ago the Earl of Tankerville, in a series of articles he wrote for the *Field*, made allusion to the deerhound. He said many that he saw "were beautiful, swift, and powerful. Some are able to pull down a stag single handed, but the bravest always gets killed in the end. The pure breed have keen noses as well as speed, and will follow the slot of a wounded deer perseveringly if they find blood. The most valued are not necessarily the most savage, for the latter (the reckless ones) go in and get killed, whilst the more wary, who have taken the hint after a pug or two, are equally enduring, and will hold their bay for any indefinite time, which is a merit of the first importance."

Lord Tankerville continues, that he was informed of a remarkable deerhound, belonging to a poacher in Badenoch, that never missed a deer. In due course he obtained the hound, and called it Bran. Later on it saved the life of a keeper from the furious attack of one of the wild bulls of Chillingham. After being delivered to his new home, Bran was placed in the kennel, and it was thought that the pallisades with which it was surrounded were sufficiently high to prevent any dog getting over them. However, Bran did succeed in scaling them, and Lord Tankerville, having paid his money and lost his dog, was considerably upset, and never thought of seeing the

hound again. However, in a few days the
"poacher" brought back the errant Bran, who
had, in fact, reached his old home before his master,
who was considerably astonished, on reaching his
cottage, to see his old companion rush forward
to meet him. The distance between Chillingham
and the man's cottage was about seventy miles,
and to take the shortest route, which Bran no
doubt did or he would have caught his master on
the road, he must have swum Loch Ericht.

Naturally modern dog shows have done much to
re-popularise the deerhound, now that he is so
seldom required for that purpose for which, shall I
say, nature first intended him. How little he is used
in deer stalking may be surmised by a list that
appears in Mr. Weston Bell's monograph of the
variety (1892). Here some fifty-eight forests are
named, and in but about seven of them is the deerhound kept. The collie is now more frequently
trained and used to track the wounded stag, because
he works more slowly, and is therefore less liable to
unduly scare and alarm the deer. From the earliest
institution of dog shows, classes have been provided for the deerhound, and these have resulted
in a number of excellent animals being benched of
a uniformity and quality that our excellent friend
Charles St. John would scarcely have thought

The Deerhound.

possible, and Archibald Macneill would have deemed incomprehensible.

There is no handsomer dog than the deerhound—he has the elegance of shape, the light, airy appearance of the greyhound, a hard, crisp, and picturesque jacket, either of fawn or grey brindle, an eye as bright as that of the gazelle, but loving, still sharp and intelligent; and a good specimen has not a bad feature about him. His disposition is of the best; he is sensible and kindly; and friends of mine to whom I gave a puppy, on its death refused to be consoled by any other dog than one of the same variety.

"It's a blooming lurcher," is the yokel's idea of a deerhound, an opinion in which the cockney corner man evidently coincides. Either will pass a rude remark about your aristocratic canine companion. The Scotsman away from home, be he out at elbows, or otherwise, pays compliments to the dog. If his shoes are down at the heels, the chances are he is the sole survival of a chieftain of some great clan, and, on the strength of your possession of one of his native quadrupeds, will seek to allay his thirst, or penchant for Glenlivat, at your expense. Still, I do not fancy that the deerhound is quite so popular as a companion over the border as he is on this side the border. Englishmen have paid greater attention to his breeding; the honours to be gained at shows make it worth while their doing so; and, being more difficult to rear than most other dogs, he requires greater care in bringing up, and, if not allowed continual exercise, will become crooked on his fore legs, and out at the elbows—ungainly enough in little dogs, but a terrible eyesore in big ones. They will not rear well in a kennel.

It has been said the deerhound is uncertain in his temper with children; in some cases this may be so, but not in all. Again, it has been stated that when a puppy he will chase anything that moves in front of him—sheep, poultry, &c. What puppy will not? All young dogs are alike in this particular, and if not carefully watched will, like your favourite little boy or girl, be for ever getting into mischief.

Deerhounds, like all dogs, require careful early training, and when once broken off sheep and other " small deer," are as safe and reliable in the fields as any other of the canine race. As a fact, I believe that both pointers and setters, greyhounds, and even the collie himself, is as " fond of mutton " as the often maligned dog about which this article is being written. Many dogs have been spoiled by their manners being neglected during their puppyhood; no doubt others will be so in the future, and it is a pity that one so docile, handsome, sagacious, and aristocratic as the deerhound, should obtain an evil

The Deerhound.

name through the negligence or over-indulgence of its owner.

As already stated, dog shows have been of infinite advantage in raising the deerhound to its present popularity, though prior to this epoch, what Sir Walter Scott writes of his Maida and other favourite hounds, with Landseer's fine paintings, had made the general public anxious to see such handsome hounds in the flesh. The first show at Birmingham, in 1860, provided two classes for them, but there were few entries, and both leading prizes were taken by Lieut.-Colonel Inge, of Thorpe, near Tamworth, who, at that time, possessed a capital strain of deerhounds. Later on the numbers increased, and in 1862 there were ten competitors in the dog class, but they were a mixed lot, though the winner, called Alder, bred by Sir John Macneil, was a splendid specimen, which again took leading honours two years later. The succeeding show had, for some reason or other, a capital entry, sixteen in the one class, six in the other, and these included several dogs from the Highlands, one of the latter, called Oscar, now beating Alder, who looked old and worn, and was past his best.

About this period Lord Henry Bentinck took great pride in his deerhounds, and kept a fine kennel of them. In 1870 they were sold by auction in

McDowell's rooms, Edinburgh, when sixteen hounds realised 296*l*. 16*s*. The highest figures were 50 guineas for the thirteen-year-old Factor, 40 guineas for Elshee, 30 guineas for Fury, the others bringing 30, 26, 20, and 19 guineas respectively. Mr. McKenzie, Ross-shire; Mr. J. Wright, Yeldersby House, Derby; Mr. Menzies, Chesthill; Mr. Grant, Glenmorriston; Colonel Campbell of Monzie; Mr. Wright-Omaston; Lord Boswell; Mr. W. Gordon, Guardbridge, Fifeshire; Lord Bredalbane; the Duke of Sutherland; Mr. Spencer Lucy; Mr. George Cupples, author of "Scotch Deerhounds and their Masters"; and Dr. Hadden, have at one time or another had good deerhounds in their kennels, as well as many others of the older Scottish families. The Dukes of Richmond and Gordon for generations kept a fine kennel of deerhounds, and the remnants thereof, which included a couple or two of grand old hounds, were brought from the Highlands to Aldridge's in London, where they were sold by auction in 1895, realising sorry prices, varying only from one guinea to six guineas each.

In 1869 we find a Cameron of Lochiel sending to Curzon Hall and taking a first prize with Torum, who afterwards became the property of Mr. H. C. Musters. Torum had been sent from the Highlands because he was too big for work, and Mr. Donald

Cameron was surprised at his winning, for his hound stood 32in. in height, and weighed 120lb. The following year he sent Pirate and Shellock, brother and sister to Torum, and both much better than he in symmetry as well as in work. However, size again told, as it so often does now, and Torum won once more, with Pirate second, whilst the bitch was first in her class. Sir St. George Gore was a frequent exhibitor, and in 1865 he showed a deerhound that was almost smooth, a big coarse, ugly greyhound in appearance, that of course did not take a prize. Mr. H. C. Musters, Captain Graham, of Rednock; Mr. J. H. Beasley, Northampton; Mr. G. W. Hickman, Birmingham, and a few others who admired the fine form of the Scotch hound, were exhibiting about 1870. The following year had Mr. Dawes' Warrior, who won so many prizes up and down the country, mostly in variety classes. However, prior to him came one or two exceptionally good hounds, Mr. Beasley's bitch Countess especially so; nor must Mr. Hickman's excellent dog Morni be omitted, for he was not only good to look at, but could boast a lineage which contained some of the bluest blood of the day. Indeed, it was said by many good judges that Morni was far ahead of any deerhound they ever saw, and that, even with the accident to his stern, which necessitated his retirement after three years' successes, he was good enough to beat the best. Another almost perfect deerhound was Mr. Hickman's Lord of the Isles, of whom a Cameron of Lochiel said he was beyond criticism. The head of this splendid hound is printed on the little pamphlet issued by the Deerhound Club, and which contains its rules. Unfortunately Mr. Hickman only obtained one litter of puppies by him, but of these Fingal was sire of more good hounds of one uniform type than perhaps any other dog of the variety who has succeeded him; to wit, Enterprise, Earl II., Ensign, Esquire, Rossie Blake, Brian, Bruar, Beppa, Blue Bonnet, and some few others.

Lord of the Isles, bred by Mr. H. P. Parkes, in 1875, was a grandson of Morni, and during his show career was pretty well invincible. Tara, a daughter of Cuchullin and Morna, all with Morni for their sire, were "lions" in their day; and Mr. Hickman subsequently owned Barra, Princess Marjorie, and many more, which were always well able to at any rate hold their own, at the Birmingham, London, Warwick, and other large shows where they were entered. Following a few years later was that fine old hound Bevis (Mr. Hood Wright's), so sober and sedate that in his declining years he took to the stage, and appeared with great success

The Deerhound.

at one or two of the Sheffield pantomimes at Christmas.

There are now, at least a dozen shows held annually, at which classes are provided for this variety, and naturally new breeders have sprung up. Mr. J. Harriott Bell, of Rossie, Perthshire, has got together a kennel containing a number of splendid deerhounds (this kennel was originally established by Mr. E. Weston Bell, whose untimely death was much regretted); and Mr. W. H. Singer, of Frome, Somerset; Mr. Walter Evans, Birchfield Birmingham; Mr. R. H. Wright, Frome; Mr. W. Gibbons, Stratford-on-Avon; Mr. A. Maxwell, now of Bedford, formerly of Croft, near Darlington; Major Davis, Bath; Miss Rattray, Swindon; the Duchess of Wellington; Mr. M. Goulter, Hungerford, Mr. W. C. Grew, Moseley, Birmingham; and Mr. H. Rawson, Midlothian, all possess deerhounds of the highest merit. Perhaps the best of their race during most recent years have been or are: Sir Gavin, Fingall II., Earl II., Ensign, Shepherd, Swift, Enterprise, Royal Lufra (a beautiful headed bitch, for which excellence she won a special prize at Bath a few years ago), Rossie Blue Bell, Rossie Blue Bonnet, Rossie Beppa, Selwood Morven, and Mr. Jenner's Dinah; the latter one of the old sort, not too big, abounding in character, and possessing a charming look out. And there are many others, almost if not equally good to look at, on the show bench.

The deerhound, in colour, should be either brindled in various shades, blue, or fawn; white is detrimental, though a little on the chest or feet does not matter very much. Pure white dogs are occasionally found, but it is not a deerhound colour, any more than it is that of a collie, though Mr. Morton Campbell, jun., of Stracathro, near Brechin, had a white hound of considerable beauty; it was obtained from the Highlands, and its pedigree is unknown. I prefer the darker shades of colour; the darker brindles are very attractive, and, in actual work, it is a colour that tones well with the surrounding rocks and dark heather. The largest and heaviest dogs are not to be recommended, either for work or otherwise, they cut themselves on the rocks, and are not nearly so active and lithe on the rough ground as the lighter and smaller specimens. The dog should not, at any rate, be more than about thirty inches at the shoulder, the bitch from one to two inches less. One or two specimens have been shown, and won prizes too, that measured up to thirty-two inches, and even an inch more, and it is said that Bran, figured in "Dogs of the British Isles," was thirty-three inches! At the Kennel Club's show in October, 1896, Mr. W. C. Grew showed an eighteen

The Deerhound.

months puppy called Kelso which measured $32\frac{3}{4}$ inches in height. This was certainly the best big deerhound I ever saw, for there was no coarseness about him, and he was thoroughly symmetrical, although losing somewhat in character on account of his rather light coloured eyes. He won all the prizes he could win, including one given to the best deerhound in the exhibition.

The following heights and weights of some of the best deerhounds of the modern standard may be interesting, and all are excellent specimens in every way, and perhaps equal to anything that has yet been seen. Mr. Walter Evan's Fingal II. stands $29\frac{3}{4}$ inches at shoulder, and weighs 87lb.; his Earl II., $28\frac{3}{4}$ inches and 81lb.; Duke of Brewood, $30\frac{1}{4}$ inches, weighs 88lb.; and his bitch, Enterprise, stands 29 inches, and weighs 85lb., a big weight for a bitch. Mr. W. H. Singer's well-known dog, Swift, is 79lb. weight, and 30 inches at the shoulder; and his bitch, She, weighs 72lb., and stands $26\frac{1}{2}$ inches.

> With eyes of sloe,
> And ears not low;
> With horse's breast,
> And deep in chest;
> And broad in loin,
> And strong in groin;
> And nape set far behind the head—
> These were the dogs that Fingal bred.

In general form the deerhound should be like a greyhound: ears similar, loins likewise, legs and feet equally good. In his character he differs from the smooth hound considerably, as he does in coat, which is hard, crisp, and close, not too long, whilst silkiness on the top knot, and elsewhere, is not desirable. In galloping or running he carries his head higher than a greyhound, nor does he lay himself down so closely to his work; he appears, indeed, to be on the look out for contingencies, and does not, as a rule, go at his greatest pace, unless actually required to do so. He hangs back, as it were—maybe to avoid a stroke from the stag, or to look out for the proper place to seize. One hound will seize one part, one another. " Bran's point of attack was always at the shoulder or fore leg, whilst Oscar had a habit of biting at the hind leg, above the hock, frequently cutting through the flesh and tendons in an extraordinary manner, and tumbling over the deer very quickly," says St. John in his " Highland Sports."

His endurance is great, his scent keen, and Ronaldson Macdonnel, of Glengarry, instances one hound which, held in a leash, followed the track of a wounded stag, in unfavourable rainy weather, for three successive days; then the quarry was killed. The story goes, that this stag was wounded within

The Deerhound.

three miles of Invergarry House, and was traced that night to the Glenmoriston. At dusk, in the evening, the stalkers placed a stone on each side of the last fresh print of his hoof, and another over it; and this they did each night following. On the succeeding morning they removed the upper stone, when the dog recovered the scent, and the deer was that day hunted over a great part of the Glenmoriston ground. On the third day it was retraced on to Glengarry, where a shot at close quarters brought the unprecedented drag to a conclusion.

When hunting, the deerhound runs mute, as he does when coursing, but when the stag is brought to bay, the hound opens, and by his "baying" or barking, attracts his master to the spot, where, maybe, in some pool, with a steep rock at his back, the noble monarch of the glen bids defiance to his foes.

In puppyhood, the deerhound is delicate, and difficult to rear, that scourge known as distemper carrying him off in large numbers. This is, no doubt, owing to continued inbreeding, but with our increasing knowledge of canine ailments, and some slight introduction of fresh blood, which may perhaps come through the Irish wolfhound and his Great Dane cross, the mortality is decreasing.

During 1892 a club to look after the welfare of

the deerhound was established, and issued the following description of him :

Head.—The head should be broadest at the ears, tapering slightly to the eyes, with the muzzle tapering more decidedly to the nose. The muzzle should be pointed, but the teeth and lips level. The head should be long, the skull flat, rather than round, with a very slight rise over the eyes, but with nothing approaching a stop. The skull should be coated with moderately long hair, which is softer than the rest of the coat. The nose should be black (though in some blue-fawns the colour is blue), and slightly aquiline. In the lighter-coloured dogs a black muzzle is preferred. There should be a good moustache of rather silky hair, and a fair beard.

Ears.—The ears should be set on high, and, in repose, folded back like the greyhound's, though raised above the head in excitement without losing the fold, and even in some cases, semi-erect. A prick ear is bad. A big thick ear hanging flat to the head, or heavily coated with long hair, is the worst of faults. The ear should be soft, glossy, and like a mouse's coat to the touch, and the smaller it is the better. It should have no long coat or long fringe, but there is often a silky, silvery coat on the body of the ear and the tip. Whatever the general colour, the ears should be black or dark-coloured.

Neck and *shoulders.*—The neck should be long—that is, of the length that befits the greyhound character of the dog. An over-long neck is not necessary nor desirable, for the dog is not required to stoop to his work like a greyhound, and it must be remembered that the mane, which every good specimen should have, detracts from the apparent length of neck. Moreover, a deerhound requires a very strong neck to hold a stag. The nape of the neck should be very prominent where the head is set on, and the throat should be clean-cut at the angle and prominent. The shoulders should be well sloped, the blades well back, and not too much width between them. Loaded and straight shoulders very bad faults.

Stern.—Stern should be tolerably long, tapering, and reaching to within 1½in. off the ground, and about 1½in. below the hocks. When the dog is still, dropped perfectly straight down, or curved. When in motion it should be curved, when excited in no case to be lifted out of the line of the back. It should be well covered with hair, on the inside, thick and wiry, underside longer, and towards the end a slight fringe not objectionable. A curl or ring tail very undesirable.

Eyes.—The eyes should be dark; generally they are dark brown or hazel. A very light eye is not liked. The eye is moderately full, with a soft look in repose, but a keen, far-away look when the dog is roused. The rims of the eyelids should be black.

Body.—The body and general formation is that of a greyhound of larger size and bone. Chest deep rather than broad, but not too narrow and flat-sided. The loin well arched and drooping to the tail. A straight back is not desirable, this formation being unsuitable for going up-hill, and very unsightly.

Legs and *feet.*—The legs should be broad and flat, a good broad forearm and elbow being desirable. Forelegs, of course, as straight as possible. Feet close and compact, with well-arched toes. The hind quarters drooping, and as broad and powerful as possible, the hips being set wide apart. The hind legs should be well bent at the stifle, with great length from the hip to the hock, which should be broad and flat. Cow hocks, weak pasterns, straight stifles, and splay feet very bad faults.

Coat.—The hair on the body, neck, and quarters should be harsh and wiry, and about three or four inches long; that on the head, breast, and belly is much softer. There should be a slight hairy fringe on the inside of the fore and hind legs, but nothing approaching "the feather" of a colley. The deerhound should be a shaggy dog, but not over-coated. A woolly coat is bad. Some good strains have a slight mixture of silky coat with the hard, which is preferable to a woolly coat, but the proper coat is a thick, close-lying, ragged coat, harsh or crisp to the touch.

Colour.—Colour is much a matter of fancy, but there is no manner of doubt that the dark blue-grey is the most preferred. Next comes the darker and lighter greys or brindles, the darkest being generally preferred. Yellow and sandy, red or red fawn, especially with black points, *i.e.*, ears and muzzles, are also in equal estimation, this being the colour of the oldest known strains, the M'Neil and the Chesthill Menzies. White is condemned by all the old authorities, but a white chest and white toes, occurring as they do in a great many of the darkest coloured dogs, are not so greatly objected to, but the less the better, as the deerhound is a self-coloured dog. A white blaze on the head, or a white collar, should entirely disqualify. In other cases, though passable, yet an attempt should be made to get rid of white markings. The less white the better, but a slight white tip to the stern occurs in the best strains.

Height of dogs.—From 28in. to 30in., or even more if there be symmetry without coarseness, but which is rare.

Height of bitches.—From 26in. upwards. There

can be no objection to a bitch being large, unless too coarse, as even at her greatest height she does not approach that of a dog, and, therefore, could not have been too big for work, as over-big dogs are. Besides, a big bitch is good for breeding and keeping up the size.

Weight.—From 85lb. to 105lb. in dogs; from 65lb. to 80lb. in bitches.

The club did not issue the numerical value of the various points, but I should place them as follows:

	Value.		Value.
Head and skull	15	Legs and feet	10
Eyes and ears	10	Coat	8
Neck and chest	10	Stern	5
Body, including loins	10	Colour	5
Thighs and hocks	12	General symmetry	15
	57		43

Grand Total 100.

CHAPTER IX.

THE GREYHOUND.

Not one of our British dogs has had such justice done to him by writers on canine matters as the greyhound. He has always been popular, and, being probably the oldest of his race, no doubt quite deserves all that has been said and written of him. So far back as the second century, A.rian gives us a long and painstaking work on coursing, which, in 1831 was admirably translated from the original Greek into English by George Dansey. In 1853 that great authority on the greyhound, "Stonehenge," produced his excellent and reliable work, and I fancy the latter will survive as the best of all for very many years to come.

Whether, in the first instance, our earliest dogs hunted by sight or scent I am not going to attempt to decide here. Both forms of "venerie" may have been followed at the same period; the deer and the hare hunted by sight, the wolf, stag, or other beast, by scent. The earliest coursers, dating back to what may be called the uncivilised period of our history, were assisted by nets, and then by bows and arrows, in taking the game, for at that period there were few cultivated stretches of land, free from forest, of sufficient extent to allow the long courses common at the present day. However that may be, greyhounds pretty much of the shape and form they are found now were known prior to King Canute's time, when no one of less degree than a "gentleman"—possibly a freeholder—was permitted to keep greyhounds.

Mr. Gardner Wilkinson, in his great work on Egypt, gives copies from the Egyptian monuments of dogs used in coursing being taken to the ground in slips, and loosened therefrom in the modern manner, and no pains were spared to properly train the hounds for this sport. Two of these are similar to our greyhounds, though perhaps shorter on the legs, two are more like our modern pointer or foxhound, others resemble a Borzoi or Russian wolfhound, whilst a fourth type is like a big coarse, smooth-coated Irish wolfhound. These were the hounds kept at the time of the Pharoahs. Centuries before the Christian era Xenophon had used greyhounds for coursing which had been sent by the Romans from Britain, and Ovid describes the " greedy Grewnde coursing the silly hare in fields without covert."

The Greyhound.

In the British Museum there is a fine old sculpture of two greyhounds fondling each other, and this was taken from the ruins of Antoninus, near Rome. In Dansey's translation of Arrian there is an excellent engraving of this beautiful work, and other sculptures of even an earlier period are to be found, in which the greyhound type of dog is predominant. Confined however, to the "gentleman," coursing could not become very popular, especially when even he "was not allowed to take his greyhound within two miles of a royal forest unless two of its toes were cut off." Even so late as 1853 each greyhound had a tax to pay of 22s. each, whilst other dogs, maybe of equal value, could be kept at a charge by the State of from 15s. 4d. to 8s. 2d. each.

However, still keeping to old times, we find our old sporting sovereign King John, receiving, in 1203, "two leashes of greyhounds," amongst other valuables, in return for the renewal of a grant to a certain right, and the same monarch repeatedly took greyhounds in lieu of money where fines or penalties had been incurred and forfeitures to the Crown became due. Two of these are on record, one being "five hundred marks, ten horses, and ten leashes of greyhounds;" the other "one swift running horse and six greyhounds." Thus early, we read of a brace (two) and a leash (three) of greyhounds, when ordinary hounds were known in "couples." It has been said, though there is no proof in support of the assertion, that the "Isle of Dogs," some four miles from the city of London, obtained its name from the fact that certain of our monarchs had kennels of greyhounds and other dogs there.

In the times of the earlier King Edward, Kent must have had some notoriety for the excellence of its greyhounds, for, according to Blount's "Ancient Tenures," the land owners in the manor of Setene (Sittingbourne) were compelled to lend their greyhounds, when the King went to Gascony "so long as a pair of shoes of 4*d*. price would last."

The erudite Froissart tells the following story of Richard II. which, maybe, redounds as little to the credit of the wretched sovereign as to the dog; for the one proved grossly superstitious and the other exhibited a degree of faithlessness that one does not expect to find in a hound. The king had a favourite greyhound called Mithe, his constant attendant, and so attached to his master that it would follow no one else. One day Henry, Duke of Lancaster and the king were talking together, when suddenly Mithe left his royal master and commenced to fawn upon the duke, whining and showing such pleasure as he had never before done to a stranger or even to a guest. Lancaster expressed his astonishment at the

The Greyhound.

behaviour of the greyhound, but the king said, "Cousin, this bodeth great good for you, as it is an evil sign for me. That greyhound acknowledgeth you here this day as King of England, as ye shall be, and I shall be deposed. Mithe knows this naturally, so take him; he will follow you and forsake me." And the story concludes that ever after the dog forsook the weak and vacillating Richard II., became the companion of his "cousin," and, in the end, affairs turned out as the king had prognosticated.

Henry VIII. was fond of coursing, and records are extant of his losing money therein by bets, which he made with Sir William Pickering, Lord Rochford, and others. The Royal coursing meetings sometimes took place in Eltham Park. There appears to be a peculiar fatality attending these royal attachments to the greyhound; for we have Charles I. with one as a companion. "Methinks," said he to Sir Philip Warwick, "I hear my dog scratching at the door. Let in Gipsy." Whereupon Sir Philip, who opened the door and let in the monarch's favourite, took the boldness to say: "Sire, I perceive you love the greyhound better than you do a spaniel?" "Yes," replied the King, "for they equally love their masters, and yet the hound does not flatter them so much." This unfortunate monarch met his death on the scaffold.

But let us leave such a troublous period, and at once enter upon that epoch in the history of the greyhound when he was used much in the same fashion as he is to-day. In Elizabeth's reign the first rules and regulations as to coursing were drawn up at the instance of the Duke of Norfolk, and they are very similar to those of the present day. That dog which led to the hare, won, if no other points were made; the hare had to have twelve score (?) yards law; two wrenches stood for one turn; a go-by was equal to two turns. If a dog that led and beat his opponent stood still in the field, and refused to go further he lost the course; if, by accident, a dog was run over in his course, the trial was void, and he who did the mischief had to make reparation. There were other regulations likewise, but this short summary will show how closely they approach the rules in force at the present time.

In 1776, the Earl of Orford established the Swaffham (Norfolk) Coursing Club, the earliest of its kind, and contemporary writers tell us this was the turning point in the popularity of the sport. In 1798, the club numbered twenty-four members, there being one vacancy, and in addition there were the lady patroness, the Marchioness of Townsend;

vice patroness, Countess of Cholmondeley; assistant vice patroness, Mrs. Coke, and one honorary member, the Earl of Montraith. Following Swaffham in 1780 the Ashdown Park Meeting was established by Lord Craven, Lord Sefton, and Lord Ashbrook, and this exists at the present time, and is by far the oldest established coursing meeting we possess. The Altcar Club, established in 1825, and the Ridgway Club, in 1828, still amongst the leading meetings of the year, are well supported, and appear to have a long and useful existence in front of them. Swaffham was resuscitated on more than one occasion, and in 1892, and ever since, meetings have been held there. Other old fixtures that may be mentioned were Malton, in 1781; Louth, 1806; Newmarket, 1805; Midlothian, 1811; Ardrossan, established a few years later, and, although there is no specific date given, Mr. W. F. Lamonby, the keeper of the "Stud Book" believes that the Biggar meeting was in existence prior to the present century, but like many other of the early gatherings, it has long been discontinued.

Mention has already been made of Lord Orford, a nobleman of great sporting proclivities, and of unusual eccentricities. If reliance can be placed upon the "Sportsman's Cabinet," published in 1803, and I believe there is nothing to the contrary, it contains some particulars of greyhound coursing just prior to that date that may be of interest. His lordship's bitch Czarina is said to have won forty-seven matches without being beaten. She had no puppies until about thirteen years old, when she gave birth to eight, all of which lived and coursed. The last match that Czarina ran took place when her owner, confined to the house, was supposed to be watched by an attendant. However, just as the two greyhounds were slipped, Lord Orford, looking wild as he was, and ill, came on to the field riding his piebald pony, and no one could restrain him from his anxiety to view the course and gallop after the dogs to see his favourite bitch win, which she did. The trial was barely over when Lord Orford fell from his pony, and, pitching on his head, expired almost immediately.

Afterwards his greyhounds were sold, and Czarina with the pick of the kennel purchased by Colonel Thornton, at prices ranging from thirty guineas to fifty guineas apiece. These appear to be pitiful sums when compared with the 850 guineas Fullerton produced in the sale ring in 1888, and, though the matches run by Czarina cannot be compared with the work done by the late Colonel North's crack, both having, comparatively speaking, a similar record, the two may be placed side by side.

The Greyhound.

Major Topham's pure white dog Snowball, up to the close of last century, was said to be the best greyhound yet produced, and was a cross between the Norfolk and Yorkshire strains, each equally fashionable at that time. Snowball won ten pieces of plate and forty matches, and his owner accepted every challenge that was made for him to run, irrespective of the kind of country, rough hills, abounding with fences, or otherwise. Whether the greyhounds of that day had greater staying powers than those of the present time, or were not so handy with their teeth, or the hares were stronger, we know not, but Snowball's chief performance was in a course "extending over four miles without a turn, including a hill half a mile (*sic*) in height, twice ascended." He is said to have won this trial with his sister, whom he beat, killing the hare close to Flexton. A dog like Master McGrath would have saved himself such a long trial by reason of his extraordinary skill with his teeth. Now, a greyhound must not only be fast, but a "good killer," to prove of extraordinary merit. Courses of four miles, "up and down a high hill twice," would quite preclude any modern greyhound getting to the end of a stake, when perhaps he might have four or five courses to run before being returned the winner. Major, a brother to Snowball, and both out of Czarina.

already mentioned, was said to be the faster of the two, but without the stamina of his brother; still he was successful in his matches, which at that time were much more common than they are now, when coursing meetings are more numerous.

The latter quickly attained the position they hold at the present day, for they afforded capital sport to the million at a minimum cost; they were the means of producing first-class dogs, and as now a man to keep a greyhound need not of necessity be a "gentleman," or of extraordinary means, coursing obtained a hold on the public second only to those gatherings which took place on the racecourse. Even at this time, say about 1850, the licence to keep a greyhound cost more than it did for any other dog, viz., 12s. 6d. This was an arrangement that the growing liberality of our Government soon abolished, and after various changes a greyhound has to pay but the 7s. 6d. duty, just the same as though he were a mongrel terrier. I do not know that anyone objects to this, or has hitherto looked upon the equalisation of the dog licence as specially dishonourable to those of the canine race which can lay claim to an ancient lineage.

Although a few years ago an attempt at a change in the general arrangements and conduct of

The Greyhound.

coursing meetings was made by certain private companies, who gave large prizes, and arranged stakes for which the entry fee was £25, and of which more later on, they did not shake the popularity of our great gathering—that known as the Waterloo, and run over the flats at Altcar, not far from Liverpool.

No doubt this Waterloo meeting, which was established in 1836, and has been continued yearly ever since, is the most popular one of the kind ever held—the chief prize is valued at £500, the stake being made up of entrance fees by sixty-four subscribers at £25 each. A portion of the money goes to two minor stakes, the "Plate" and the "Purse," competed for by dogs beaten in the two early rounds of the Cup. It must be stated, however, that during the first year the Waterloo Cup was an eight-dog stake; in 1837 sixteen dogs ran, and from 1838 to 1856 thirty-two dogs competed. From the latter date till now the arrangements have been as they are at present. Here, as a rule, the best dogs in England, Ireland, and Scotland compete, and for an owner of greyhounds to win "the Cup" is an honour as high as that achieved by a racing man who wins "the Derby"—the Waterloo Cup is the blue ribbon of the leash. It may be said that there is actually no cup, but the winner of the honour, in addition to the stake already mentioned, receives a silver collar which he retains until the meeting following the one at which he won the stake.

Going back not many years there are met with such well-known names as Cerito, winner of the Waterloo Cup three times when a thirty-two dog stake; Hughie Graham, Larriston, Judge, King Lear, Captain Spencer's handsome dog Sunbeam, Mr. Blackstock's Maid of the Mill, Canaradzo, Cardinal York, Sea Rock, Roaring Meg, Chloe, Mr. G. Carruthers' Meg, Brigadier, Lobelia, Sea Cove, Bit of Fashion, Miss Glendyne, Greater Scot, Herschel, Mr. Pilkington's Burnaby; Bab at the Bowster, Pretender, Chameleon, Muriel, Peasant Boy, Gallant Foe, with Coomassie (only $44\frac{1}{2}$lb. weight), the smallest greyhound that ever won the "Cup," and she did so twice. Of course there were other great greyhounds, but the blood of those above, or of many of them, will be found in the pedigrees of the most successful dogs of the present day.

The advent of Lord Lurgan's Master McGrath, as a puppy, in 1868, caused a great sensation. He was a rather coarse animal in appearance, but he could gallop faster than any dog he ever met, and was extremely "handy" with his teeth, *i.e.*, he usually

The Greyhound. 239

struck and held his hare after the first wrench or two. Thus he invariably made his courses short, while his subsequent opponents were consequently handicapped by longer trials. This son of Dervock and Lady Sarah, who was bred by Mr. Charles Galway, of Waterford, ran unchallenged through the Cup that year, and in 1869; in 1870 he was beaten by Lady Lyons (Mr. Trevor's, but running in Colonel Goodlake's nomination). The following year he succeeded in leading and beating every dog he came against, and had the honour of winning three Waterloo Cups out of four times trying— a feat which everyone thought would never be equalled.

Master McGrath was fêted; he was taken to Windsor and introduced to the Queen, money would not buy him, and he died quietly in his kennels, in Ireland, at Brownlow House, near Lurgan in December, 1871. So popular were the victories of the great Irish dog with the people generally, that it was said the advent of another Master McGrath would do more to suppress sedition in Ireland than any Land Act or Home Rule Bill any Government might offer. This celebrated greyhound was black, with a few white marks on him; he weighed only 54lb., and, as already stated, was considered to be actually invincible in the work that he had done, winning in public thirty-six courses out of thirty-seven in which he competed.

But there was the Irish dog's equal, indeed, more than his equal, to come, and in 1888 Mr. James Dent, a Northumberland courser, who had already proved very successful with his kennel, had a puppy by Greentick—Bit of Fashion, by his favourite Paris by Ptarmigan—Gallant Foe; Paris was of the same litter as Princess Dagmar, who won the Waterloo Cup in 1881. This puppy, Fullerton, believed to be exceptional in speed and cleverness, before competing in the Waterloo Cup, was purchased by Colonel North (who died in 1896), at that time entering heartily into the sport of greyhound coursing. Eight hundred and fifty guineas was the sum given for the puppy, the highest price, stated publicly, ever paid for a greyhound, though privately, it has been said, much higher sums have been obtained.

A statement appeared that one of Colonel North's dogs, Young Fullerton by Greentick—Bit of Fashion, and not sired by the dog his name would imply, had been sold by auction for 1050 guineas. This was incorrect, as the dog was not sold, and still remains in Colonel North's family. Fullerton's trials were so good that he started second favourite for the Waterloo Cup in 1889, and, as the great Irish

The Greyhound. 241

dog had done a few years before, fairly spreadeagled all comers, and ultimately divided with his kennel companion Troughend. In 1890 Fullerton won outright; he did likewise in 1891, and being kept back for the following season's Waterloo, notwithstanding an indifferent trial that he had run in public, started once more a warm favourite and eventually won his fourth great victory.

But Fullerton's historical career was not yet ended. Placed at stud his list was speedily filled at the unprecedented fee of forty guineas, his worldwide reputation being indicated from the fact that several nominations were received by cablegram from the United States. He failed as a sire, so was again put in training and reserved to appear once more on Altcar's plain for the Waterloo Cup in 1893. No greyhound of his age, which was now six years, by those best able to judge was considered to have the remotest chance of running through such a stake without defeat. Still Fullerton was so popular with the public that he again started a very great favourite. How he struggled through his first course and was beaten in his second by Mr P. B. Keating's Full Captain—running in the nomination of Captain M'Calmont—is now a matter of history, and so, almost ignominiously, did the great greyhound close his career on the coursing field. He had placed stakes to the value of £1910 to the credit of his owner.

More misfortunes than the great one at Waterloo awaited Fullerton, for in March of the same year he was lost near London, and not recovered for some days, when he was found wandering about in a half starved condition by a walking postman. The grand old dog was taken to Eltham, Colonel North's residence, and there led a happy life until the death of his gallant owner early in 1896. Later he was presented to his breeder Mr. E. Dent, is still the favourite at Short Flatt Tower, and late in the same year was on view at one of the local dog shows in Northumberland. Shortly afterwards, "Vindex," the coursing correspondent of the *Sportsman,* told us that Fullerton, when having a ramble, came across a hare, which he chased and killed, running his course as truly and well as a puppy would have done. In all, this extraordinary greyhound ran thirty-three courses in public and only sustained two defeats, they being in the final of the puppy stakes at Haydock Park, where, after being hard run, he was beaten by Greengage, owned by Mr. Gladstone, and, as above stated, in the second round of the Waterloo Cup by Full Captain. Fullerton, a brindled dog, with a little white on him, scaled about 65lb. weight when in training, and he, with Master

McGrath, form the subject of the illustration immediately preceding this chapter. I need hardly draw attention to the great difference in build and general formation of the two best greyhounds that ever ran.

It is rather difficult to compare the respective merits of these two great greyhounds, which I have mentioned at considerable length because of their unsurpassed excellence. The Irish dog was certainly the better killer; maybe not quite so fast as the Northumbrian dog, who in his 1892 Waterloo also exhibited determination and gameness that must stamp him in that particular as second to none —nor did he lack the latter quality when defeated the following year. As an old dog Fullerton did not go quite so well as when in his prime, but he was as keen as ever, if not quite so perfect in covering his game. The year of Fullerton's defeat was a rather peculiar one so far as the Waterloo Cup was concerned, for the winner proved to be Count Stroganoff's Texture, a bitch that had been purchased at Rymill's Repository for 110 guineas, when she went into the possession of her fortunate owner, who is a Russian nobleman. Thus, low prices do not always mean inferior merit, and in the same season Ruby Red, who won at Carmichael, had been purchased just before for 13 guineas.

Mr. Russel's Red Rover and Rosary, who were successful at the same gathering, had been included in a London sale, and, not reaching their reserve of thirty pounds, returned to their old kennels, where they soon far more than paid for their keep.

There was another extraordinary dog, or rather bitch, that flourished between the years 1867—1870, by many good judges considered even superior to Lord Lurgan's and Colonel North's great dogs; but she was not, though her courses were run on a greater variety of ground than were those of either of the "cracks" already mentioned. Both were, it may be said, "bottled" up for the great meetings. But Mr. Blanchard's red or fawn bitch Bab at the Bowster, by Boanerges—Mischief, when brought out went in reality as well at Altcar as she did at the Scottish National, where she won the Douglas Cup on two occasions. She also ran second for the Waterloo Cup, won the Great Scarisbrick Cup twice, and during the three years she was to the fore had sixty-two courses to her credit and losing but five. "Bab" was a handsome animal, weight 47lb., though perhaps not quite as speedy as Fullerton and Master McGrath, was quite their equal in cleverness, and well deserves her place here, for no other greyhound won so many courses in public. One celebrated performance of hers may be noted. This was at the Brigg meeting, in the Elsham Cup. Mr. Blanchard's bitch had a terrific course when running a bye, and after the trial had ended the hare got on to the railway line, and here she was run along the hard and rough "permanent way" for at least a mile before puss was killed. Although Bab at the Bowster was much exhausted when taken up, she divided the Cup next day. Some of these Lincolnshire hares were very strong, and, like those of Stranraer, Ridgway, and a few other places, often enough ran their pursuers to a standstill. Very different from those at our "inclosed meetings"!

It will be seen from what has been written that not one of this leash of celebrated greyhounds was of exceptional size. The late Colonel North's dog is the biggest of the lot. It is seldom indeed that the over-sized dog, even one so big as Fullerton, is good; he may be fast enough, but, as a rule, is awkward and ungainly when next the hare, and cannot turn in such little space as the smaller dog, who nicks in, keeps close on the scut of puss, and wins the course. Still, here, as elsewhere, a good big one will beat an equally good little one, the difficulty being to find a good big one. At the Altcar meeting in November, 1896, Mr. Leonard Pilkington ran two puppies, between which there was an extraordinary disparity in size, Pontarlier scaling 72lb. and Pescara just half that weight. Both ran well, and are, undoubtedly, high-class greyhounds.

About twelve years ago, inclosed meetings for greyhounds were inaugurated, and I believe, during the time the most important ones continued, they seldom flourished. Considerable harm was done by them to the sport of coursing. They were g te-money meetings, run in inclosures, with hares that might have been turned down "the night before the race," for anything publicly known to the contrary. Puss was sent through an opening, near to which the slipper stood; he let her get away, then slipped his dogs. The hare had, perhaps, a distance of 800 yards to go before she reached a refuge, into which her pursuers could not enter. Usually she escaped; before doing so she might be turned a few times, but a very fast hare could reach the covert without being turned or wrenched by either dog. A thousand-pound stake was to be won at one meeting, at Kempton Park, not far from London. Big prizes were also provided at Haydock Park near Liverpool, where they did their best to breed their own hares, and at Gosforth, near Newcastle. However, with the exception of that at Witham, not one of them has proved pecuniarily successful, and

The Greyhound. 247

it and the Massereene Park (Ireland) gathering are the most important of the survivors. They are, however, not encouraged by the older class of coursing men, who consider them too much like the rabbit coursing with terriers and whippets, so popular in the North of England, and affording more a test of pace than of the actual all-round merits of a greyhound.

The pedigree of the greyhound has for many years had considerable attention. The National Coursing Club, established in 1858, rules all matters appertaining thereto; and no dog can win a prize at any coursing meeting that has not been duly registered in the "Greyhound Stud Book," which costs a few shillings only, and those of "unknown pedigree" cannot compete at all.

The Council of the National Coursing Club is decided by election, those minor clubs with over twenty members each having the privilege of being represented in what may be called the coursing parliament. In 1895-6 there were forty-one members of the council.

Although a well-known coursing authority, named Thacker, started a coursing calendar about 1840-1, the present calendar was not commenced until 1857, "Stonehenge" being its first editor, and succeeding him, and until 1891, "Robin Hood" (Mr. C. M.

Browne) "occupied the chair." At his death the duty devolved upon Mr. B. C. Evelegh. of the *Field*, writing as " Allan-a-dale." The first keeper of the " Greyhound Stud Book " was Mr. D. Brown, well known as " Maida " in the columns of *Bell's Life* and the *Field* for many years. During eleven years Mr. Brown most ably conducted the registration affairs of the National Coursing Club, and his retirement, on the grounds of ill-health, is a distinct loss to the " Stud Book." Mr. W. F. Lamonby, also on the coursing staff of the *Field*, is, as I write, keeper of the " Greyhound Stud Book." For a great many years Mr. Lamonby has been, and still is, well known by his contributions written over the name of " Skiddaw."

The recent publication of the Coursing Calendar contained reports and particulars of fifty-nine meetings for the season 1894-5. From this the extent of the sport may be judged, though some years ago its popularity appeared to be seriously threatened by legislation that gave a tenant the peculiar privilege to kill ground game on the land he farmed, irrespective of agreement to the contrary with his landlord. Though hares are scarcer in some parts than they were, the sport has not, in reality, suffered very much, nor with the support it receives on all hands, is it likely to do so in the near future.

And more recent legislation, affording hares a certain close time, during which they are not to be sold, may be the means of reviving some meetings that had already become defunct.

The greyhound as a "show dog" is a failure, rather than otherwise. With few exceptions, the best animals in the field have not possessed that beautiful shape and elegance of contour that is attractive in the ring. Master McGrath was as ugly a dog to look at, from this point of view, as could be imagined; Fullerton is better, but his appearance is by no means taking. Mr. J. H. Salter has had one or two good dogs in the field that could win on the bench, though Mr. T. Ashton's Jenny Jones was, perhaps, the most notable exception to the general rule, she having been so consistent a performer as to be heavily backed for the Waterloo Cup of 1888. This, however, she failed to win, though running into the last four, when she was beaten by Herschel, a dog of great reputation in the field, and, later, at stud. As a bench bitch she was about as good as anything of her day, which has been proved under many good judges. She died in 1894. In December, 1891, Mr. H. T. Clarke, of Abingdon, made what I fancy is a record, for his black dog, Carhampton, then over three years old, won second prize at Birmingham show, and the following week ran through a nine-dog stake at the Cliffe Coursing Meeting. A most unusual occurrence, for a greyhound in condition to run is not in a fit state to compete successfully on the show bench. Another "bench winner" and good performer was Mr. H. C. While's Maney Starlight, who was first at Birmingham in 1894-5, and won a stake at Newport, Salop, early in 1896. Her sister Scandia was also a good-looking bitch, and clever likewise, she taking part in the Waterloo Cup in 1895.

Bab at the Bowster was handsome enough for exhibitions—very much the stamp of Jenny Jones,—and Lauderdale, who for a long time, when shown by Mr. T. Sharples, was perfection in shape and form, and a fast dog too, but it was said, "his heart was in the wrong place." The best show of greyhounds is usually to be seen at Darlington at the end of July, and the committee there have usually a "coursing" man to judge them.

Allusion has been made to Fullerton competing in the Waterloo Cup in his fifth season. Another old runner is Mr. J. McConnochie's Maut, who, when seven years old, ran a capital course at the Mid-Annandale Meeting in October, 1896, being unfortunate in being beaten in the second round through the hare favouring her opponent. As a rule a dog in his second season is at his best, and it is

The Greyhound.

exceptional to find one running on with any great degree of success until his fourth season.

At the present time, the spring of 1897, there are a number of particularly strong kennels of greyhounds, and none more so than that of Messrs G. F. and C. J. F. Fawcett, of Lancashire, who, during the past few years, have been peculiarly successful — as a rule with dogs of their own breeding. In 1895 they ran second in the Waterloo Cup with Fortuna Favente, Mr. Pilkington's Thoughtless Beauty being the winner; but the following year they won the trophy outright with Fabulous Fortune. In 1891 the same kennel ran up with Faster and Faster, and achieved a similar position in 1892 with Fitz Fife. In addition, they have won at all the leading meetings, and are likely for some time to come to hold a leading hand in the sport of coursing.

Mr. Leonard Pilkington, St. Helen's, is almost equally successful, he winning the Waterloo Cup in 1888 with Burnaby, and in 1895 with Thoughtless Beauty, which was, however, run in the nomination of Mr. Carruthers. In 1886 his very fast and clever bitch, Penelope II., was runner up for the cup. In his kennel there are dogs and puppies of sufficient quality to lead one to believe that his successes have not yet been exhausted. The expenses of keeping a kennel of greyhounds are very high, and, although many of the stakes to be won are valuable, coursing can only be considered an expensive amusement, and we fancy that neither Messrs. Fawcett or Mr. Pilkington, with all their successes, have made it pay. In one season—1885-6—the latter won in stakes about £1900, and this included the Kempton Park £1000 stake, which was placed to the credit of the St. Helen's courser by means of his dog Phœbus. In 1894 the same owner's stakes amounted to £1100, but in the following year they did not reach £800. But the expenses of training, railway fares, &c., would, doubtless, far more than swallow up such sums, large though they seem. I should not be at all surprised to find Mr. Pilkington's total of £1900 for the season a record one, notwithstanding the recent triumphs of Messrs. Fawcett.

In Scotland, Sir W. Anstruther, Sir R. Jardine, Mr. J. Russel, Mr. W. Patterson, and others, hold first-class dogs in their kennels. Ireland as coursers has Mr. G. J. Alexander, Mr. F. Watson, Mr. Swinburne, Captain Archdale, Mr. R. M. Douglas, and many others, most of whom have had or will have greyhounds which can hold their own anywhere. Gallant little Wales is not without her representatives, of whom the Marquis

The Greyhound.

of Anglesea and Mr. T. Jenkins, Carmarthen, may perhaps be at the head. From Russia we have had Count Stroganoff competing successfully with hounds trained and bred in this country. Other leading kennels are those of Lord Masham, Yorkshire; Hon. O. C. Molyneux, Windsor; Mr. W. H. Smith, Kidderminster; Mr. J. Trevor, Lichfield; Sir T. Brocklebank, Lancashire; Dr. J. H. Salter, Essex; Mr. R. F. Gladstone, Lancashire; Colonel Holmes, Essex; Mr. J. Quihampton, Hants; Mr. F. E. C. Dobson, Durham; Messrs. Smith, Suffolk; Sir W. Ingram, M.P., Kent; Sir Humphrey de Trafford, Lancashire; Mr. H. Brocklebank, Lancashire; Mr. G. Bell Irving, Sussex; Mr. W. Paterson, Dumfries; Mr. R. Paterson, Biggar; Mr. H. Hardy, Cheshire; Mr. R. V. Mather, Lancashire; Mr. M. G. Hale, Suffolk; Mr. T. P. Hale, Suffolk; Mr. F. Waters, Lancashire; Mr. T. Graham, Cumberland; Mr. Hamar Bass, M.P., Derby; Mr. J. Haywood, Sussex; Mr. C. E. Marfleet, Lincoln; and Messrs Reilly, Cambridgeshire.

The following are the points and description of the greyhound as compiled by "Stonehenge," and adopted generally by all coursing men at the present day.

The head should be fairly large between the ears,

the jaw lean, but by no means weak, as, if it were so, he would not be able to hold his game, and there should be little or no development of the nasal sinuses; the eye full, bright, and penetrating, a good eye is a *sine quâ non;* ears small, and folding down when at rest, but raised in semi-prick fashion when animated; teeth strong and the mouth level (many of the show greyhounds are overshot, which gives the dog an extra long and smartly cut jaw); neck fairly long and a trifle arched rather than otherwise.

The shoulders must be well placed, as oblique as possible; the chest fairly deep, and as wide as may be consistent with speed. A "narrow-fronted," shallow-chested greyhound is no use. There should be good length from the elbow to the knee, compared with that from the knee to the ground. Feet hard and close, not so round and cat-like as in the foxhound, and with the toes well defined or well developed.

The loins strong and broad; back powerful, and, in the speediest and best dogs, slightly arched.

Hind quarters very muscular; stifles strong and well bent—a straight stifled dog cannot gallop; hind legs well turned and shapely, and, as in all speedy animals, somewhat long, looking by their curve even longer than they actually are; the tail

The Greyhound.

is generally fine and nicely curved, but some strains carry more hair than others.

Colours vary—blacks, brindles, reds, fawns, blues, or slates, and these colours mixed with white. One hue is as good as another, though white is considered indicative of a certain amount of weakness— still there have been good dogs almost pure white, Snowball, Scotland Yet, and Canaradzo to wit.

In disposition the greyhound is, as a rule, kindly and amiable; dogs in high training are apt to be unreliable, and during exercise may fight and seriously injure each other.

The following are the points:—

	Value.		Value.
Head and eyes	10	Hind quarters	20
Neck	15	Feet	15
Chest and fore quarters	20	Tail	5
Loin and back ribs	15	Colour	0
	60		40

Grand total, 100.

Weights vary, and, as already stated, a competitor at a meeting in 1896 had two puppies running, one of which weighed 72lb., the other but 36lb., and yet both went fast and approached the end of stakes. The smallest bitch to win the Waterloo Cup was Coomassie, who scaled 44lb., and we doubt if a heavier dog than Fullerton, who weighed 66lb., ever won the great prize. Thus, a greyhound may weigh anything between 36lb. and 75lb.

The points of the course are as follows :—

Speed: which shall be estimated as one, two, or three points, according to the degree of superiority shown. The *go-by:* Two points, or, if passed in the outer circle, three points. The *turn:* one point. The *wrench:* half a point. The *kill:* two points, or, in a descending scale, in proportion to the degree of merit displayed in that kill, which may be of no value. The *trip*, or unsuccessful effort to kill, or where a greyhound flecks the hare and cannot hold her, one point. There are also penalties for refusing to fence; where a dog, from his own defect, refuses to follow the hare at which he is slipped ; and where he stands still.

Of course, in dealing with a trial between two greyhounds, very much rests with the judge, and there is no doubt that the two judges of the generation are Mr. G. Warwick, who officiated at Waterloo for thirteen consecutive years, and his successor, Mr. James Hedley, who, since Mr. Warwick's retirement, has done duty at the same meeting for twenty-three years without a break. Almost as much depends upon the slipper, and after the celebrated Tom Raper, who died in 1893, and who was *par excellence* in his line for a quarter of a century, T. Wilkinson followed him, and now T. Bootiman is the leading exponent of this arduous and difficult department of greyhound coursing.

A good many greyhounds have from time to time been shipped to America and to many of our colonies, but coursing of late has not made any great headway outside Great Britain. In Australia at one time it seemed progressive; there was a "Waterloo Cup" run for, and at great expense hares were imported from this country, the trials taking place in enclosed grounds. I believe a great deal of money was expended in promoting the sport, which, although of a high class, was ultimately allowed to lapse. As a fact, the Colonists did the thing so well at the commencement that their Waterloo Cup was worth as much as ours, and they had Mr. G. Warwick, our crack judge at that time, over to officiate at the inaugural meeting, which took place in 1874, and at other meetings which took place later on. However, the importation of greyhounds was beneficial, inasmuch as their crosses enabled the colonists to produce a strong, heavily-made, fleet-footed dog, very useful in kangaroo hunting; indeed, a variety of the canine race which is perhaps of more use than any other in the Antipodes.

Although greyhound coursing has never made great headway on the Continent, meetings of a semi-

S

private nature are periodically held in France, at which one of our best English judges, Mr. Brice, officiates. He has also been invited to St. Petersburg and Moscow for a similar purpose, and there he has had his duties varied by being asked to give his opinion on the trials of Russian hounds, Borzoi, when slipped to the common wolf of the country. It need scarcely be stated here that in Russia the sport of coursing is only participated in by the princes and nobles, with which that country abounds, and whose wealth is prodigious.

CHAPTER X.
THE WHIPPET.

WITH, I believe few exceptions, the whippet or snap dog has not been included as a distinct variety in any book on English dogs. Still, it is now, and has been for some time, quite a variety of itself, and amongst the colliers and other working men in the north of England, including Lancashire and Yorkshire, none is so popular or provides so much amusement.

Originally the "whippet" was a small dog—a cross between the Italian greyhound and some terrier or other, partaking in general appearance more of the greyhound cross than of the terrier. Thus, in many parts of the north, the dog is still called an "Hitalian," the local pronunciation of the name of that country from which it is supposed the fragile toy dog first came. He is also known as a "running" dog, the reason for which will be obvious, and is likewise called a "snap" dog because of his ability to snap or hold quickly and smartly a rabbit or any other small animal.

The whippet in perfection is a miniature greyhound, built on the lines of a Fullerton or of a Bab at the Bowster, but smaller in size. It is kept specially for running races and for coursing rabbits on enclosed grounds arranged for the purpose, and for which it undergoes a course of training suitable to the circumstances. These coursing and running matches may be considered the popular pastime amongst a very large class in the mining and manufacturing districts northwards in the neighbourhood of Newcastle, in Durham, Lancashire, and Yorkshire especially.

Several attempts have recently been made to extend the popularisation of the whippet, especially so far as its running powers are concerned. The Kennel Club, for the first time in 1892, gave it an entry in the Stud Book, and classes have been provided for it at several south country shows. Such had repeatedly appeared in the catalogues at Darlington and elsewhere in the north, but they seldom filled satisfactorily, and as a "bench dog" I need scarcely say the whippet is not likely to be any greater success than the greyhound. The entries made in the Stud Book are few, and most of the dogs there are minus a leading part of their history—namely, their pedigrees.

About the time the Kennel Club acknowledged

The Whippet.

the whippet, attempts were made to form clubs with more or less "tone" about them to encourage dog racing, but none of them got beyond an initial stage, although they were no doubt considerably assisted by the publication by Mr. L. U. Gill, of Freeman Lloyd's "Whippet or Race Dog," a very complete compendium of all that appertained to that dog and its sport. Then at the Ladies' Kennel Association show in 1895, held in the Ranelagh Club grounds, whippet racing formed one of the attractions (?). It, however, fell flat, and generally the attempt to popularise this sport with the better class of people in the south of England has, to say the least, not been a success. Its surroundings have not, as a rule, been of the highest in the social scale, nor have the rabbit coursing matches and tests of speed always been conducted by its owners in the fairest way possible.

Various tricks are tried by the unscrupulous to prevent an opponent's dog winning, and a trainer or his friend has to be a sharp man in his line, to run successfully the gauntlet of all that is placed in his way during a match for money where such dogs compete. And it must be confessed that, notwithstanding the fairness, honesty, and firmness of the owners of the enclosed grounds where dog races and coursing take place, and of the umpires and referees, the general spirit of the sport is not the most wholesome in the world. Of course, these remarks are not applicable to all owners of whippets —many of whom are as straightforward and good sportsmen as ever owned a dog — but there can be no doubt that the popularity of the variety has been kept back and will continue to be so by those "black sheep" to whom allusion is made.

As I have said, the whippet ought not to be a big dog, weighing, from 12lb. to, say, about 25lb. when in training. However, some of them are much heavier than this, and many of the so-called champion rabbit coursers reach 40lb. in weight or even more. I have known a thoroughbred greyhound take part in one of the big handicaps that are held during the season in the neighbourhood of Manchester and elsewhere. It scarcely remains for me to say that these bigger dogs are the direct cross with the greyhound, and some of them are built on such lines, and contain so much greyhound blood, as to be scarcely distinguishable from the real article.

Such animals are fast, clever with their teeth, and oftener than not run straight into their rabbit, "holding" it without a turn, the one that does so winning the trial, irrespective of the capacity it shows for working, turning, or making the points as in coursing hares. The law allowed varies from anything between 30 and 70 yards, and directly the rabbit is dropped the dogs are slipped, the latter being done by a skilful man, specially appointed for the purpose. Handicaps are made according to the weight or height of the dog; in Newcastle-on-Tyne and the surrounding districts, the latter being the custom—the dog being measured from the top of the shoulder blade to the pad of the foot—whilst in Lancashire and Yorkshire handicap by weight is preferred. In all cases a dog has to allow a bitch three yards start. These customs or rules likewise apply to dog racing, as dealt with later on. In some of the more important handicaps, each couple of dogs, as they are drawn together, have to compete the best out of five or even more courses. In minor affairs, one rabbit for each trial is made to suffice.

Private matches between two dogs are frequently run, and such often enough create as much interest as the handicaps, notably when two "cracks" are competing. Here the conditions may vary somewhat, the start given the rabbit being specially named, and the number of courses being usually the best of twenty-one, or, perhaps, of thirty-one; a certain interval, generally five minutes, being allowed between each trial.

However, if the whippet is to become generally

popular, it will not be by means of an ability to kill rabbits. The dog racing by him will be more likely to find favour with the public. Those who are not connected with the sport will be surprised to find the hold it has obtained amongst the working classes in the north. There are repeatedly from one hundred and fifty to over three hundred such dogs entered at one competition, the trial heats of which, three dogs taking part in each heat, being run as a rule one Saturday, the finals the Saturday following. This day is a half-holiday with the miners and workpeople, hence its selection, but other meetings are held on the recognised Bank holidays, and sometimes on the Monday.

Dogs of all sizes compete in the same stake, they being handicapped according to height or weight, if unknown; otherwise according to their performances, weight, &c., of course, likewise being taken into consideration. The most useful size of the whippet is, probably, a dog scaling about 20lb. or so, and the pace such an one can go for a comparatively short distance is extraordinary, 200 yards having been covered in $12\frac{1}{2}$ seconds. It is generally considered that a dog about 15lb. is the speediest animal in proportion to its weight.

Before these dogs have attained sufficient proficiency to take part in a handicap or match, they must undergo a certain tuition, during which they come to run at their greatest speed. All preliminaries being arranged, the dog makes an appearance at one of the many "running" grounds. Here a course is laid out on the cinder path, the distance usually being 200 yards. At one end the various handicaps are marked out, three dogs start in a heat, and each, as in ordinary pedestrianism, has a side allotted to it by draw or otherwise. The starter is behind the dogs, pistol in hand. A friend of the owner holds his dog on the mark, the owners or trainers run in front of their dogs up the course calling to them, and dangling something attractive—a chicken's or pigeon's wing, perhaps, or a piece of rag, a towel or an old shirt; rabbits and live stock are not allowed. These owners or trainers having reached the limit of the course, the pistol is fired, the dogs are slipped, and at their full pace urge on to the goal where their trainers await them. Near there the judge is placed, who quickly and promptly pronounces which dog wins, and so the fun goes on. The rules are stringent to a degree, as all rules ought to be (subject even to no appeal in a court of law), and any man slipping his dog before the pistol is fired is disqualified, not only for that heat, but for the whole stake. The sport is exciting enough, and if it does not attract the thousands that gather to see the "final" of a Sheffield handicap, the attendance is usually quite large enough to be pleasant. I need scarcely say that the training of these running dogs is made a "profession," and a skilled man is well paid for his work.

There are dogs that will not run these races to the best of their ability, some preferring to have a growl or fight with an opponent; others, more kindly disposed, seeking to romp and play. To guard against such canine breach of discipline, an arrangement can be made by erecting long strips of canvas, and between each strip a dog runs, thus quite out of sight of its opponent, until the judge and goal are reached. This plan is frequently adopted, as some of the very best animals, after competing repeatedly under the ordinary system, become either careless or quarrelsome, and refuse to "try," contenting themselves by running alongside an antagonist, and losing the race by a head, and the owner's weekly wage and more at the same time.

Some time ago, Mr. T. Marples wrote an exhaustive article on coursing and running by whippets. He says that "at times, especially in winter, when snow has to be cleared from the ground which is harder than usual, many of these dogs run in what are called 'stoppers'—leather gloves that are placed over the claws of the fore feet, the latter being apt to be injured by the suddenness with which the dogs stop at the end of the race." These are, of course, only required where the racing is done on a cinder-path, and would be quite out of place on grass during rabbit coursing.

As to handicapping, the same writer tells us that as a rule a dog 15lb. weight is taken as the basis of the handicap, and he is given or takes three yards, according to size, irrespective of the allowance for sex alluded to earlier on. However, when the dogs "reach about 27lb. in weight, they are pretty much equalised, just as an increase is given to small dogs down to about 8lb. in weight. For instance, a dog of 15lb. would give one of 14lb. three yards start; but one of 13lb. would receive seven yards from the 15lb. dog, and in all likelihood a 10lb. dog would receive from eighteen to twenty yards in the two hundred. Then, in turn, the 15lb. dog would receive three yards from the 16lb animal, and from one up to 20lb. the 15lb dog would receive ten or twelve yards start," irrespective, of course, of penalties for previous successes. Novices are usually given an advantage of about 2lb.

The above seems a somewhat complicated arrangement, but it is thoroughly understood by the handicappers.

I need scarcely say that these whippets when in

training are fed on the best food that can be provided; they are kept warm, sleep in the house in a cosy corner, and are muzzled and sheeted when outside. Their owners are for the most part working men, and instances are not isolated where their wives and children have gone with empty stomachs, whilst the dogs and their masters regale on rump steaks and chops cut from a leg of mutton.

Perhaps it may be mentioned that during the past twenty years or so the sport with "running dogs" and "rabbit coursers," as conducted in the north, has flourished amazingly, and personally I regret that it has done so to the detriment of the more manly pedestrian exercises, wrestling, and the clever game of knur and spell.

The points and general description of the whippet are, excepting so far as size is concerned, identical with those of the greyhound as they appear on a preceding page, though occasionally comparatively rough coated or wire-haired whippets are met with. Such, of course, show breeding back to the wire-haired terrier, or perhaps to some cross-bred "lurcher," a few of which are still kept for poaching purposes in various parts of the country. Need I mention that for rabbit coursing staying power as well as pace is required in a whippet, whilst for racing speed alone is the desideratum.

CHAPTER XI.
THE IRISH WOLFHOUND.

SOME there are who believe that this historical hound became extinct soon after the last wolf was killed in Ireland, which happened in 1710. Others hold the opinion that it never became extinct at all; but survives in the Scotch deerhound, with which they say it was identical. A third division have equally strong opinions, something between the two, which are to the effect that so recently as eighty or ninety years ago very few real Irish wolfhounds remained, and these not readily traceable back to the oldest strains; and some advocate the smooth greyhound as the true article. Then, to complicate matters still further, the Great Dane has become mixed up in the controversy, and one great authority has stated that the original wolfhound, or the dog from which he sprang, was brought over to Ireland in the sixth century, B.C., by the Celts, during their migration from the shores of the Black Sea. It has also been urged that the wolfhound and the Great

Dane, as we know them now, had a common origin, and that they were the foundations of the mastiffs and other large dogs which, at a later period, had in a measure made Great Britain famous for its powerful and ferocious varieties of the canine race. Many authorities of the past generation write to prove that the Irish wolfhound, if not a Great Dane, was a smooth-coated creature very like him; and additional evidence that such was the case is to be found in the following instance.

Some eight or nine years ago, I was shown by the Earl of Antrim a life-sized painting of an enormous hound which had been in his family for about a hundred years. Through generations this had been handed down as a true Irish wolfhound, a noble creature that had saved the life of one of his lordship's ancestors under peculiar and extraordinary circumstances, so the faithful creature had its portrait painted. Now this dog was a huge southern hound in appearance, marked like a modern foxhound, with long pendulous ears, possibly an animal identical with the *mâtin* of old writers. The painting, which I believe is in the Kennel Club, gives the idea that the subject had, in life, stood about thirty-four inches high at the shoulders.

It was but natural, when I introduced this interesting discovery to the public through the columns of the *Field*, that discussion and controversy thereon would arise, and such was the case. Little new material as to the history of the Irish dog was elicited, and it was to be regretted that Lord Antrim could afford no further particulars as to the animal to which attention was first drawn.

The following is one of the many stories extant of the Irish wolfhound " at home." " In the mountainous parts of the county Tyrone, some time in the sixteenth century, the inhabitants suffered much from the wolves, and gave from the public fund so much for the head of one of these animals. There lived an adventurer, who, alone and unassisted, made it his occupation to destroy these ravagers. The time for attacking them was long after dark, and midnight was fixed upon for doing so, as that was their wonted time for leaving their lairs in search of food, when the country was at rest and all was still; then, issuing forth, they fell on their defenceless prey, and the carnage commenced. There was a species of dog for the purpose of hunting them called the wolf dog; the animal resembled a rough, stout, half-bred greyhound, but was much stronger. In the county Tyrone there was then a large space of ground inclosed by a high stone wall, having a gap at each of the two opposite extremities, and in this were secured the flocks of the surrounding farmers.

Still, secure though this fold was deemed, it was entered by the wolves, and its inmates slaughtered. The neighbouring proprietors having heard of the noted wolf hunter above mentioned, by name Rory Carragh, sent for him, and offered the usual reward, with some addition, if he would undertake to destroy the two remaining wolves that had committed such devastation. Carragh, undertaking the task, took with him two wolf dogs and a little boy twelve years of age, the only person who would accompany him, and repaired at the approach of midnight to the fold in question. 'Now,' said Carragh to the boy, 'as the two wolves usually enter the opposite extremities of the sheepfold at the same time, I must leave you and one of the dogs to guard this one, while I go to the other. He steals with all the caution of a cat, and you will not hear him, but the dog will, and will give him the first fall. If, therefore, you are not active enough when he is down to rivet his neck to the ground with this spear, he will rise and kill both you and the dog. So good night.' 'I'll do what I can,' said the little boy, as he took the spear from the wolf-hunter's hand.

"The boy immediately threw open the gate of the fold, and took his seat in the inner part, close to the entrance, his faithful companion crouching at his side, and seeming perfectly aware of the dangerous business he was engaged in. The night was very dark and cold, and the poor little boy, being benumbed with the chilly air, was beginning to fall into a kind of sleep, when at that instant the dog, with a roar, leaped across, and laid his mortal enemy upon the earth. The boy was roused into double activity by the voice of his companion, and drove the spear through the wolf's neck as he had been directed, at which time Carragh appeared, bearing the head of the other."

One might have expected to find something reliable and convincing as to what the Irish wolfhound really was in the "Sportsman's Cabinet," published in 1803. Here we have an excellent engraving from a picture by Reinagle, of a huge dog, an enormous deerhound in fact, the identical creature popular reputation stated such a dog to be. Unfortunately the letterpress describes quite a different animal— more of the Great Dane type than of the deerhound. And so the authorities who wrote at the time differed quite as much on the matter as do the admirers of the variety at the present time.

To Captain G. A. Graham, of Dursley, Gloucestershire, we owe considerable gratitude for the trouble he has taken to resuscitate the Irish wolfhound. Enthusiast though he be, he is not like so many other

T

enthusiasts, led away to say things he cannot prove, or, indeed, to lay claim to his hounds being descended in a direct line from those animals which may have or may not have killed the last wolf near Dingle over 200 years ago. The gallant gentleman acknowledges that the breed in its original integrity has disappeared, but he believed, when first writing on the subject twenty years since, that so much of the true strain remained that, with the aid of the modern deerhound, and with judicious management, the breed in its "pristine grandeur" could be recovered.

The difficulty, to my mind, would be to exactly define the original Irish wolfhound. The popular idea—and this is not always correct—was of a big powerful dog, with a wire-haired or rough coat, built on the lines of a deerhound, but altogether a heavier and stronger animal. What height a full-grown specimen should be there is a diversity of opinion. Old writers have said he was as big as a donkey; others that he stood from 36 inches to 40 inches at the shoulders. In the museum of the Royal Dublin Society there are two skulls of wolf-hounds dug out of barrows by the late Dr. Wilde. The dimensions of them have been very useful to those who believed in the bigness of the wolf-hound. Unfortunately for the side of the latter,

The Irish Wolfhound.

these skulls, when carefully measured and compared with others of living dogs, deerhounds, wolfhounds, and greyhounds, could not have been possessed by animals more than 29 inches high at the shoulders.

However, it is not my province here to say what kind of an animal the historical Irish deerhound was, whether there were two, three, or four varieties, or whether any dog that would tackle and hunt a wolf was from the moment he did so called a wolfhound. This would only be similar to that which occurs in our own days; for have we not the ordinary foxhound called a staghound or a buckhound when he is entered to hunt the deer?

Mr. G. W. Hickman, of Birmingham, has written most exhaustively and carefully on the subject on one side; so have Mr. H. Richardson, Captain G. A. Graham, Mr. R. D. O'Brien, Limerick, and others on another side. I have to deal with "Modern Dogs," and so the wolfhound, as he is now resuscitated, must be described by me. There is no doubt that by careful crossing between certain dogs obtained from Ireland about 1841 with the deerhound and the Great Dane, an animal of a certain distinctive type has been obtained, which, in its turn, breeds perhaps quite as truly, up to a certain standard, as most other canine varieties. Captain

G. A. Graham, who must be said to be the chief supporter of the modern variety, says that his own strain "he can trace back to those had by Richardson in 1841-42, though not beyond 1862 from father to son. He says the breed had been kept up by Mr. Baker, of Badylohm Castle, and Sir John Power, of Kilfane, from 1840 to 1865, or thereabouts. He further says that on good grounds it was believed that "these dogs were descended from Hamilton Rowan's so called, last of his race, Bran by name, a fine dark grey, rough hound, that was his constant companion." Captain G. A. Graham had a grandson of Kilfane Oscar, a dog he obtained from Sir Ralph Payne-Gallwey, and from this he traces the purity of the blood as far back as it will go. He advocated a cross with the Great Dane and deerhound, and latterly, on the popularisation of the Borzoi, or Russian wolfhound, has suggested a third cross with that variety.

Some of the Irish wolfhounds seen at modern exhibitions are extremely fine animals, docile and quiet as they recline on their benches, and by no means quarrelsome, evidently quite contented with their lot. Indeed, they possess an excellent reputation as companions, especially such as are not the first cross between the two modern varieties already alluded to. I think it was at Brighton show in

1895, that Mr. W. K. Angelo showed a particularly fine " Irish wolfhound," Goth II., who stood 34 inches at the shoulders, and weighed 134lb. at eighteen months old. An extremely handsome hound this, which, on inquiry, I found had the Borzoi Korotai for his grandsire on one side, and besides he included deerhound and Irish wolfhound blood. In addition his grandsire, on his dam's side, was an imported " Siberian wolf dog or sheep dog." This hound, and others of the same strain in Mr. Angelo's kennels, have been and are used successfully in Scotland for coursing deer.

Never having been the fortunate possessor of any Irish wolfhounds, and being desirous of obtaining the best information about them as companions, I wrote to a friend who at times had kept two or three of them, and who would gladly give me his opinion. That friend says the Irish wolfhound is very good with children, is the best domestic pet of any big dog, and none more useful in a quiet country place. He never had a case of anyone being bitten by his Irish dogs, though, from their size and appearance, they are a great deterrent to bad characters and the tramping fraternity generally. Some of the strains that contain the Great Dane first cross are not quite of the same disposition as the others, being not nearly so dignified in their demeanour, and inclined to steal whenever an opportunity is afforded them so to do. They are exuberantly affectionate, seldom at rest a moment, but still not quarrelsome. The finer strains are generally more lethargic, stately, and sedate; strong in their attachments to an individual, and extremely quiet and good-tempered with other dogs; the latter often approaching to softness. Still, when roused and angry, they can give a good account of themselves, and punish their enemy severely. In no degree are they quarrelsome for they are quite as reliable in temper as the modern deerhound.

This is not a bad character for a dog that one requires to be an every-day companion either in town or country; and certainly, so far as I have studied and noticed the variety, I must agree with the excellent testimonial the Irish wolfhound receives from one who has kept him for half a generation.

This dog has been recommended as likely to be useful with "big game," not elephants and hippopotami, but with wolves, hyenas, and such inferior animals as are to be found in South Africa and other great hunting countries. Whether they would do so well as either the pure Dane or the Deerhound is an open question. They are not sufficiently smart and active to cope successfully with powerful beasts of prey, though perhaps, if brought up to the work and at an early age trained to hunt, they would be able to do as well as any other breed of dog. But it is folly for a young fellow to obtain a hound of any of these varieties—Great Dane, deerhound, or Irish wolfhound—from some of the show kennels, rush him over to the Cape, or into the interior of Africa, and expect him to take as kindly to hunt " the king of the forest " or the leopard as he would to accepting a biscuit from the hand of some fair mistress. An Irish wolfhound requires to be properly entered to game just as carefully as do the pointer, setter, and retriever; and generations passed in kennels or in the drawing-room have no tendency to improve him as a destroyer of wild animals when they come in his way.

A modern Irish wolfhound is in appearance just a big and rather coarse deerhound, and, previous to giving his description as drawn up by the Wolfhound Club, the following statistics of the height and weight of some of the best specimens will perhaps not be without interest:—Captain G. A. Graham's Brian, figured in " Dogs of the British Isles," stood $30\frac{1}{2}$ inches at the shoulder, and weighed 128lb.; Dhulart was 31 inches at the shoulder and 126lb. weight; Banshee, $29\frac{3}{4}$ inches and 101lb. weight; Mask, $30\frac{1}{4}$ inches, and 106lb. weight; Tara, 29 inches and about

100lb.; Fintragh, 29¾ inches, and 110lb. weight. Colonel Garnier showed a particularly fine young dog at the Kennel Club's Show at Islington in 1888, which unfortunately died soon after the exhibition. The hound, called Merlin, stood 33 inches at the shoulders, and, though unfurnished, scaled 150lb. He was fawn in colour, and undoubtedly the finest specimen of the race I have seen or has yet appeared at any of our shows. Already have I referred to Mr. Angelo's Goth II., who at eighteen months old measured 34 inches at the shoulder, and scaled 134lb. Another hound of Mr. Angelo's, called Torrum, and who has killed several deer, is 33 inches at the shoulders; whilst Mr. Trainor's Thuggum Thu, shown at the Kennel Club's Show in October, 1896, was quite 34 inches in height, and a well-made dog, too, but, like all of his cousins, inclining very much to the deerhound type. Another very good specimen is Mr. Crisp's Bran, bred by the Earl of Caledon, and standing 33 inches at the shoulder. He is a steel brindle in colour, but, unlike Thuggum Thu, who inclines to the deerhound, shows his Great Dane descent, though in jaw and other particulars he excels. Perhaps a better bitch has never been shown than Captain Graham's Sheelah, described by one admirer of the variety as the best bitch he ever saw. She was about 30 inches at the shoulders,

The Irish Wolfhound.

wheaten in colour, with a few black hairs intermingled, and with black points, and showed neither undue deerhound or Great Dane blood. Moreover, she proved an excellent brood bitch, being dam of Dhuart and Mr. Hood Wright's Starno, both excelling in type, which is so difficult to find in the present generation.

It is rather unfortunate that so fine a dog has not attracted popular fancy. Had it done so, there would have been as much a run on the Irish wolfhound as there has been on other and perhaps less deserving varieties. The club to look after its interests is fairly successful, but there is a sad lack of enterprise amongst the general public. Even the natives of the Emerald Isle themselves have refused to answer the call, although, in the national emblem of Erin, an Irish wolfhound is lying beside the harp, and, as a rule, the prizes at Dublin for the national breed of dogs are swept away by the Saxon invader. Their terrier they patronise, but neglect the wolfhound and the Kerry beagle. Had it not been for a Scotsman, Captain G. A. Graham, this canine relic of a mighty race might even now be extinct. To prevent its becoming so, earnest admirers of the dog, such as he, with the Hon. Miss Dillon; Colonel Garnier; Mr. W. K. Angelo, Brighton; the Earl of Caledon; Mr. Hood Wright, Frome; the

Rev. H. L. O'Brien, Limerick; Mr. Bailey; Mr. G. E. Crisp; Mr. Playford, Ipswich; Mr. J. Trainor, Liscard; Mr. Williams, Llangibby; Mr. W. Allen, Cardiff; and some few others, do their best, and usually possess some few specimens of the article as genuine as it can be obtained. Most of the bigger shows provide classes for Irish wolfhounds, but the competition therein is never strong, and the chief prizes are usually taken by one or other of the gentlemen to whom allusion has been made.

The following is the description of the variety as drawn up by the Club:

1. *General appearance.* — The Irish wolfhound should not be quite so heavy or massive as the Great Dane, but more so than the deerhound, which in general type he should otherwise resemble. Of great size and commanding appearance, very muscular, strongly though gracefully built; movements easy and active; head and neck carried high; the tail carried with an upward sweep, with a slight curve towards the extremity. The minimum height and weight of dogs should be 31in. and 120lb.; of bitches, 28in. and 90lb. Anything below this should be debarred from competition. Great size, including height at shoulder and proportionate length of body, is the desideratum to be aimed at, and it is desired to firmly establish a race that shall average from

The Irish Wolfhound. 283

32in. to 34in. in dogs, showing the requisite power, activity, courage, and symmetry.

2. *Head.*—Long, the frontal bones of the forehead *very* slightly raised, and *very* little indentation between the eyes. Skull, not too broad. Muzzle, long and moderately pointed. Ears, small and greyhound-like in carriage.

3. *Neck.*—Rather long, very strong and muscular, well arched, without dewlap or loose skin about the throat.

4. *Chest.*—Very deep. Breast, wide.

5. *Back.* — Rather long than short. Loins, arched.

6. *Tail.*—Long and slightly curved, of moderate thickness, and well covered with hair.

7. *Belly.*—Well drawn up.

8. *Fore-quarters.*—Shoulders muscular, giving breadth of chest, set sloping. Elbows well under, neither turned inwards nor outwards. *Leg.*—Forearm muscular, and the whole leg strong and quite straight.

9. *Hind-quarters.*—Muscular thighs, and second thigh long and strong as in the greyhound, and hocks well let down and turning neither in nor out.

10. *Feet.*—Moderately large and round, neither turned inwards nor outwards. Toes well arched and closed. Nails, very strong and curved.

11. *Hair.*—Rough and hard on body, legs, and head; especially wiry and long over eyes and under jaw.

12. *Colour and markings.*—The recognised colours are grey, brindle, red, black, pure white, fawn, or any colour that appears in the deerhound.

13. *Faults.*—Too light or heavy a head, too highly arched frontal bone; large ears and hanging flat to the face; short neck; full dewlap; too narrow or too broad a chest; sunken or hollow or quite level back; bent fore-legs; overbent fetlocks; twisted feet; spreading toes; too curly a tail; weak hindquarters, cow hocks, and a general want of muscle; too short in body.

CHAPTER XII.

THE BORZOI OR RUSSIAN WOLFHOUND.

THERE is no dog of modern times that has so rapidly attained a certain degree of popularity as that which is named at the head of this chapter. A dozen years ago it was comparatively unknown in England; now all well-regulated and comprehensive dog shows give a class or classes for him, which are usually well filled, and cause quite as much interest as those for our own varieties. Indeed, the Borzoi is a noble hound, powerful and muscular in appearance, still possessing a pleasant and sweet expression, that tells how kindly his nature is. He is one of the aristocratic varieties of the canine race, and the British public is to be congratulated on its discernment in annexing him from the Russian kennels, where, too, his reputation is of the highest.

In the early days of our dog shows, Borzois, then known as Siberian and Russian wolfhounds, and by other names, too, occasionally appeared on the benches. Most of them were similar in type to those we see now, and no doubt have a common origin with the ordinary Eastern or Circassian greyhounds, occasionally met with in this country. But the latter were usually smaller and less powerful than their Russian relative. According to the "Kennel Club Stud Book" a class for "Russian deerhounds" was provided at the National dog show held at the Crystal Palace in 1871. This was not the case, but a foreign variety class was composed almost entirely of Russian hounds, and one of them, Mr. S. T. Holland's Tom won the first prize. Lady Emily Peel and Mr. Macdona were exhibitors at the same show.

It will be nearly thirty years since the Czar of Russia presented the Prince of Wales with a couple of his favourite hounds, Molodetz and Owdalzka. These his Royal Highness exhibited on more than one occasion, and bred from them likewise, Mr. Macdona having presented to him one of the puppies. History repeated itself when in 1895 H.R.H. the Princess of Wales was presented with a splendid hound called Alex, from the Czar's kennels, which has met with a considerable amount of success at several leading shows. In 1872 Mr. Taprell Holland showed an excellent hound in the variety class at Birmingham, for which he obtained a prize. Even before this, specimens of the

Borzoi (sometimes called Siberian Wolfhounds) were met with on the benches at Curzon Hall. In 1867, Mr. J. Wright, of Derby, had one called Nijni; and three years later the same exhibitor benched an excellent example of the race in Cossack, a grandson of Molodetz, already mentioned as having belonged to the Prince of Wales, and being from the Imperial kennels. Perhaps the earliest appearance of all on the bench was in 1863, when the then Duchess of Manchester showed a very big dog of the variety at Islington, and bred by Prince William of Prussia. I have the authority of Captain G. A. Graham for stating that this hound was 31 inches at the shoulders, quite equal in size, as he was in power, to some of the best specimens now on our shores.

Thus, after all, this fine race of dog is not quite such a modern institution in our country as would be imagined, though the earlier strains, I fancy, must have been lost, possibly on account of the inter-breeding consequent on an inability to obtain a change of blood. Communication between the eastern and western divisions of Europe is now much more rapid and easier of accomplishment than in the early days of dog shows.

Advancing a few years, Lady Charles Kerr occasionally sent some of these Russian hounds to the exhibitions, but most of them were small and somewhat light and weedy—far from such powerful animals as the best that are with us to-day, and even they in height do not reach that which belonged to the late Duchess of Manchester, and already alluded to. Of course, long before this, the dog, in all his prime and power, was to be found in most kennels of the Russian nobles. Some of them had strains of their own, treasured in their families for years. Such were mostly used for wolf-hunting, sometimes for the fox and deer, and bred with sufficient strength and speed to cope with the wolf—not, indeed, to worry him and kill him, but, as a rule, to seize and hold him until the hunters came up.

In 1884 a couple of Borzois, which even then we only knew as Russian wolfhounds, were performing on a music-hall stage in London, in company with a leash of Great Danes. The latter were, however, the cleverer "canine artistes," though the former the handsomer and more popular animals. I fancy their disposition is too sedate to make them eminent on the boards, resembling that of the St. Bernard and ordinary Highland deerhound, neither of which we have yet seen attempting to emulate the deeds of trained poodles and terriers in turning somersaults and going backwards up a ladder.

A correspondent, writing to the *Field* in 1887, gives the following description of the Borzoi, and it is so applicable to him at the present time as to be worth reproducing here. He says this Russian hound " Is one of the noblest of all dogs, and in his own land he is considered the very noblest, and valued accordingly. Like all things noble that are genuine, he is rare; and, like many other highly-bred creatures, the genuine Borzoi is, from in-breeding, becoming rarer every year. By crossing, however, with the deerhound and other suitable breeds, the race will no doubt be kept alive with stained lineage.

" From the earliest times, the great families of Russia have bred the Borzoi jealously against each other for the purpose of wolf hunting, but there are now few really good kennels of the breed. There are, I believe, various kinds of Borzois—the smooth, the short-tailed, &c.—but by far the handsomest, and the only one of which I have personal knowledge, is the rough-haired, long-tailed strain. Of these I have seen but very few good specimens in England, and, in fact, have seen prizes given at shows to very inferior specimens entered in the foreign class under his name. The true Borzoi is shaped like a Scotch deerhound, but is a much more powerful dog. In height he should be from 26in to 32in., with limbs showing great strength, combined with terrific speed power. Indeed, their speed is greater than that of an English greyhound. This quality is clearly shown by the long drooping quarters, hocks well let down close to the ground, and arched loins of such power and breadth as to give the dog almost a hunched appearance. The coat is silky, with a splendid frill round the neck, well-feathered legs, and a tail beautifully fringed on the under side. The carriage of the tail is peculiar, as it is almost tucked between the hind legs, so straight down does it hang until at the end it curls slightly outwards with a graceful sweep; but this, like the bang tail of the thoroughbred racehorse, adds to the beauty of the quarters. The depth of these dogs through the heart is quite extraordinary, giving them, with their enormous strength of loin, a very powerful appearance, and it seems strange that they do not possess more staying powers than they are generally accredited with. The head is very beautiful, being nearly smooth, and with immense length and strength of jaws, armed with teeth which make one feel glad to meet the Borzoi as a friend. The eyes are bright and wild, and have the peculiarity of varying in colour with the colour of the dog. Thus, a white dog marked, with lemon eyes; a mouse-coloured, eyes of the same tinge, and so on.

"The favourite colour of all, and by far the rarest

for these dogs, is pure white, but this is seldom met with. The usual colour is white, marked with fawn, lemon, red, or grey more or less mixed. Perhaps the prettiest features of all in the Borzoi are its ears, which are very small, fringed with delicate silky hair, and should be pricked with a half fall-over like a good collie's. In his movements he much resembles a wild animal, and has quite the slouching walk and long sling trot which is a characteristic of his born enemy, the wolf. Yet to see a Borzoi trot out with his long swinging action, and then just break into a canter, has always reminded me of a two-year-old cantering down to the post. The muscles on the quarters, thighs, and arms should be well developed, as these dogs are intended, and in fact used, to course the wild wolf. Strong must be the muscles, long the teeth, and indomitable the pluck of the Borzoi, who has to encounter single-handed the wild wolf in his own haunts. No doubt the Borzoi, on such occasions, remembers the well-known fact that the favourite meat of the wolf is dog, and acts accordingly. It is usual, however, to employ two Borzois to course a wolf, and it is only the best specimens that can be trusted to account for one single-handed."

Perhaps, before going more fully into the Borzoi as a British dog, the following extract from an article by Mr. F. Lowe, who a few years ago spent some time in Russia, will give an idea of the extent of the kennels of the Borzoi hounds, and the value placed upon them in their native country. He says: " In the south of Russia, from which I have just returned, I had the good fortune to be the guest of a keen and well-known sportsman, Mr. Kalmoutzky, who, since coming into the inheritance of a magnificent property of something like twenty square miles, has built kennels which I should say are not surpassed in any country—being very large in size, and as near to perfection in detail as can well be imagined. The lodging houses, numbering three, are benched on two sides, and at each end there is a room for a man; three kennelmen being allowed for each kennel, two of them on duty night and day. This gives nine kennelmen to the kennels and, with five other officials, the number of men employed on it are fourteen. It is necessary to have men in attendance at all times, as the wolfhounds are very quarrelsome, and terrible fighters. Each kennel has a large yard of more than three-quarters of an acre. In addition to the above, there are commodious kennels for puppies (and these buildings are heated with hot air), cooking houses, and a hospital. There is telephone communication from all the kennels to Mr. Kalmoutzky's house, and he expects everything to be in readiness for a hunt in ten minutes from the time he sends his orders.

" In the kennels above described can be seen perhaps the finest pack of wolfhounds in the world, numbering twenty-two couples. They form a magnificent collection, their owner having spared no expense in getting the best to be found in Russia, and of the oldest blood. Some of them have cost £300 each; and the estimated worth of the pack is considerably over £5000.

" A perfect wolfhound must run up to a wolf, collar him by the neck just under the ear, and, with the two animals rolling over, the hound must never lose his hold, or the wolf would turn round and snap him through the leg. Three of these hounds hold the biggest wolf powerless; so that the men can dismount from their horses and muzzle the wolf to take him alive.

" The biggest Scotch deerhounds have been tried, but found wanting; they will not hold long enough. And to show how tenacious is the grip of the Russian hounds, they are sometimes suffocated by the very effort of holding. Some of them stand 32in at the shoulder, are enormously deep through the girth, and their length and power of jaw are something remarkable. They have a roach back, very long, muscular quarters, and capital legs and feet. In coat they are very profuse, of a soft, silky texture, but somewhat open.

"I took the journey to Russia with eleven couples of foxhounds, as additions for Mr. Kalmoutzky's pack. I had cases made to hold two hounds, so that I had eleven of these big packages, which went as my personal luggage, the weight being a ton and a quarter. It took me exactly seven days to get to my destination, from Dover *via* Paris, Vienna, and Jassy; and I was met in right regal state, as there was a carriage and four for myself, another for Mr. Kalmoutzky's steward, and five waggons, each drawn by four horses, for the hounds, with seven chasseurs to take charge of them.

"We had nearly forty miles to drive; and the hardy little Russian horses did this at a hard gallop, over plains, with no roads, and there were no changes. We were just under four hours doing this wild journey; and my good friend and host, who did not expect me to arrive so early, had gone out on a wolf-seeking expedition; but on his return, the first thing, after a most hearty welcome, was to inspect the kennel, with which I was, of course, greatly delighted. He would not show me the wolfhounds at this moment, as that inspection was reserved until after dinner, when they were all brought into his study, one by one, and their exploits separately recorded. Noble looking fellows they are; and by their immense size and powerful frames, of much the same formation as our English greyhound, they are admirably adapted to course big game. They look quiet, but the least movement excites them; and in leading them even through the hall, from the study, there was very nearly a battle royal or two. The Russian chasseurs, though, beat any men I have ever seen in handling a hound; and their influence, apparently all by kindness, is extraordinary. I noticed that even the puppies at play made for the same spot in trying to pull each other down— namely, by the side of the neck under the ear; and this mode of attack seems instinctively born in them. The wolf's running is perfectly straight, and if he attacks it is straight ahead; he will only turn if caught in a manner to do so; and a dog laying hold of him over the back or hind quarters would be terribly punished. The clever wolfhound never gets hurt, no matter whether he or the wolf attacks first; and some singular trials of this sort have taken place.

"Recently, a very big wolf, that had been captured with much difficulty, was matched against any two hounds in Russia. The challenge was accepted, and the wolf placed in a huge box in an open space.

The moment the trap was pulled the wolf stood and faced the spectators; on the hounds being slipped on him he attacked them; but they avoided his rush, and pinned him so cleverly that the wolf was muzzled and carried off without the least difficulty; whereupon an enormous price was paid for one of the hounds.

"The Russian style of hunting would not meet all our English views of sport; but there is doubtless a deal of excitement about it Mr. Kalmoutzky's domain is entirely on a plain, with scarcely any woodlands at all. It is all like a "sea of grass," the going being as good as on Newmarket Heath, with here and there the land turned up in cultivation, but looking much like patches in the vast expanse; so also did the reed beds of 300 or 400 acres each, and these are the coverts for the wolves and foxes. These reed beds are mostly eight or nine miles apart, so English foxhunters could see what a gallop could be had here; better than Dartmoor or Exmoor, as the turf is perfect, no rough ground, and the hills little more than undulations.

"Special hunts would have been arranged on my behalf, but, alas! like our own frozen-out sportsmen, I had to be disappointed, as frost and snow interfered. However, one morning I was given an insight into wolf coursing, by one that had been previously captured being let loose on the snow. First a very noted hound was slipped to show how one could perform single-handed. The start given to the wolf was about 200 yards, and in about 600 yards the hound had got up, and in the next instant had taken hold by the neck, and both seemed to turn head over heels in a mass. The next course two hounds were slipped, and these ran up to the wolf one on each side, catching him almost at the same moment; the foe was then powerless, and seemed to be as easily muzzled as a collie dog.

"I remarked to my host that I did not think the hounds seemed to go quite as fast as our greyhounds, and he replied, 'No, they do not. We have tried them, and the greyhound is the faster; but none of your breeds have the hold of our hounds.'

"The plan of a regular hunt was fully described to me. It is decided to draw a reed bed, and very quietly a mounted chasseur with three wolfhounds is stationed on some vantage ground near. Other points are guarded in the same manner, and then the head huntsman rides into the covert with a pack of foxhounds. The oldest wolves will break covert at almost the first cheer given to hounds; but the younger ones want a lot of rattling. However, the keen eyes of the men and hounds soon detect wolves stealing away; the three hounds are then slipped, a gallop begins, and generally, in the course of a mile or less, the wolf is bowled over. The chasseur then dismounts, cleverly gets astride the wolf, and collars him by the ears, the hounds still holding on like grim death. Another chasseur rides up, slips a muzzle on the wolf, which is then hauled on to one of the horses, tightly strapped to the Mexican sort of saddle, and taken off to a waggon in waiting near. Foxes are similarly coursed and killed with foxhounds, the latter being stopped at the edge of the covert."

The following account of a wolf hunt, from the pen of an English officer, will perhaps be found interesting, as it deals with one or two matters not alluded to by Mr. Lowe :

" Some years ago, while I was in the Russian service, the officers of a cuirassier regiment gave ' ours ' a chance to see these fine dogs work. We had been trying to hunt wolves with our pack of boarhounds, but with little success. Occasionally we shot one, but, though our dogs could bring the biggest boar to bay, they were useless in tackling wolves. Several of the boldest and fiercest hounds had been crippled by the savage brutes.

" One day a courier rode over with an invitation for all of us to go to Bielowicz two days later. The Czar's wolfhounds were expected to arrive at the lodge at that date, and fine sport was promised. 'Don't trouble to bring any weapons,' the letter ran, 'for these are the dogs we have told you so much about, and they are to do all the work.

"Of course we all clamoured to be allowed to go, and gained our point with our good-natured colonel. As there were fifteen of us then on duty, it was arranged that three parties of five should each take three days off, for it took two days to go there and back. My party got off first, and by riding all day we reached the lodge before night. The cuirassiers gave us the best of welcomes and a fine dinner, to which the chasseur en chef was also invited. The gentleman had for twenty years had charge of the Czar's wolfhounds.

"After dinner he ordered his men to bring in some of the best dogs for our inspection. An attendant dragged them in one at a time, not without some trouble; but as soon as they saw the chasseur they became as quiet as lambs, and did anything he ordered. He was very proud of them, and gave us interesting details of their prowess. One huge fellow, called Dimitri, had the repute of being able to catch and hold the largest wolf single-handed, and the chasseur promised to show him off to us the next day.

"As the coverts to be drawn were seven miles

away, we took an early start. Twelve chasseurs, each leading a fine wolfhound, rode in advance; four attendants, with a pack of common hounds, followed. Next came a big iron cage drawn by four horses, in which the captured wolves were to be put; for, while small and inferior wolves are killed, all the largest are kept for the young wolfhounds to practise upon.

"As soon as the common hounds were sent into the underbush, hares and foxes came rushing out, but the boars and wolves were harder to start. The chasseurs had taken up good positions along the edge of the forest, where a stretch of open plain offered a splendid chance to see the fun if any wolves were driven out. I kept with the man who had charge of Dimitri.

"With ears erect and nose in the air, this fine dog seemed to take as much interest in the sport as any of us. Though the barking and baying hounds in the coverts came nearer every second, he never moved a muscle nor made a sound. Suddenly a big, black wolf rushed out of the scrub, gave one glance around, then started off for the next covert a mile away.

"All the dogs tugged at their leashes; but not till the wolf had a clear start of two hundred yards did the head chasseur's bugle ring out. It was

The Borzoi or Russian Wolfhound. 301

Dimitri's call; and as he was loosed, he gave one fierce howl and then bounded silently away.

"With such tremendous energy did he start that his feet hardly seemed to touch the ground. Every leap seemed longer than the last; and as he grew smaller in the distance, he looked like a big rubber ball bouncing over the plain. In less than a minute he had overtaken the wolf and seized him by the neck under the right ear. A cloud of dust flew up as dog and wolf rolled over and over; but when it cleared away, we saw that Dimitri had brought the beast to a standstill. His chasseur had followed him as quickly as his horse would run. On coming up the man jumped down, and, getting astride of the wolf, fastened a strong muzzle over its jaws, secured a chain round round its neck and dragged the now skulking animal back to where the cage stood.

"In the meantime other wolves had been started, and several of the dogs were hard at work. When two were loosed in pursuit of one wolf, they ran alongside of him, one on each side, until a favourable opportunity offered, when, with a sudden snap, one would seize the creature. As the wolf turned to try to free himself, the other would get a grip that prevented him from moving at all.

"So surely and neatly did these dogs do their work that not one was bitten, although no animals can do quicker or more damaging work with their jaws than wolves.

"Seven wolves were driven out of that covert, but only two were thought to be worth keeping. They were put in the cage, and we moved on to the next likely spot. In the course of the day the dogs caught sixteen wolves, not one got away when fairly out of cover, and we returned to the lodge with five fine live wolves.

"While discussing the ways of wolves that evening after dinner, one of us ventured to express a doubt whether even Dimitri could successfully face a wolf at bay. The speaker was satisfied that the dog could seize and hold a running wolf, but did not believe he could avoid the savage attack such an animal makes when cornered. Before we left next morning he was convinced of his error. The largest captured wolf was turned loose in an inclosed yard, and Dimitri was set on him. Seeing himself trapped, the wolf did not wait for the dog to attack, but rushed straight at him.

"The two animals met and closed, rolling over and over; but when the struggles ceased, Dimitri had the wolf securely by the neck, and had not received a scratch. Our friend, the chasseur en chef, offered to bring out other hounds that could do this feat as well as Dimitri; but we were convinced.

As our time was up, we departed, regretting that we could not take a few of the Czar's wolfhounds away with us."

Following the publication of Mr. Lowe's article some correspondence ensued, and Colonel Wellesley forwarded an interesting communication he had received from Prince Obolensky on the subject. His Royal Highness, who has a famous strain of Borzoi of his own, and may be taken as a leading authority on the breed, says:

"The dogs that have been catalogued at various shows in England for the last three years are pure Borzoi, and have come originally from the best kennels in Russia. For instance, Krilutt, Págooba, Sobol, Zloeem, and others were not ordinary working hounds, but dogs that were admired in their native country, both on the show bench and in the field. Págooba, for example, who is of exceptional size for a bitch, has several times pinned wolves single-handed.

"The English traveller mentions the size—viz., 32in.—of the dogs he saw as tremendous. There are exceptional cases where the Borzoi has stood very near that height. At the dog show in Moscow this year a dog called Pilai measured $31\frac{1}{2}$in., or 80 centimètres; but the average height is from 28in. to $29\frac{1}{2}$in. It often proves to be the case, however, that, for working purposes, the smaller dog shows itself to excel in speed, pluck, and tenacity.

"For wolf hunting I personally prefer the English greyhound, acclimatised here (*i.e.* born in Russia from English parents); but I am also a great admirer of the Russian rough-coated Borzoi. I may claim to know something about the latter, because for many years I have bred and hunted them, and my dogs are the lineal descendants of those bred by my grandfather, General Bibikoff, who was himself renowned for his sporting proclivities, and for the excellence of his breed of dogs. So valued is that strain now, that it can be found in most of the best kennels in Russia."

In addition to sport with Borzois obtained in the above manner, occasional meetings are held where hares are coursed; and "bagged," or rather "caged," wolves treated in a similar manner. Judging, however, from what I have been told of such gatherings, they are by no means desirable or of a high class, so need not be further alluded to here.

It is but natural that with the popularisation of a new variety of dogs, some discussion should take place thereon. In the present instance, an attempt was made upon the name of the hound, but as the word Borzoi had obtained general acceptance, was easy to pronounce, and not too long to puzzle even a child, the "raid" failed. It is now adopted by the Kennel Club, by the chief Russian authorities, and no doubt that hound once known as the Russian wolfhound will remain the Borzoi to the end of his days. On this matter, Prince Obolensky says: "I am glad to see English sporting papers adopting the Russian name for this breed, for the word itself (Borzoi *mas.*, Borzaia *fem.*) means 'swift and hot-tempered;' and though poets sometimes apply the expression to a high-spirited steed, it is, with this exception, always applied to greyhounds only; for this reason the English greyhound is called, in Russia, 'Angliskaia Borzaia,' or English Borzoi."

Some little time before the above was published, Lieutenant G. Tamooski, writing from Merv, proposed the term "Psovi," which means literally "thick coated," as a fit name for the dog as it is known in this country, because he says "Borzoi" means any coursing hound whatever.

The Duchess of Newcastle, Colonel and the Hon. Mrs. Wellesley, the Duke and Duchess of Wellington, Mrs Morrison, of near Salisbury; Lady Innes Kerr, Mr. A. H. Blees, Mrs. Coop, Mrs. W. B. Stamp, Mrs. E. H. Barthropp, Mrs. M. E. Musgrave, Mrs. G. W. Fitzwilliam, Miss A. M. Head, Mrs. Young, Miss M. Thompson, and many others, have given particular attention to the Borzoi, and they, with

Mr. K. Muir, an English resident in Moscow, who brought over with him, during a visit to this country, a couple of excellent hounds, own, or have owned, animals perhaps as good as can be found in any Russian kennel. Their best specimens are much stronger, and more powerful than most of those seen at our earlier shows. Mrs. Wellesley's Krilutt was measured to be 30in. at the shoulders, and pretty nearly 100lb. in weight, and Mr. Muir's Korotai was half an inch taller, and said to be 110lb. in weight. Both were Russian born, and proved their ability to win prizes at St. Petersburg and Moscow, as well as in our own country. Like the rest of their race, they are "thick coated dogs"—the smoother ones are not liked in this country—not so hard in their hair as the English deerhound, but the jacket is closer, and, if not so straight, is perhaps the more weather-resisting of the two. As the Russians themselves say that the two kinds of coat, thick and comparatively smooth, appear in puppies of the same litter, there is no other conclusion to arrive at, that they are one and the same variety. At any rate, they are allowed to be so in this the land of their adoption.

Considerable interest was taken in the extraordinary collection of this hound that appeared at the Agricultural Hall, Islington, in February, 1892.

Here, many classes had been provided, the result being an entry of about fifty. These included a splendid team from the "Imperial Kennels," most of which belonged to the Grand Duke Nicholas. However, three were actually the property of the Czar, including a beautiful bitch called Lasca, and a couple of dogs, Oudar and Blitsay. Oudar was a particularly fine hound, and though in bad condition, consequent on his long journey from St. Petersburg, he stood well with the best of our previously imported dogs, and in the end gained second honours in perhaps as good an open class as was ever seen anywhere. He stood 30½in. at the shoulders, and scaled about 105lb.

Most of these Russian dogs were sold, some of them for high prices, Oudar realising £200, the bitch already named as much, and the then Lord Mayor of London was presented with a handsome specimen. Their "caretaker" had instructions to sell the lot, but none for less than £20 apiece. The strains in this country have been improved by these importations, and any fears as to degeneracy from inter-breeding may now be set at rest. Another big dog of the race was Colonel Wellesley's Damon, 30¾in. at the shoulders, and about 110lb. in weight, but when we saw him he did not quite equal in symmetry and general excellence such dogs as

X 2

Krilutt, Oudar, Korotai, and may be of another dog, imported by Mr. Summerson, of Darlington, called Koat, afterward H'Vat.

To dwell a little more upon the very best specimens seen in England—Krilutt and Korotai, with Oudar and Ooslad, have been and still are equal to anything I have seen. The latter, a fawn hound, is rather smaller than the others, but on one occasion, at least, he beat Korotai, a decision with which I did not agree; for if Ooslad was a little finer in the head, his opponent beat him in coat, colour, power, size, and in all other particulars. Korotai was a white dog with slight blue markings. It is said that when in Russia he had run down and overpowered a wolf. His strain was of the highest and most valued pedigree, and I certainly liked him the best of any of his race I had seen until Oudar came on to the scene. However, at the show already alluded to, the latter was not in good condition, and suffered defeat; Korotai winning chief honours in an extraordinary fine lot of dogs. Krilutt had been in the challenge class; Oudar was first in a division for novices, and at the present time he is well cared for in the kennels of The Duchess of Newcastle at Clumber, and, although now over eight years old, is able to take more than his part against the best on the show bench. At the present time there are over fifty Borzois at Clumber, of which Velasquez and Velsk, by Korotai—Vikhra, are perhaps the best couple ever bred in this country. Tsaritsa, bred by Count Stroganoff, also deserves special mention, a bitch by many good judges considered the best of her sex ever exhibited.

Argos (Mr. O. H. Blees's), a black and tan in colour, was also a very nice hound, excepting so far as the colour goes, which is not good. The owner of the last named Borzoi, who is a Russian, has repeatedly been an exhibitor in this country, and at the Kennel Club's show, in 1891, he took first, second, and third prizes in dogs, but was not so successful in bitches, where Mr. F. Lowe won, with a powerful and excellent specimen he had brought with him from Russia, and called Roussalka. She would, no doubt, have been useful here, but, unfortunately, died soon after the show. Colonel Wellesley's bitch, Págooba, and Mr. R. B. Summerson's dog Koat, afterwards H'Vat, were hounds of high class.

Of these many excellent specimens, Colonel Wellesley must have the honour of being first in the field with Krilutt, who made an early appearance —and a most successful one it was—at the Kennel Club show, when held at the Alexandra Palace in 1889—the year of the bloodhound trials. Krilutt had come with a great reputation as the winner of a silver medal at Moscow, and quite bore out all the good words that had been said of him. Exquisite in coat and colour—the latter white with light markings of pale fawn—he stood taller than any other dog in his class, and up to this period and for some time after was certainly the best Borzoi I had seen. Since, two or three have appeared that are, I believe, quite his equals. Whether it is worth while mentioning a dog named Zloeem, which, a year later, had been purchased in Russia by an American gentleman, Mr. Paul Hacke, is an open question. However, it was said that Zloeem could lower the colours of Krilutt and all other opponents, and at Brighton and the Crystal Palace was produced for the purpose of doing so. How completely he failed is now a matter of history—a second-rate dog only when at his very best. Since the above dogs flourished many good specimens have appeared, notably H.R.H. the Princess of Wales's Alex, who has been particularly successful on the bench; Mrs. Coop's Windle Courtier, the Duchess of Newcastle's Velasquez, Vikra, and Milkha; Mrs. Kate Sutton's Vera III., Mrs. Barthropp's Leiba, Mrs. Musgrave's Opromiot, Mrs. Stamp's Najada, and some others, the names of which do not occur to me.

It might be well to mention that considerable

risk is run by the loss of these dogs immediately after their arrival in this country. To my personal knowledge, three or four deaths have so taken place. No doubt the changes of food, in their manner of living, and in other surroundings, bring on a complication of disorders not unlike ordinary distemper. That handsome bitch, Roussalka, brought over by Mr. F. Lowe, died soon after it left his kennels—it cost its new owner £100; and Mr Muir's Korotai had a narrow escape, lying at death's door for several days. Being a dog of strong, hardy constitution, and well nursed, he contrived to pull through.

The usual colours of the Borzoi are white with markings of fawn in varying shades, of blue or slate, sometimes of black and tan. The latter is not considered good, nor are the whole colours which are occasionally seen—fawn and black and tan. Some of the white dogs are occasionally patched with pale brindle, which, however, is not so well defined in its bars or shades as that colour is found on our greyhounds and bull dogs. Many persons object to the brindle or " tiger-coloured " marks, and Colonel Tchebeshoff, one of the great authorities on the breed, disqualifies black, and black and tan, and white with black spots, as indicating descent from English or Oriental greyhounds. Still, against this opinion there is a famous picture, in the possession of the Czar, of four Borzois chasing a wolf. At least one of these animals has the appearance of being black and tan, with an almost white face, very broad white collar and chest, white stern and hind quarters.

The size of the Borzoi and his coat will have been surmised from what has already been written. His general appearance will be seen from the illustration. As a companion he is highly spoken of, but, like all other dogs, he must be brought up for the purpose for which he is intended. In most of the Russian kennels he is kept solely for hunting a savage animal (by a few only to be used for fox and hare), and to do so successfully must be savage himself. Those which have been reared in this manner, and not had the benefit of civilising home influences, are not to be trusted any more than would one of our own foxhounds. But, as I have said, properly brought up and educated, he will be found as companionable as the best—no fonder of fighting than the deerhound, faithful as the collie, and as handsome and picturesque as either. His naturalisation with us is accomplished, and I can see no reason whatever why he is any more likely to be eliminated from "Modern Dogs" than the St. Bernard. He will be used here as a purely fancy variety; there are no wolves for him to kill, hares and rabbits are out of his line, and deer must be left for the big foxhound and the Highland deerhound.

I have written of the Borzoi as we know him here, and as he will in the future be known, taking no account of the various strains said to be in the Czar's dominions, and the following description of him, translated from the Russian by M. A. Boldareff, a member of the Imperial Hunt, Moscow, and which appeared in the *Stock Keeper* in July, 1896, will be found interesting :

" The general appearance of the Borzoi is noble and elegant. This is shown in the shape of the head, the silkiness and brilliancy of the hair, and even in the gait, which should be full of energy and grace. The different points of the dog, taken separately, have no value in the general appearance; the dog may have defects in head properties, in the body, in the legs, the coat may be too short, but nevertheless its air of nobility and elegance, its blueblood aspect, will indicate purity of breeding. Only pure blood and careful breeding for several generations will impart this look, which excites the admiration of connoisseurs of Borzois and all other lovers of dogs.

" It is a pity that nowadays many of our sportsmen

surrender general appearance for perfection in other points, so that the Borzoi of high and noble quality is becoming rare.

"The pure race of the Borzoi is principally characterised by the shape of the head, the ear, and by the tail. Many breeders concentrate their attention upon the head, and disdain the tail.

"We find, on the contrary, that the tail is one of the most characteristic points of race, because its thinness, its elasticity, and its shape, which resembles a reaping hook (*a*), among all the Russian breeds (we consider the Crimean and Caucasian varieties as Russian) belong exclusively to the Borzoi (*b*).

"Muzzle slightly arched and forehead prominent are typical of the Borzoi, but when the arch is too pronounced or the forehead too prominent, they are faults.

"The skull must be long, oval to the sides, and have a small slip to the back part of the head, finishing by a prominency sharp enough and well pronounced. Every other form is not typical.

"The muzzle is long, thin, and clean, the nostrils

(*a*) A comparison very popular among Russian hunters.

(*b*) The writer forgets the greyhounds of Poland, whose tails are exactly of the same shape as the Borzoi, only covered with very short hair.

rather large and slightly projecting over the lower jaw. The nose must be black (*a*).

"The eye must be full, and of oblong shape (an oblique eye is a defect, and a round one is not typical); it must be of a dark colour in a dark lining (*b*). Its expression is austere, but certainly not when indoors or when the dog is caressed, but at liberty or while hunting.

"The ear is small, thin (its thinness is a proof of high blood), having the form of a wedge. It must be very mobile, and is sometimes carried erect like a horse's ear (*c*).

"This last quality is one of the best proofs of high birth. The hair that covers the ear must be very short, soft as satin, and must not grow in bunches. The dog should carry its neck like an English greyhound, but the Borzoi's neck is shorter, and is not so straight. The shoulders should be flat and well seen; the elbows must not be turned outwards, but should be clear of the sides of the dog.

"The arch of the back of a dog must be quite

(*a*) A nose not sufficiently black, even when it has the colour of flesh, must not be considered as a proof of bad race. It is simply a symptom of poorness of blood.

(*b*) A light eye and the absence of a dark lining represent the same defect as a light nose.

(*c*) A favourite comparison with Russian amateurs.

regular and make no impression of a hump. The arch seems higher than it really is, because the hind part of the dog is higher than the fore part. The bitch has the back less arched, but even a high arch must not be considered as a great defect.

"The ribs of the Borzoi must descend as low as the elbow They can be either flat or round, their form depending upon the breadth of the back; but they must never be too round (*a*). The ribs must gradually get smaller to the stomach. The stomach is drawn in and quite hidden behind the groin. The groin of a dog must be small; the less the better. A bitch must have it longer.

"The hind quarters are long and broad. The dog is more sloping than the bitch. A short and drooping loin is a great defect, because it forces the hind legs to be quite straight (*b*).

"The fore legs are quite straight. The bone must be flat from the side, and not round. The foot resembles that of a hare (*c*), with toes of medium length. On each toe grows a bunch of hair, long

---

(*a*) Not so round as the sides of an English greyhound.

(*b*) Many huntsmen begin to prefer a sloping loin. The reason is that this form was common to the majority of coursing winners in Russia.

(*c*) Comparison generally used by Russian amateurs. We consider a cat foot a fault for Borzois.

and thin (*a*). The under part of the paw is of an oblong form.

"The hind legs are parallel one to another, slightly set back (not too much).

"The thighs are flat, with very broad bones. The muscles are flat, long, and firm.

"The tail is thin, but strong in its beginning, growing gradually thinner and thinner to the end; it must be elastic, have the form of a sickle, and be of medium length. Its upper part is covered with curly hair, but the hair on the lower part is long and slightly undulated.

"The hair of the dog is curly on the neck, slightly wavy on the back of the dog—as far as the loins—and again more wavy on the thighs, much shorter on the sides, but falls long and satin-like from the chest.

"Personally, we admit as typical colour of the hair only white, grey, yellow, and white spotted with grey and yellow (*b*)."

In Russia, although judging dogs by points is in vogue, the procedure connected therewith is arranged on different lines to that followed in this country.

(*a*) Not for dogs in field condition.

(*b*) All our amateurs were quite astonished when we heard that a black dog (I think its name was Argos) was proclaimed champion in England. This colour is one of the first proofs of a great deal of Crimean or Caucasian blood.

For instance, forty-five is taken as the complement indicating perfection, and each point of the dog is given five, no particular one having a greater number allowed than another. However, to modify this the various points are placed in order of precedence, according to the Russian standard, they being as follows: Hind legs, fore legs, ribs, back, general symmetry, muzzle, eyes, ears, tail.

In 1892 a Borzoi club was established in Great Britain, and the following is their description of the hound :

Head.—Long and lean. The skull flat and narrow; stop not perceptible, and muzzle long and tapering. The head from the forehead to the tip of the nose should be so fine that the shape and direction of the bones and principal veins can be seen clearly; and in profile should appear rather Roman nosed. Bitches should be even narrower in head than dogs. Eyes dark, expressive, almond shaped, and not too far apart. Ears, like those of a greyhound : small, thin, and placed well back on the head, with the tips, when thrown back, almost touching behind the occiput.

Neck.—The head should be carried somewhat low, with the neck continuing the line of the back.

Shoulders.—Clean, and sloping well back.

Chest.—Deep, and somewhat narrow.

Back.—Rather bony, and free from any cavity in the spinal column, the arch in the back being more marked in the dog than in the bitch.

Loins.—Broad and very powerful, with plenty of muscular development.

Thighs.—Long and well developed, with good second thigh.

Ribs.—Slightly sprung at the angle of the ribs; deep, reaching to the elbow, and even lower.

Fore legs.—Lean and straight. Seen from the front they should be narrow, and from the side broad at the shoulders and narrowing gradually down to the foot, the bone appearing flat and not round as in the foxhound.

Hind legs.—The least thing under the body when standing still, not straight and the stifle slightly bent.

Muscles—Well distributed, and highly developed.

Pasterns.—Strong.

Feet.—Like those of a deerhound, rather long; the toes close together and well arched.

Coat.—Long, silky (not woolly), either flat, wavy, or rather curly. On the head, ears, and front legs it should be short and smooth; on the neck, the frill should be profuse and rather curly; on the chest and rest of body, the tail, and hind quarters, it should be long. The tail should be well feathered.

Tail.—Long, well feathered, and not gaily carried.

Height.—At shoulder of dog, from 28 inches upwards ; of bitches, from 26 inches upwards.

Faults.—Head, short or thick ; too much stop; parti-coloured nose ; eyes too wide apart ; heavy ears, heavy shoulders; wide chest; "barrel" ribbed ; dew claws ; elbows turned out, wide behind.

The colour ought to be white, with blue, grey, or fawn markings of different shades, the latter sometimes deep orange coloured, approaching red. Pale brindled marks on the white ground are often found, and are not objectionable, and fawn dogs with or without black muzzles are not unusual. Whole colours are unsatisfactory. The lighter marked animals are the handsomest and the most admired in this country, though, as stated earlier on, one or two heavily coloured dogs of great merit have been shown here.

One Russian admirer of the breed gives some of the characteristics of the Borzoi as follows : "The structure of the body of a pure bred Russian Borzoi astonishes everybody by its thinness, elasticity, and form of the bones. The muscles are not hard and cushion-formed, but on touching, nearly elastic and long-stretched, which enable these dogs to reach any other animal at a short distance with a few leaps. They have a soft, silky, and glossy coat, the

The Borzoi or Russian Wolfhound.

hair never hanging down in short hard locks. The character of the dog is mostly morose, but as a pet his intelligence mostly increases, but the most astonishing thing is his sharp-sightedness and rage against other animals when hunting."

According to our English notion of awarding points I should make those of the Borzoi as follows:

	Value.		Value.
Head and muzzle	15	Thighs and hocks	10
Ears and eyes	10	Legs and feet	10
Neck and chest	10	Stern	5
Back and loins	15	Coat	5
Ribs	10	General symmetry	10
	60		40

Grand Total, 100.

The height for a dog should be from 27 inches to 31 inches at the shoulder; a bitch about two inches smaller. Weight, a dog, from 75lb. to 105lb.; a bitch, from 60lb. to 80lb.

I do not know that measurements are, as a rule, any great guide in determining excellence, still the following figures relating to the well-known Krilutt, and published in the *Dog Owner's Annual* for 1892, will give some idea as to what a perfect Borzoi ought to be when analysed statistically in inches: "Length of head, 11½ inches; from occiput to between shoulders, 11½; between shoulders to between hips, 23; between hips to set on of tail, $6\frac{1}{4}$; length of tail, 21 inches; total length, $73\frac{1}{4}$ inches. Height at shoulders, $30\frac{1}{4}$ inches; girth of chest, 33; of narrowest part of "tuck-up," 22; girth above stifle bend, 13; round stifle, $11\frac{1}{2}$; round hock joint, $6\frac{1}{2}$; below that joint, $4\frac{1}{2}$; round elbow joint, $8\frac{1}{4}$; above that point, $8\frac{3}{4}$; girth, midway between elbow and pastern, $6\frac{1}{2}$; round neck, 17; girth of head round occiput, $16\frac{1}{2}$; girth between occiput and eyes, $16\frac{1}{4}$; girth round the eyes, $13\frac{3}{4}$; and girth of the muzzle between eyes and nose, 9 inches. Weight about 98lb.

As to the above, Captain Graham tells me he measured Krilutt carefully on more than one occasion, but could not make him more than $29\frac{3}{4}$ inches at the shoulders, and I have made his full height bare 30 inches.

It may be said that I have not entered with sufficient fulness into the history of the Borzoi, as he is known in Russia, and given the names of the various strains some writers claim there are in his native country. We are, however, contented with the animal as we have him here, and to tell his admirers that there is a strain of the hound, known as the Tchistopsovoy Borzoi, another as the Psovoy Borzoi, that the Courland Borzoi is extinct, and other such matter, would be a little too confusing.

And really so much has appeared about this dog since his popularisation in this country that is of doubtful truth, care ought to be taken in what is reproduced.

One recent writer tells us that, even so far back as 1800, certain Borzoi of the Courland strain were sold for from 7,000 to 10,000 roubles apiece, which, in our money, cannot be computed at less than from 1000*l*. to 1500*l*. a head! No wonder that so valuable a hound has become extinct (on the principle that the best always die), and it is interesting to learn that, at a time when we in England were giving 50*l*. each or little more for our very best hounds, more than twenty times that sum was being paid in Russia for similar quadrupeds.

Still the Borzoi always did flourish in the dominions of the Czar, and the Imperial kennels at St. Petersburg usually contain from fifty to sixty full grown Borzois and almost as many puppies. There are fourteen men kept to look after and to train them to their proper work, and the nature of this I have already stated. Whatever may be urged to the contrary, it must further be said that, in pace and general excellence for hare coursing purposes, this Russian hound is far behind our own good greyhound; but, as already stated, it is not our admiration for him as a sporting dog which has made him fashionable. His shape and elegance have made his fortune here, nor, so far as the present outlook is concerned, is it likely to wane in the near future. Perhaps before this volume is in the hands of the public a special exhibition of Borzoi will have taken place, for arrangements for holding one at Southport, Lancashire, are in progress, and it will be under the auspices of the Borzoi Club. Her Grace the Duchess of Newcastle has consented to judge, and, no doubt, the novelty of a canine exhibition of the kind will ensure its success, especially as it will be the first occasion upon which a lady of such social distinction and noble family has officiated in the judging ring.

CHAPTER XIII.

THE GREAT DANE.

HERE is a dog, not an English animal, but one thoroughly acclimatised to the rigours of our climate, and fairly naturalised. Still, it seems as it were only the other day (it is nearly thirty years since) that "Stonehenge" (Mr. J. H. Walsh) refused to give it a place in the first edition of his "Dogs of the British Isles," which Mr. F. Adcock then requested him to do.

I do not think that this dog (under which name, following the Great Dane Club's good example, I include boarhounds, German mastiffs, and tiger mastiffs) has made great progress here. Fifteen years since he appeared in a fair way to become a favourite. The ladies took him up, the men patronised him, but the former could not always keep him in hand. Handsome and symmetrical though he may be, he had always a temper and disposition of his own, which could not be controlled when he became excited. Personally, I never considered the

Great Dane suitable as a companion or as a domestic dog. He might act as a watch or guard tied up in the yard, or, may be, could be utilised in hunting big game, or in being hunted by it in return, but he always seemed out of place following a lady or gentleman. When the early orders came into force in London and elsewhere, commanding all dogs to be muzzled or led on a chain, the Great Dane received a severe blow. Muzzling amazed him, and made him savage, the restraint of chain or lead was not to be borne. The dog pulled; his fair mistress had either to free him from the chain or be overpowered. She did the former, and her unmanageable pet chevied a terrier across the road, and the mischief was done.

In that suburb in which I reside the Dane was numerous enough before the various rabies scares and the muzzling orders. He could not be confined with safety, so he had to be got rid of, and where once a dozen boarhounds reigned not one is now to be seen. This is, I think, an advantage few owners of dogs find fault with, for he, when not under control, was fond of fighting, and his immense strength and power gave him a great advantage over any other dog. Some twenty-five years or so ago, in the ring at a provincial show in Lancashire, Mr. Adcock's then celebrated Great Dane, called Satan, got at loggerheads with a Newfoundland, and the latter, poor thing, was shaken like a rat, and would soon have ceased to live, excepting in memory, had not three strong, stout men choked off the immense German Dog.

This was about the time he was being introduced to this country, or may be, rather, re-introduced, for I am one who believes that a hundred years ago there was in Ireland a Great Dane, not a wolfhound proper, but an actual Great Dane, just as he is known to-day. Hence the confusion that has arisen between the two varieties. From paintings and writings of a past generation there is no difficulty in making out this dog to be as old as any of the race of canines that we possess, but as he is brought forward here as a British dog, his history before he became such would be out of place. However, it may be said that M. Otto-Kreckwitz, of Munich, a great authority on the breed, says that "the nearest approach to the German Dogge (the Great Dane) of our time is one which is represented on a Greek coin from Panormos, dating from the 5th century B. C., and now in the Royal Museum, Munich. This dog with cropped ears is exactly our long-legged elegant Dogge with a graceful neck." The same authority takes exception to the name of the Great Dane on the grounds that, as he is now, he was actually made in Germany and thus should be called the German Dogge on the same principle that we have the English Mastiff.

Amongst our earliest specimens of the race, Satan, already alluded to, must take a leading place, though his temper was so bad. He was a heavily made, dark coloured dog, with a strong head and jaw, that would not be at all popular with the present admirers of the variety. However, his owner, Mr. F. Adcock, was an enthusiast, and by his patronage of the dog, and his subsequent establishment of a Great Dane Club, did more than any other man to bring the strain prominently before the British public.

It was not, however, until 1884, that special classes were provided for them at Birmingham, the Kennel Club having acknowledged them in their stud book the same year. However, at both places he, a year previously, had classes given him, but as a " boarhound," and since, with his name changed to " Great Dane," " boarhounds " and " German mastiffs " have become creatures of the past.

I have a note of a big black and white dog, shown by Sir Roger Palmer, about 1863 or 1864, which was said to be 35 inches at the shoulder, 200lb. weight, and a Great Dane! I never saw a dog of this variety approaching this size, and at that

The Great Dane. 329

time a two hundred pound weight dog had not been produced. Satan himself, a very heavy dog, would not be more than, perhaps, 150lb. at most.

Coming a little later, we find that in June, 1885, a dog show, devoted entirely to Great Danes, was held at the Ranelagh Club Grounds, near London. This was just at the time when the animal was reaching the height of his popularity here, and a noble show the sixty hounds, benched under the lime trees in those historic grounds, made. Never has such a collection of the variety been seen since in our island, and, need I say, never such a one previously. The great fawn dog, Cedric the Saxon, was there, perfect in symmetry, and a large dog; carefully measured, he stood $33\frac{1}{4}$ inches at the shoulder. With Captain Graham, I took the heights of several of these big dogs on that occasion, and it was extraordinary how the thirty-five and thirty-six inch animals dwindled down, some of them nearly half a foot at a time.

The tallest and heaviest hounds we made a careful note of were Mr. Reginald Herbert's Leal, who stood $33\frac{3}{4}$ inches at the shoulders, and weighed 182lb.; M. Riego's brindled dog, Cid Campeador, who stood exactly $33\frac{1}{2}$ inches, and his weight was 175lb. This couple were the tallest dogs of their race I had up to that time seen, but, at Brighton show in 1895 I weighed and measured a dog called Morro, the property of Mr. Woodruffe Hill. He stood fully 34 inches at the shoulders and scaled 190lb. Height is a great consideration in the breed, the club's standard being from 30 inches to 35 inches for a dog, and from 28 inches to 33 inches for a bitch.

It would appear that, within the last eighty years or so, considerable improvement must have been made in the size and power of the Great Dane. Sydenham Edwards, who wrote of him in 1803, said he was usually about twenty-eight inches in height, though, occasionally, he would be found thirty-one inches. The same writer goes on to describe him: " Ears, usually cropped; eyes, in some, white, in others yellow, or half white or yellow. A beautiful variety, called the Harlequin Dane, has a finely marked body, with large or small spots of black, grey, liver colour, or sandy-red, upon a white ground . . . . The grand figure, bold, muscular action, and elegant carriage of the Dane, would recommend him to notice, had he no useful properties; and thus we find him honoured in adding to the pomp of the noble or the wealthy, before whose carriage he trots or gallops in a fine style; not noisy, but of approved dignity, becoming his intrepid character he keeps his stall in silence." Edwards further says this dog must be muzzled, to prevent him attacking his own species.

Contrary to the above statement we have that of Richardson, who, writing about 1848, says the Great Dane is a dog of gigantic stature, standing from thirty to thirty-two inches in height at the shoulders, or even more. He says the ears are short, and drop down very gracefully. At the present time they are big, and hang down in a fashion so ungainly, that until quite recently it was the custom to crop them, an operation that was best performed when the puppies were about three weeks old, and when suckling their dam. One large breeder, Mr. E. H. Adcock, followed this custom successfully, and the wounds were soon healed by the contact of a mother's tongue. Others "cropped" their puppies when three or four months old, some still later, when the dog was more matured, say at eight or nine months, but at that time it was a nasty job, and a terribly unpleasant one, to him who took it in hand. Happily this cropping is illegal nowadays, and is only alluded to here as one of the follies of a fast passing away generation.

Perhaps it was the custom to have these dogs shorn of part of their ears that led to their, comparatively speaking, non-popularisation, for it is difficult to find proficient operators, who run the risk of fine or imprisonment if the cruelty they perpetrate be brought to the notice of the authorities.

A few years ago, I was attending one of the Crystal Palace dog shows, and engaged in conversation with a man, well known as a skilful performer on the ears of terriers and other dogs. Walking past the benches where the Danes were chained, we were startled by a terrible growl and furious lunge, a huge brindled dog springing up and making violent attempts to reach the man to whom I was talking. Luckily for him the chain and collar and staple held. I never saw so much ferocity depicted on the face of any animal whatever, as there was on the countenance of that Great Dane. It would have been bad for that man had it got loose. Need it be said, we soon gave it a wide berth. "What was the meaning of that?" said I to the fellow, who was, in reality, very much frightened and shaken by the occurrence. "Well," said he, "I know the dog, he was badly 'cropped,' and about five months ago, Mr. ———— called me down to his place to 'perform' on his ears again. We had a terrible job with him, and I guess the dog just recognised me, and wanted to have his revenge. I shall have nothing more to do with cropping 'boarhounds,'" continued the

The Great Dane.

whilom operator, " nor do I think I shall go near his bench ; no, not if I knows it ! "

I fancy from the above and other experiences I have gained, that no other variety of British dog possesses the same strength of mind, and is so ready to resent a supposed injury as he. It is dangerous to thrash some of them; they may turn on you, or will surlily growl ; and in fighting with any opponent they are not always able to discriminate between the hands of their master (who may be interfering in the combat) and the throat of an opponent. Still, faithful and intelligent, many of them are thoroughly trustworthy when their master is about—not always in his absence. They possess great power and activity, and are most symmetrically built. The Great Dane is usually a good water dog, but there are some which will not swim a yard.

As we know him here as a companion and a guard only, no more than passing allusion need be made to him as a sporting dog, to hunt the wild boar and chase the deer. That he was used for these purposes long before he came to be a house dog there is no manner of doubt, for his portraits can be recognised in all the great pictures of hunting scenes that took place in the Middle Ages. This is the reason I place him in the group of Sporting Dogs.

That he is thoroughly amenable to discipline I found some few years ago, in 1884, during a visit to the Oxford Music Hall, in London. Here Mr. Fred. Felix, a well-known trainer, had a group of performing dogs, which included three Great Danes, and all good specimens, especially the best trick dog in the lot, who no doubt gloried in his name of Grandmaster. These dogs went through a variety of performances in an extraordinarily kindly and willing manner, jumping through hoops, walking on their hind legs, sitting on chairs, jumping over each other's backs, with all the docility and more of the freedom than the poodle would have displayed.

Grandmaster made some astonishing leaps, and two of the hounds had a "make-believe" fight, growling, seizing each other, and rolling on the stage as they might have done in a less friendly strife. The latter was a performance I have not since seen attempted, and must be a most difficult thing for a trainer to teach. I do not know when I was better pleased with a group of performing dogs than I was with these Great Danes. I have seen other showmen performing with them in a cage of lions, and similar dogs formed a portion of "a happy family" of wild beasts that a few years since proved a great attraction at the Crystal Palace.

Again it is not unusual for the Dane to be trained to find truffles, a well known edible fungus which grows underground.

A friend of mine who has kept the variety for years, and still owns some exceedingly fine specimens, says the Dane appears to have a peculiar dislike to pigs of any kind, and coming across either one or a " sounder" is pretty certain to lay himself out to attack them. This scarcely gives the impression that he has had any connection with Ireland, where the pig is so common.

As special attention has been called to the Great Dane as a companion, allusion to that dog belonging to Prince Bismarck may not be out of place; still Tyras, the dog, was, in his palmy days, not a very much greater favourite than his master came to be later on. Maybe, the happiness of two countries was on at least one occasion placed in jeopardy by the action of the German Chancellor's hound. It has been said that a somewhat spirited conversation was proceeding between Bismarck and the Russian Prime Minister Gortschakoff. The latter, gesticulating rather more violently than usual, led Tyras, who lay reposing on the rug, to suspect an attack on his master, so, springing at the proud Russian, he brought him to the floor. Apologies were profuse and accepted. Prince Gortschakoff was not bitten, only frightened, and the peace of Europe remained undisturbed.

A writer in the *Kennel Gazette* gives the following interesting description of Prince Bismarck's favourite dog: I reproduce it here, as it will assist my readers in arriving at the character and disposition of the ordinary Great Dane:

"Of all the dogs that have a place in history, Tyras, the noted Ulmer dog of the German Chancellor, is the only one whose death has been deemed of sufficient interest to be cabled round the world as an event, not merely of European, but of cosmopolitan interest. Indeed, the record of Tyras hardly ended with his life, for the cable has since told the world that the first visitor to Prince Bismarck on his recent birthday was the youthful emperor, who brought as a present another dog, of the type of the lamented Tyras. For nearly sixty years Prince Bismarck has owned specimens of the Great Dane, and generally has had one or more of unusual size. His first hound, acquired while living with his parents at Kniephof, was one of the largest ever seen, and was an object of awe to the peasantry of the district. This dog afterward accompanied his young master to the college at Göttingen, where he speedily made his mark. Once when Bismarck was summoned to appear before the rector for throwing an empty bottle out of his window, he took with him his enormous hound, to the great dismay of the reverend dignitary, who promptly found refuge behind a high-backed chair, where he remained until the hound had been sent out of the room. Bismarck was fined five thalers for bringing this " terrific beast " into the rector's sanctum, in addition to the punishment meted out to the original offence.

" As a law student and official at Berlin, during his travels in many lands, throughout his diplomatic career at Frankfort, St. Petersburgh, Paris, and elsewhere, as well as at Varzin and at Friedrichsruh, Bismarck has always had the companionship of one or more of his favourite dogs. Probably the one to which he was most attached was Sultan, which died at Varzin in 1877. Tyras, who was of unusual size, and of the slate colour, which is most popular in Germany, was then quite a young dog, and he was the constant companion of his illustrious owner till the time of his death, sharing his walks, his rides, his business, and his meals, and keeping guard in his bedroom at night. Owing to his uncertain temper, he was not often seen in the streets or gardens of Berlin.

" He was, indeed, regarded more as belonging to

the "Pomeranian Squire" side of the Prince's life than to his official establishment. At Varzin or Friedrichsruh, however, the two were inseparable. No sooner was the most absolutely necessary business of the morning dispatched, than the Reichskanzler sallied off with the "Reichshund" at his heels, and for the rest of the day, the long light coat, and the battered felt hat of the famous statesman, were not greater objects of interest than the huge dog which followed him everywhere, on horseback or on foot."

At the present time the best Great Danes in England are owned by Mr. Reginald Herbert; Mr. R. Hood Wright, Frome; Mr. and Mrs. H. L. Horsfall, Diss; Mr. C. Petrywalski, London; Mr. R. Leadbetter, Berkshire; Mr. S. Pendry, Windsor; Mr. R. Coop, St. Helen's, and some few others. He is not in many hands, and, although the entries in the Kennel Club's stud book keep up their numbers fairly well, the old Great Dane Club itself had but twenty-seven members when it ceased to exist in 1895, consequent on the rule the Kennel Club adopted with regard to the abolition of cropping. Another club was immediately started, and at the time of writing, it has over forty members. Now the classes at Birmingham, the Crystal Palace, Brighton, Liverpool, &c., secure entries quite equal in number to any since the introduction of the Dane in this country, the new club evidently popularising the Dane as a show dog.

Perhaps the best all-round Great Dane we have had here was the brindled bitch Vendetta, first exhibited by Mr. Reginald Herbert, and sold by him to Mr. Craven for a large sum. She was not a particularly big bitch, though perhaps taller and heavier than she looked by reason of her lovely symmetry. She stood $31\frac{1}{2}$ inches at the shoulder and weighed 140lb.; but in general form and correctness of type of head, without lippiness or hound-like appearance, she was pretty nearly perfect. Windle Princess (Mr. Coop's) is another beautiful bitch, and again not a very big one. Mr. E. H. Adcock's Ivanhoe, a richly coloured brindle dog, has repeatedly and deservedly won prizes at our leading shows. Mr. Wilbey's Hannibal the Great was thought to be the best of his year, an enormous animal of immense power, but perhaps a little heavier and too mastiff-like in head to quite please some of our insular prejudices. He came to this country with a reputation as the best of his race in the land of his birth, which was Germany. This dog unfortunately got strangled in his kennel in August, 1892. Other good dogs are, or were, a Belgian dog, Herr Dobbelmann's Bosco Colonia, fawn in colour, who won prizes at the

Agricultural Hall in 1897; War Cry, Corsica, Harlequin Nero, Bouchan, Sea King, Leal, Baron of Danes, Norseman, Queen of Saxony, Windle Princess, Earl of Warwick, Windle Queen, Selwood Sambo and Selwood Ninon, Count Fritz, Hannibal of Redgrave, Mammoth Queen, Snow King, and Senta Valeria, the latter a harlequin bitch of great excellence which, when shown by M. Aaron, took leading honours at the Crystal Palace in 1895; she is now the property of Mr. R. Leabetter.

As to the heights and weights of prominent winners, the following may, perhaps, not be without interest:—Norseman was 33 inches at the shoulders, weight 155lb.; Sea King, 32½ inches, weight, 168lb.; eal 33¾ inches, weight, 182lb.; Young Leal, 33½ inches, weight, 154lb.; Prince Victor, 33 inches and 150lb. weight; Cedric the Saxon, 33½ inches and 170lb. weight; Baron of Danes, 33½ inches and 155lb. weight; Ivanhoe, 33 inches and 168lb. weight; Marco, 34 inches and 190lb. weight; Earl of Warwick, 33 inches and 175lb. weight; Dorothy, 30½ inches, 125lb. weight; Challymead Queen, 30½ inches and 125lb. weight; Corsica, 31 inches and 140lb. weight; and Ranee, 29 inches, 105lb. weight.

The original Club had a hard and fast rule absolutely disqualifying any dog with cankered teeth or with a joint or more removed from the end of the tail. These disabilities have, however, been removed by the new club, who elect to leave disqualification or otherwise for such defects altogether in the hands of the judges. I do not know that Danes are more afflicted with "cankered" teeth than any other dogs ; but, with respect to their "tails," cases have occurred where a dog has had a joint or two amputated, in order that the appendage did not curl at the end. The sore or bare place remaining was accounted for by the hound dashing his stern against the kennel walls or benches, a habit which frequently causes trouble to the caudal extremity of some big smooth-coated dogs.

As to cropping, the rule of the Kennel Club is to the effect that no dog born after March 30th, 1895, can, if cropped, win a prize at any show held under Club Rules.

The standard of points and description of the Great Dane as adopted by the new club are as follows:

1. *General Appearance.*—The Great Dane is not so heavy or massive as the mastiff, nor should he too nearly approach the greyhound in type. Remarkable in size, and very muscular, strongly though elegantly built, movements easy and graceful; head and neck carried high ; the tail carried horizontally

with the back, or slightly upwards, with a slight curl at the extremity. The minimum height and weight of dogs should be 30 inches and 120lb.; of bitches, 28 inches and 100lb. Anything below this shall be debarred from competition. Points: General appearance, 3; Condition, 3; Activity, 5; Height, 13.

2. *Head.*—Long, the frontal bones of the forehead very slightly raised, and very little indentation between the eyes. Skull not too broad. Muzzle, broad and strong, and blunt at the point. Cheek muscles, well developed. Nose large, bridge well arched. Lips in front perpendicularly blunted, not hanging too much over the sides, though with well-defined folds at the angle of the mouth. The lower jaw slightly projecting—about a sixteenth of an inch. Eyes, small, round, with sharp expression and deeply set, but the " wall " or " china " eye is quite correct in harlequins. Ears very small and greyhound-like in carriage, when uncropped. Points, 15.

3. *Neck.*—Rather long, very strong and muscular, well arched, without dewlap, or loose skin about the throat. The junction of head and neck strongly pronounced. Points, 5.

4. *Chest.*—Not too broad, and very deep in brisket. Points, 8.

5. *Back.*—Not too long or short; loins arched, and

The Great Dane.

falling in a beautiful line to the insertion of the tail. Points, 8.

6. *Tail.*—Reaching to or just below the hock, strong at the root, and ending fine with a slight curve. When excited it becomes more curved, but in no case should it curve over the back. Points, 4.

7. *Belly.*—Well drawn up. Points, 4.

8. *Fore-quarters.*—Shoulders, set sloping; elbows well under, neither turned inwards nor outwards. Leg: Fore-arm, muscular, and with great development of bone, the whole leg strong and quite straight. Points, 10.

9. *Hind-quarters.*—Muscular thighs, and second thigh long and strong, as in the greyhound, and hocks well let down and turning neither in nor out. Points, 10.

10. *Feet.*—Large and round, neither turned inwards nor outwards. Toes, well arched and closed. Nails, very strong and curved. Points, 8.

11. *Hair.*—Very short, hard and dense, and not much longer on the underpart of the tail. Points, 4.

Colour and Markings.—The recognised colours are the various shades of grey (commonly termed "blue"), red, black, or pure white, or white with patches of the before-mentioned colours. These colours are sometimes accompanied with markings of a darker tint about the eyes and muzzle, and with a line of the same tint (called a " trace ") along the course of the spine. The above ground colours also appear in the brindles, and are also the ground colours of the mottled specimens. In the whole-coloured specimens, the china or wall eye but rarely appears, and the nose more or less approaches black, according to the prevailing tint of the dog, and the eyes vary in colour also. The mottled specimens have irregular patches or " clouds " upon the above-named ground colours; in some instances the clouds or markings being of two or more tints. With the mottled specimens, the wall or china eye is not uncommon, and the nose is often parti-coloured or wholly flesh-coloured. On the continent the most fashionable and correct colour is considered to be pure white with black patches; and leading judges and admirers there consider the slate coloured or blue patches intermixed with black as most undesirable.

Faults.—Too heavy a head, too slightly arched frontal bone, and deep " stop " or indentation between the eyes; large ears and hanging flat to the face; short neck; full dewlap; too narrow or too broad a chest; sunken or hollow or quite straight back; bent fore-legs; overbent fetlocks; twisted feet; spreading toes; too heavy and much bent, or too highly carried

The Great Dane.

tail, or with a brush underneath; weak hind-quarters, cow hocks, and a general want of muscle.

STANDARD OF POINTS.

	Value.		Value.
General appearance	3	Belly	4
Condition	3	Tail	4
Activity	5	Fore-quarters	10
Head	15	Hind quarters	10
Neck	5	Feet	8
Chest	8	Coat	4
Back	8	Size (Height)	13
	47		53

Grand total, 100.

Scale of Points for Height divided as follows:

Dog of 30 in., or Bitch of 28 in.			Points	0
,, 31 in.	,,	29 in.	,,	2
,, 32 in.	,,	30 in.	,,	4
,, 33 in.	,,	31 in.	,,	6
,, 34 in.	,,	32 in.	,,	9
,, 35 in.	,,	33 in.	,,	13

So much for the Great Dane, Ulmer dog, German boarhound, German dogge, or whatever his owner likes to call him. I have been told that I am not one of his staunchest admirers, and that the foregoing chapter is a little biassed against him. I do not think this is the case. I am certainly no advocate for keeping these enormous dogs as companions, and, although they find favour in what may be called their native country, and some foreigners keep them as house dogs here, they are not generally popular as such. Their great activity, muscular development and power should make them of particular use where dogs are required for big game hunting, and, being pretty hard in constitution, they are certainly better adapted for the purpose than our British mastiff, or the converted bulldog. Perhaps the Great Dane might cross efficiently with the latter, and produce a more powerful dog than the ordinary bull-mastiff cross, which is often bred and trained as a watch dog and as an assistant to the game-keeper in such districts where a dog is required by him on his rounds at night.

INDEX.

	PAGE		PAGE
Adcock, Mr. E. H.	331	*Baily's Magazine*	35
Adcock, Mr. F.	327	Bagot's (Lord) Bloodhounds	33
Agassæos, the	7	Bampfylde, Hon. C.	128
Aldenham Piper (harrier)	128	Barnaby (bloodhound)	23, 31
Alder (deerhound)	213	Bassett, Mr. C. H.	114
Alex (Borzoi)	286	" Bavarian Mountain bloodhound "	44
Alexandra Palace Show in 1889	309		
"Allan-a-Dale" (Mr. B. C. Evelegh)	248	Beagle packs	148
		Beagle, proper work for	152
Allen-Jefferys', Mr., harriers	123	Beagle, size and points of	149
American Bloodhound Club	44	Beagle Studbook	147, 156
Amery's, Sir John Heathcote, Staghounds	114	Beagle, the, an ancient dog	133
		Beagle, used for covert shooting	143
Angelo, Mr. W. K.	277, 280	Beagle, the, Kerry	152
Anglesea's, Marquis of, harriers	129	Beagle, wire-coated	146
		Beagle, varieties of	152
Anne's, Queen, Staghounds	111	Beagles at Brighton	143
Argos (Borzoi)	309	Beagles at the shows	139
Arrian's work on coursing	226	Beagles beating coverts	140
Ashdown Park Meeting, establishment of	233	Beagles' ears	142
		Beagles in the South of England	140
Ashton, Mr. T.	249		
Athol, Duke of	169	Beagles kept by Royalty	134
Ayris, Harry	92	Beagles, pack of small	134
		Beagles, the, and the coachman	135
Bab at the Bowster (greyhound), her performances	244	Beard, Mr. Steyning	126
Badminton Hounds	81	Beckford, Peter	59

Index.

	PAGE
Beeswing (bloodhound)	23
Belhus (bloodhound)	23
Bell, Mr. J. Harriott	217
Bell's, Mr. Weston, monograph of the deerhound	210
Belvoir Hounds, origin of	58
Benson, Mr. John	168
Bentinck, Lord Henry	92
Bentinck's, Lord Henry, deerhounds	213
Berkeley, Grantley	38
Berners, Dame Juliana	7, 122
Bevis (deerhound) on the stage	216
Bismarck, Prince (Great Danes)	335, 356
Blackmore Vale Hounds	81
Blees, Mr. O. H.	309
Blencathra Hounds, great run with	62
Blew, Mr. W. C. A.	57
Blitsay (Borzoi)	307
Bloodhound bitch tracking poachers	12
Bloodhound characteristics	2, 51
Bloodhound Club in America	44
Bloodhound kennels, some good	34
Bloodhound, points of	45
Bloodhound, the modern	36
Bloodhound, the origin of	1
Bloodhound trials at Boxmoor	20
Bloodhound trials at Warwick	16
Bloodhound trials in 1889	17
Bloodhound used as a cross	2
Bloodhound as companion	33, 38, 40
Bloodhounds as crosses	36
Bloodhounds hunting	3, 8, 10, 12, 17, 20, 35, 41
Bloodhounds in the Southern States	3

	PAGE
Bloodhounds in the streets	10
Bloodhounds must be quietly handled	36
Bloodhounds of 1897	38
Bloodhounds, pack of	34, 35
Bloodhounds sent to Jamaica	6
Bloodhound's voice, the	39
Blount's "Ancient Tenures"	230
Blue Belle (beagle)	142
Blueberry (bloodhound)	23, 31
Blue Ransom (foxhound)	81
Boar Hound (Great Dane)	328, 345
Boece, Hector	109
Boddington harriers, the	128
Boldareff, M. A., on the Borzoi	313
"Book of St. Alban's," the	122
"Boot, clean," hunting	20
Bootiman	7, 257
Border thieves	3
Borzoi a Russian name	305
Borzoi as a companion	312
Borzoi, British breeders of the	305
Borzoi, colours of the	311
Borzoi, description of, by M. A. Boldareff	313
Borzoi, description of, from the *Field*	289
Borzoi, different strains of	322
Borzoi, first exhibited	287
Borzoi kennels at St. Petersburg	323
Borzoi, Mr. F. Lowe on	292
Borzoi new to England	285
Borzoi or Russian wolfhound	285
Borzoi, points for judging	317
Borzoi, the Princess of Wales'	286
Borzoi, some good specimens	310
Borzoi, value of the	307, 323

Index.

	PAGE
Borzois at the Agricultural Hall in 1892	306
Borzois at the shows	286
Borzois coursing hares	304
Borzois hunting the wolf	293-303
Borzois in Russia	288
Borzois, Mr. Kalmoutzky's pack of	292-298
Borzois on the stage	288
Borzois, the best seen in England	308
Borzois, the Prince of Wales's	286
Bosco Colonia (Great Dane)	339
Boswell on the deerhound	204
Boxmoor, bloodhound trials at	20
"Brach," the, in Arthurian legend	133
Bran (deerhound anecdote)	209
Bran (Irish wolfhound)	280
Brice, Mr.	258
Bromley, Sir Henry	167, 170
Bronwyd beagles, the	148
"Brooksby" on the foxhound	75-81
Brookside harriers, the	126
Brough, Mr. E.	18, 31, 34, 37, 41
Bruce, King Robert, and the "white faunch deer"	201
Buckhounds, the Royal	111
Buckley's, Mr., Welsh hounds	181, 182
Burnaby (greyhound)	251
Cackett, Mr. E. J.	141
Caius, Dr.	122
Cameron of Lochiel's deerhounds	214
Cambridge's, Mr. H. P., beagles	140
Campbell, junr., Mr. Morton	218

	PAGE
Canteleu, Le Comte de, on the foxhound	34, 87
Carhampton (greyhound)	249
Carlisle otter hounds, the	167
Carrick, Mr. J. C.	158, 167
"Carted" deer	110
Cedric the Saxon (Great Dane)	329
Century Magazine, the	41
Charles I. and his greyhound	231
Charlton hunt, the	57
Chaucer (bloodhound)	14
Cheriton, Mr.	169
Cheshire Beagle Hunt Club	148
Chesshyre's, Mrs., beagles	139
Christ Church, Oxford, beagles	148
Cid Campeador (Great Dane)	329
Clarke, Mr. H. T.	249
"Clean Boot" hunting	20
Cliffe Coursing Meeting	250
Clift, Mr. Harry	168
Clumber, Borzois at	308
Coachman and the beagles	135
Cockermouth otter hounds, the	168
Co. Down staghounds	118
Collier, Mr. W.	169
Comins, J.	118
Coniston hounds, extraordinary runs	52, 61
Constable's (Sir Talbot) hounds	124
Contest (foxhound)	99
Corbet, Mr. Reginald	57, 93
Cossack (Borzoi)	287
Countess (deerhound)	215
"Couples" of hounds	230
Coursing abroad	257
Coursing clubs, establishment of	232
Coursing club, the earliest	232
Coursing Calendar	247

	PAGE
Coursing fixtures, early	233
Coursing in enclosures	246
Coursing in early times	227
Coursing judges and slippers	256
Coursing meetings of the present day	236
Coursing rules in Elizabeth's time	232
Cowen, Colonel	34
Crane's, Mr., rabbit beagles	136
Craven harriers, the	128
Craven, Mr.	27
Croescade Welsh hounds, the	176
Crofton, Mr.	143
Crofton's, Mr., beagles	145
Crofton's, Mr. W. R., beagles	139
Cromwell (foxhound)	92
Cromwell (bloodhound)	37
Crony (bloodhound)	14
Culmstock otter hounds	169
Cumberland and Westmoreland foxhunting	60
Cupples, Mr. George	204
Curfew (Welsh hound)	183
Cursis Stream beagles	148
Curzon Hall Dog Show	33
"Cymru Bach" on the Welsh hound	192
Czarina (greyhound)	234
Dainty (bloodhound) discovering a dead child	19
Damon (Borzoi)	307
Dane, the Great	325, 346
Dane, the Great (Club)	328, 341
Dane, the Great (cropping)	331, 332, 338
Dane, the Great (disqualifications of)	341

	PAGE
Dane, the Great (exhibiting)	338, 340
Dane, the Great (for big game)	346
Dane, the Great (Harlequin)	330
Dane, the Great (Prince Bismarck)	335
Dane, the Great (Size of)	328, 329, 340
Dane, the Great (Useful for crossing)	346
Danes, Great (names of noted)	330, 340
Danes, Great (performing)	334
Danes, Great (Ranelagh show of)	329
Danger (bloodhound)	21, 22
Danger, Mrs.	31
Daniel, Mr. F.	143
Dansey's "Arrian"	227, 229
Darlington Show	250
Davies, Mr. Vaughan	175
Dawson, Captain	170
"Days of Deer Stalking"	206
Deer coursing	208
Deer "drives"	208
Deerhound anecdotes	200, 201
Deerhounds as companions	211
Deerhounds at the dog shows	210, 213
Deerhound Club's description	221
Deerhound colours	218
Deerhounds difficult to rear	221
Deerhounds, education of	212
Deerhounds, endurance of	220
Deerhound exhibitors	214
Deerhounds, form of, and method of attack	220
Deerhounds, heights and weights of	219

Index.

	PAGE
Deerhounds in the sixteenth century	202
Deerhounds in Scotland in the eighteenth century	203
Deerhounds in the Hebrides	205
Deerhound kennels, some first-class	217
Deerhounds little used in deer-stalking	210
Deerhounds, principal strains of	206
Deerhounds, points for judging	226
Deerhounds, prices realised by	214
Deerhound, Scotsmen's opinion of	211
Deerhounds, size of	218
Deerhounds, some owners of good	214
Deerhound, the, in Queen Elizabeth's reign	199
Deer hunting	110
Deer prepared for the chase	114
Dent, Mr. (greyhounds)	240, 242
Devon and Somerset Staghounds	112
Devon and Somerset "old pack"	114
Dhuart (Irish wolfhound)	281
"Dignity and Impudence"	41
Dinah (deerhound)	217
Dobbelman, Herr	329
Dobson, Tommy	73
"Dogs of the British Islands"	136
Dogs on the Egyptian monuments	228
Dog Owners' Annual	321
Don (bloodhound)	37
Druid (bloodhound)	38
Duster (foxhound)	97

	PAGE
Edward II.'s otter hounds	164
Edward III.'s staghounds	109
Elizabeth's, Queen, beagles	134
Fabulous Fortune (greyhound)	251
Faliscus, Gratius	7
Faster and Faster (greyhound)	251
Fawcett's, Messrs., kennels	251
Field, the, 9, 35, 44, 57, 68, 90, 123, 175, 180, 184, 209, 271, 289	
Fingal (deerhound)	216
Fitzroy, Lord Alfred	27
Fitz Fife (greyhound)	251
Foljambe, Mr. P. J. Savile	196
Forester (beagle)	141
Forster, Mr. R. Carnaby	166, 168
Fortuna Favente (greyhound)	251
Fownes', Mr., pack of hounds	58
Fox Bush harriers, the	128
Foxhunting in Cumberland and Westmoreland	60
Foxhunting season of 1896-7	106
Foxhound, the	53
Foxhound, "Brooksby" on the	75-81
Foxhound "drafts"	82
Foxhound, duties of a	59
Foxhound, Le Comte de Canteleu on the	87
Foxhound, Mr. G. S. Lowe on the	90-101
Foxhound pack, earliest	57
Foxhound packs, size of	81
Foxhound packs, their influence on the country	54
Foxhound, points of the	101
Foxhound Studbook	101
Foxhounds as otter hounds	165
Foxhounds, cost of keeping	54

	PAGE		PAGE
Foxhounds, division of large packs	81	Goth II. (Irish wolfhound)	277
Foxhounds, great runs with	60-66	Grafton (bloodhound)	41
Foxhound's homing faculty	72	Graham, Captain G. A. 273, 275, 280, 281, 287,	329
Foxhounds, management	104	Grandmaster, (Great Dane)	334
Foxhounds, number of packs	53	Grant, Dr.	169
Foxhounds of a past generation	59	Greyhound course, points of the	256
Foxhounds on the show bench	84	Greyhound, description of the	253
Foxhounds, prices of	85	Greyhound kennels, expense of	252
Foxhounds, pace of	67	Greyhound kennels, in Ireland	252
Foxhounds, "rounding" ears of	82	Greyhound kennels in Scotland	252
Foxhounds, "Stonehenge" on	83	Greyhound kennels in Wales	252
Foxhounds taken to Russia	71	Greyhound kennels, leading	253
Foxhounds, a best twelve	95	Greyhound kennels, some strong	251
Foxhounds, the smallest and the largest	81	Greyhound, points of the	255
Foxhounds, "walking" the puppies	82	Greyhound, popularity of the	227
Full Captain (greyhound)	241	"Greyhound Stud Book"	248
Fullerton (greyhound) 234, 240, 241, 242,	249	Greyhound tax	236
Fullerton's performances	240	Greyhound, the, as a show dog	249
Furrier (foxhound)	93	Greyhounds, aged, running	250
		Greyhounds (sculptured) in the British Museum	229
Gallon, Mr.	163	Greyhounds in Canute's time	228
Gamester (bloodhound)	35	Greyhounds in the classics	228
Garnier, Colonel	280	Greyhounds, King John's	229
Gaylass (Welsh hound)	179	Greyhounds, prices of 234, 240,	243
Gelly hounds, the	174	Grew, Mr. W. C.	218
George IV.'s beagles	135	Griffons, French, sent to Scotland	158
German Boarhound	345		
German Dogge	345	Gwynne's, Mr., wire-coated beagles	146
German Mastiff	345		
Gesner's "General History"	199		
Goodall (Frank) and Rummager (anecdote)	117	Hannibal the Great (Dane)	339
Goodwood Hunt, the	57	Hardy's (Colonel) beagles	136
Gore, Sir St. George	215	Hare hunting in times past	121
Gosforth Meeting	246	Hare hunting on foot	130
		Harlequin, Dane, the	320

	PAGE		PAGE
Harrier, description of	127	Inclosed meetings for greyhounds	246
Harrier, distinguishing characteristics of the	129	Inge, Lieut.-Colonel	213
Harrier packs, number of	127	Irish wolfhound, origin of the	269
Harrier pack with a "lady master"	131	Irish wolfhound as a companion	277
		Irish wolfhound (anecdote)	271
Harrier, points of the	130	Irish wolfhound breeders	281
Harriers in Lancashire	125	Irish Wolfhound Club	281
Harriers, packs of small	126	Irish wolfhound, description of	282
Harriers, size of	124, 127	Irish wolfhound difficult to define	274
Hawkstone otter hounds	166		
Haydock Park Meeting	246	Irish wolfhound, Earl of Antrim's portrait of	270
Hebe III. (bloodhound)	29, 31		
Hector II. (bloodhound)	18, 30	Irish wolfhound not very popular	281
Hedley, Mr. James	256		
Henry VIII. coursing	231	Irish wolfhound, size of	274
Herbert, Mr. Reginald	181, 329	Irish wolfhound, uncertainty as to, among writers	275
Herschel (greyhound)	249		
Heysham, Mr. G. A. Mounsey	167	Irish wolfhounds, heights and weights of	279
		"Isle of Dogs"	230
Hickman's, Mr., deerhounds	215, 275		
"Highland Sports," St. John's	207	Jaff (bloodhound)	31
		Jefferson, Mr. J. H.	180
Hill, Hon. Geoffrey, his otter hounds	166	Jenkins', Squire, pack of Welsh hounds	175
Hill, Mr. Woodruffe	330	Jenny Jones (greyhound)	249
Hodson, Mr. H. C.	38	Joachim, Mr.	141
Hogg, Mr. Lindsay	28	Johnson, Dr., his tour in the Hebrides	204
Holcombe harriers, the	125, 128		
Holland, Mr. S. T.	286	Jones, Mr. John	177
Hore, Mr. J. P.	111		
Huldman, Colonel (anecdote of bloodhound)	9	Kalmontzky, Mr.,	292-298
		Kelley, Mr. G. F.	120
Hunting horn, an ancient	57	Kelso (deerhound)	219
Hunting story, an interesting	58	Kempton Park Coursing	246
		Kendal otter hounds	167
H'Vat (Borzoi)	309	Kennedy, Captain Clarke	169
		Kennel Club Show, 1896	139
"Idstone" on the beagle	136	Kennel Club's Show in 1891	309

VOL. I.   A A

	PAGE
Kennel Club trials (1889) of bloodhounds	27
Kensington Gardens, beagle hunting in	144
Kerry beagle, points of	154
Kerry beagle, the	152
Kerr, Lady Charles	287
Keyes, Dr.	7
King John's otter hounds	163
Knowles, Mr. B. C.	29
Koodoo (bloodhound)	29
Korotai (Borzoi)	306, 308
Kreckwitz, Otto, Munich	327
Krilutt (Borzoi)	306, 308, 309, 321
Ladies' Kennel Association	261
Lady (foxhound)	93
Lamonby, Mr. W. F.	233
Landmark (Welsh hound)	181
Landseer, Sir E.	41
Langer (Welsh hound)	179
Lasca (Borzoi)	307
Lauderdale (greyhound)	250
Leal (Great Dane)	328
"Leash" of hounds	229
Legard, Sir Cecil	170
Leverarius	122
Lewis, Mr. T. P.	180
Lignum (beagle)	143
"Linehunter" on the Welsh hound	184
Lively (Welsh hound)	180
Llangibby hounds, the	176, 187
Lloyd, Freeman	261
Lomax's, Squire, otter hounds	163
Lonely (beagle)	143
Lonely II. (beagle)	143
Longford staghounds	118
Lord of the Isles (deerhound)	216
Lord, Mr.	141

	PAGE
Lord's, Mr., rabbit beagles	143
Lort, Mr. W.	141
Lounger (foxhound)	65
Lovell, Captain	119
Lowe, Mr. F., on the Borzoi	292
Lowe, Mr. G. S. on the foxhound	90-101
Lowndes, Mr. Selby	35
Luath XI. (bloodhound)	36
Macneill of Colonsay	206
Macneil, Sir John	213
"Maida" (Mr. D. Brown)	248
Major (foxhound)	235
Malcolm (deerhound)	208
Man hunting by bloodhounds 3, 8, 10, 12, 17, 20,	41
Manchester, Duchess of	287
Maney Starlight (greyhound)	250
"Manuel de Venerie Française"	34
Markland, Mr.	19
Marples, Mr. T., on whippet racing	266
Masserine Coursing Meeting	247
"Master of the Royal Buckhounds," the	118
Master McGrath (greyhound) 235, 238, 239,	249
Mâtin, the	270
Maut (greyhound)	250
Mayhew, Mr. Reginald	142
Mellbrake hounds, notable run with	61
McConnochie, Mr. J.	250
Merkin (foxhound)	67
Merlin (Irish wolfhound)	280
Merry (beagle)	141
Merthyr Old Court Welsh harriers	180

Index. 355

	PAGE		PAGE
Middleton, Lord	55	Otter hound packs, the most noted	166
Millais, Sir Everett	37		
Molodetz (Borzoi)	286	Otter hound, points	172
Monmouth, Duke of, at Sedgmoor	6	Otter hounds, royal packs of	163
		Otter hounds, some recently established packs	170
Morni (deerhound)	215		
Morro (Great Dane)	330	Otter hunting with a scratch pack	161
Mosstroopers, the	3		
Mostyn, Sir Thomas	93	Otter hound work	159
Mounter (foxhound)	68	Otter hounds, value of	168
Muir, Mr. Kenneth	306	Oudar (Borzoi)	307, 308
Musicwood (beagle)	141	Owdalzka (Borzoi)	286
Musters, Mr. H. C.	214		
		Pace of foxhounds	67
National Coursing Club	247	Págooba (Borzoi)	309
Newby Bridge, trail hunting at	67	Palmer, Sir Roger	328
		Parry, Dr. Hales	31
New Forest deerhounds	119	Payne-Gallwey, Sir Ralph	276
Nichols, Mr. E.	37	Pegler, Mr. Holmes	21
Nijni (Borzoi)	287	Penelope II. (greyhound)	251
"Nimrod" (Charles J. Apperley)	58	Penistone harriers, the	128
		Pennant concerning the deerhound	203
"Notitia Venatica"	57		
Nutt's, Mr. G. H., beagles	139, 146	Peover beagles	148
		Pescara (greyhound)	246
		Philpot, Dr.	21
Obolensky, Prince, on the Borzoi	303	Phœbus (greyhound)	252
		Piccolo (beagle)	143
O'Brien, Mr. R. D.	275	Picts and Scots, fight between	200
O'Connell, Mr. John	153		
O'Connell, Mr. Maurice	153	Pilkington, Mr. Leonard	245, 251
Ooslad (Borzoi)	308	Pirate (deerhound)	215
Opera (beagle)	143	Poachers tracked by bloodhound	12
Orford, Lord	233		
Oscar (deerhound)	213	Pontarlier (greyhound)	246
Oscar (Irish wolfhound)	276	Powell, Captain, on the bloodhound	15
Otter hound, description of	170		
Otter hounds in the north	169	Prima Donna (beagle)	143
Otter hounds on the show bench	167	Primate (bloodhound)	31
Otter hound, origin of	157	Pryse-Rice, Mrs.	131

A A 2

	PAGE		PAGE
"Psovi," a suggested name	305	Rossendale harriers, the	125
Puckeridge hounds	81	Rothschild's, Lord de, staghounds	119
Queen Elizabeth's deerhounds	199	Roussalka (Borzoi)	309
Queen of the West (bloodhound) tracking a thief	14	Royal (foxhound)	92
		Royal Rock beagles	148
		Rummager (staghound) and his master	117
Radnorshire and West Herefordshire pack	195	*Rural Almanac*, the	126, 149
Ragman (otter hound)	160, 167	"Rural Sports," Daniel's	67
Rally (otter hound)	161	Russell, Rev. John	160
Raper, Tom	256	Ryan, Mr. Clement	154
Rapture (harrier)	125	Rydal Park, trail hunting in	66
Rasselas (beagle)	141		
Reader (beagle)	143		
Red deer, chase of the wild	112	St. Clair, Henry	199
Red Rover (greyhound)	244	St. Clair, Sir William, and his deerhounds	207
Red Ruby (greyhound)	243		
Regulus (foxhound)	100	St. John, Charles, on the deerhound	207
"Reichshund," the	338		
Reinagle's picture of a wolfhound	273	Salter, Mr. J. H.	249
		Sandall, Mr. E.	140
Reynolds, Rev. E. M.	61	Satan (Great Dane)	327
Richard II. and his hounds (anecdote)	230	Sanders, Mr. R. A.	112, 114
		Scandia (greyhound)	250
Richardson, Mr. H.	275	Scarteen pack of Kerry beagles	154
Riego, M.	329	"Scotch Deerhounds and their Masters"	204
Riddlesworth (foxhound)	81		
Robert Bruce and the bloodhounds	6	Scots and Picts, fight between	200
		Scott, Sir Walter, anecdote of the bloodhound	6
Robin Hood (beagle)	143		
"Robin Hood" (Mr. C. M. Browne)	247	Scott, Mr. W. J.	29
		Scrope's "Deer Stalking"	206
Roden, Captain	34	Seavington harriers	125
Rory Carragh, the wolfhunter	271	Senhouse, Mr. H. P.	169
		Sharples, Mr. T.	250
Rosary (greyhound)	244	Sheelah (Irish wolfhound)	280
Rosebud (harrier)	125	Shellock (deerhound)	215
Roscommon staghounds	118	Siberian wolfhound	285, 287
Ross's, Dr., deerhounds	207	"Singing beagles"	149

Index. 357

	PAGE
"Skiddaw" (Mr. W. F. Lamonby)	248
Slave hunting by bloodhounds	3
"Sleeping Bloodhound," the	41
Sleuth hound, the	2
"Slough Dogs," warrant for keeping	4
Smith, Mr. Assheton	170
Snowball (greyhound), extraordinary performance of	235
Southern hounds	128
South-west Meath staghounds	118
Sperling's, Mr., harriers	125, 129
"Sportsman's Cabinet," the	233, 273
Staghound or buckhound	109
Staghound packs in England and Ireland	110
Staghound runs, some extraordinary	116
Staghounds, heights of	112
Staghounds, Her Majesty's	111
Staghounds in the reigns of Edward III. and Queen Elizabeth	109, 111
Staintondale hounds	74
Starkie, Colonel	27
Starno (Irish wolfhound)	281
"Stonehenge"	32, 38, 83, 87, 136, 140, 227, 247, 253
Strabo on the British dog	7
Stroganoff, Count, an owner of greyhounds	243
Stud Book pedigrees	38
Surbiton beagles	148
Swaffham (Norfolk) Coursing Club	232
Talbot, the	1

	PAGE
Talisman (Welsh hound)	196
Tamvoski, Lieut. G.	305
Tankerville, Earl of, on the deerhound	209
Tara (deerhound)	218
Tattersall, Mr. W.	167
Taunton, Mr. W. K.	21
Taunton Vale harriers	129
Tchebreshoff, Colonel	311
Templemore staghounds	118
Texture (greyhound)	243
Thornton, Colonel	65, 135
Thoughtless Beauty (greyhound)	251
Thuggum Thu (Irish wolfhound)	280
Tom (Borzoi)	286
Tom Finkle and his bloodhound	9
Torum (deerhound)	214
Torrum (Irish wolfhound)	280
"Trail hunting"	66, 68, 72
Trainor, Mr.	280
Trelawney, Mr.	169
"Trencher-fed" packs	73
Triumph (bloodhound)	37
Trojan (foxhound)	93
Tsaritsa (Borzoi)	309
"Tufters"	113
Twici, Edward II.'s huntsman	56
Tyras (Great Dane)	336
Ulmer Dog	336, 345
Unclean Shoe, bloodhound tracking the	32
Valiant (harrier)	128
Velasquez (Borzoi)	309
Velsk (Borzoi)	309
Vendetta (Great Dane)	338

index.

	PAGE
Voltigeur (bloodhound anecdote)	9
Wales, H.R.H. the Princess of	286
Walker, John	92
Wallace and the sleuth hounds	6
Walsh, Mr. J. H.	38
Wardell, Mr. H. P.	166
Ward Union staghounds	118
Warrior (deerhound)	215
Warwick bloodhound trials	16
Warwick, Mr. G.	256
Waterloo Cup winners	238
Waterloo Meeting, the	237
Webber's, Mr., harriers	125
Wellesley, Colonel	303, 309
Welsh hounds, character of	183
Welsh hounds compared with English	191
Welsh hounds cross	197
Welsh hound described by a Welshman	193
Welsh hound dying out, the	189
Welsh hounds hunting the "quest"	198
Welsh hounds in packs of other hounds	180
Welsh hounds, origin of	173
Welsh packs not necessarily Welsh hounds	174
"Welshman" on the Welsh hound	189
Welsh hounds, shyness of	184, 190
Welsh hounds, the earliest known	174
Welsh hounds, two types of	181
Welsh wire-haired hounds, demand for	179
While, Mr. H. C,	250
Whippets and their owners	267
Whippet handicaps	263

	PAGE
"Whippet or Race Dog"	261
Whippet, origin of the	259
Whippet, the, in the Stud-book	260
Whippets, method of handicapping	267
Whippet, the names given to	259
Whippet racing	261, 264
Whippet, size of	262
Whippet training	264
Whippet, what used for	260
Wilbey, Mr. E.	339
Wilkinson, Mr. T. (Otter hounds)	199
Wilkinson, Tom (slipper)	257
Wilkinson, Mr. Gardiner	228
Wilkinson, Mr. C.	169
William III.'s beagles	134
Wilmslow tragedy, the	19
Wilson, Mr. C. H.	35, 40
Wilton, Lord	58
Winchell, Mr.	44
Windle Princess (Great Dane)	339
Wire-coated beagles	146
Witham Coursing Meeting	246
Wolfhound, the Irish	269-282
Wolfhound skulls found in barrows	274
Wolf hunt described by an English officer	298-303
Wolfhunting by Borzois	293-303
Wolfhunter, the (anecdote)	271
Wolverton's (Lord) pack of bloodhounds	34
Woodstock and other places depopulated for deer park	109
Wright, Mr. R. Hood	18, 30, 281, 336
Wright, Mr. J.	287
Wynn, Hon. H. C.	180, 182

	PAGE		PAGE
Wynnstay Royal (foxhound)	100	Young Fullerton (greyhound)	240
		Ynysfor Welsh hounds	177
Yarborough, Lord	54		
Yates, Mr. W. C.	169	Zloeem (Borzoi)	310

Advertisements.

SPRATT'S PATENT LIMITED DOG FOODS.

PATENT MEAT "FIBRINE" VEGETABLE DOG CAKES (with Beetroot), 20s. per cwt. ; 10s. 6d. per ½-cwt.; 5s. 6d. per ¼-cwt.; 2s. 9d. per 14lb. ; 1s. 6d. per 7lb.

PERCENTAGE OF MEAT.—We make our " Fibrine " Dog Cakes with 7, 10, 20, 25, 30, and 35 per cent. of meat. Any of these percentages can be obtained, no extra charge being made up to 25 per cent. inclusive.

PATENT COD LIVER OIL DOG CAKES (large), per cwt. bag, 21s.

PATENT GREYHOUND MEAT FIBRINE DOG CAKES, per cwt. bag, 21s.

HOUNDMEAL (in three grades), Nos. 0 (for pups), 1 (Medium), and 2 (coarse), 18s. per cwt. bag.

BONE MEAL, per cwt. bag, 14s. 6d.

PATENT PUPPY CAKES, per cwt. bag, 20s. ; per 14lb. tin or box, 4s. ; per 7lb. tin or box, 2s.; and in 1s. tins. Packed also in cases, price per cwt., 23s. ; per ½-cwt., 12s. ; per ¼-cwt. 6s. 6d.

PATENT COD LIVER OIL DOG CAKES (small size) for Toy Dogs and Puppies, per cwt. case, 27s. ; per ½-cwt. case, 14s. ; per ¼-cwt. case, 7s. 6d.; per 14lb. tin or box, 4s. ; per 7lb. tin or box, 2s. ; and in 1s. tins.

YOUR TRADESMAN OR STORES WILL SUPPLY YOU.

SPRATT'S PATENT Ltd., BERMONDSEY, LONDON.

Advertisements.

Advertisements.

SCOTT ADIE,
LADIES' AND GENTLEMEN'S TAILOR,
The Royal Scotch Warehouse,
115 & 115A, REGENT ST., LONDON, W.

TRAVELLING COATS,
STALKING CAPES,
INVERNESS CAPES,
HIGHLAND JEWELLERY,
HIGHLAND SHOOTING SUITS,
HIGHLAND DRESS SUITS,
TARTAN SILKS AND RIBBONS

RUGS, MAUDS, SHAWLS AND WRAPS,
The best selection in London.
HARRIS AND SHETLAND HOMESPUNS,
HAND-KNIT STOCKINGS AND SOCKS,

The Royal Scotch Warehouse,
REGENT STREET AND VIGO STREET, LONDON, W.
TELEGRAMS: "SCOTT ADIE, LONDON."

Advertisements.

CHAMBERLIN & SMITH'S MEAT BISCUITS

Supplied to the Royal Kennels at Sandringham.

Price 16s. per cwt., bag included.
Special quotations for 5 cwt. and 1 ton lots.
Carriage paid not less than 2cwt.

EAR-CANKER LOTION for Dogs.

WORM PILLS for Dogs.

ECZEMA PILLS for Dogs.

DISTEMPER PILLS for Dogs.

TONIC PILLS for Dogs.

MANGE OINTMENT for Dogs.

Above preparations 1s. per Bottle; post free 1s. 2d.

CHAMBERLIN'S DOG SOAP,

6d. per Tablet.

CHAMBERLIN'S DOG FOOD,

For Puppies, Sick, and Dainty Feeders.

2d. per Packet.   Twelve Packets, by Parcels Post free, 3s.

PREPARED ONLY BY

CHAMBERLIN & SMITH,

Dog and Pheasant Food Manufacturers,

NORWICH, England.

Advertisements.

WESTLEY RICHARDS'
PERFECT PATENT
HAMMERLESS EJECTOR GUNS.

OVER 10,000 IN USE.

For fine workmanship, elegant form, durability, and Shooting, they cannot be surpassed. The simplest and most successful Ejector Gun yet invented. It has stood the test of eleven years' experience. Sixty thousand cartridges have been fired from one of these guns without failure or impairing the mechanism.

A FEW TESTIMONIALS.
(*From a large number.*)

" The three Hammerless Ejector Guns you made me in 1887 have given me every satisfaction, and have worked perfectly all the time."—EUSTON.

" Lord Egmont has pleasure in speaking highly of the pair of Ejector Guns supplied him by Messrs. Westley Richards & Co. They are beautifully balanced, shoot admirably, and the Ejector works easily and smoothly."

" I have given the gun supplied by you in August last a good trial, and I can only say it is as perfect as the pair I had from you in August, 1889. These guns have been in constant use, and the Ejectors work as well to-day as they did when they left your hands. I have never had the slightest trouble with the guns in any way. After such a trial as these have had, and have proved themselves so excellent, I think it only fair to tell you so."
—H. M. UPCHER.

Patent Adjustable TRY GUNS and CAREFUL FITTING at our Private Grounds
(*Half an hour's journey from New Bond Street*).
" From the shooter's point of view the ground is perfection."—*Field.*

ALL KINDS OF RIFLES, REVOLVERS, &C.
72 *page Illustrated Catalogue sent free by post on application to—*

WESTLEY RICHARDS & Co. Ltd.,
178, New Bond Street, London; or, 12, Corporation Street, Birmingham.

Advertisements.

BARNARDS LIMITED,
LONDON & NORWICH.
EVERY REQUISITE FOR DOGS, POULTRY, PIGEONS, RABBITS, &c., ON APPROVED PRINCIPLES.

New Illustrated Catalogue Post Free. Estimates given.

Highest Awards wherever Exhibited.
12
Gold, Silver, AND Bronze Medals.

New Double Kennels, No. 342, very suitable for breeding purposes. Each kennel 3ft. 6in. square, 5ft. high to eaves, runs 6ft. 6in. long, finished in the best style, £11 10s. Carriage Paid. Corrugated iron at sides, 10s. extra.

LONDON SHOW ROOMS: **23, PRINCES ST., CAVENDISH SQ., W.**
MANUFACTORY: NORWICH.

DOGS—RACKHAM'S DISTEMPER BALLS. The only cure known. Used in all the Principal Kennels. Price 1s., 2s. 6d., 5s., 10s., and 20s.; free 2d. extra.

DOGS—RACKHAM'S JAPANESE WORM BALLS, also **POWDERS.** One dose sufficient; no other medicine necessary. Price 1s., 2s. 6d., 5s., 10s., and 20s. free 2d. extra.

DOGS—RACKHAM'S TONIC CONDITION BALLS are invaluable for Greyhounds and Whippets in Training, Stud Dogs, &c. Price 1s., 2s. 6d., 5s., 10s., and 20s.; free 2d. extra.

DOGS—RACKHAM'S KATALEPRA. Cures Red Mange, Eczema, and all Skin Diseases. Price 1s., 2s. 6d., 5s., 10s., and 20s.; free 2d. extra.

DOGS—RACKHAM'S JAPAN SOAP for Washing Dogs. Prevents Skin Diseases; kills all vermin. Tablets 6d. and 1s.; post free 2d. extra.

DOGS—RACKHAM'S NORFOLK HOUND MEAL is the Best Food for all Dogs. Supplied in small or large grades. Price 16s. per cwt.

DOGS—RACKHAM'S ANTI-DISTEMPER SPECIFIC. For the Prevention and Cure of distemper. With young puppies its effects are marvellous. This remedy prevents contagion at Shows. Price 2s. 6d., 5s., 10s., and 20s. per box; post free 2d. extra.

HORSES—RACKHAM'S CONDITION BALLS, also **POWDERS.** Produce Condition, Glossy Coat, &c. Price 2s. 6d. and 5s. per box; free 2d. extra.

ADVICE GRATIS IN ALL DISEASES OF DOGS.

RACKHAM & CO., ST. PETER'S, NORWICH.

Advertisements.

THOMAS & SONS'
PATENT.
SKELETON CONTINUATIONS TO BREECHES.
(No. 28,870.)

Gentlemen having large calves and small knee bones find it difficult to get Breeches to fit them nicely without the aid of Continuations, and as these help to fill up the boots and to make the leg look clumsier still, this improvement has suggested itself to **Messrs. THOMAS & SONS**, who are always to the fore with improvements of practical utility to the Sportsman.

HUNTING and SPORTING CLOTHES of EVERY DESCRIPTION,
OF SUPERIOR CUT AND FINISH,

Including several Patented Improvements of their own unobtainable elsewhere.

THOMAS & SONS,
Sporting Tailors and Breeches Makers,
32, BROOK STREET, W.
(Corner of South Molton Street.)

Telegrams: "Sportingly," London.

Advertisements.

WORKS BY THE SAME AUTHOR.

THE NON-SPORTING Division of Modern Dogs of Great Britain and Ireland. 376 Pages and twenty-two full-page Illustrations. Price 10s. 6d.

The *Times* says: "A treatise which will, no doubt, carry high authority amongst dog fanciers."

THE TERRIERS Division of Modern Dogs of Great Britain and Ireland. 458 Pages and eighteen full-page Illustrations. Price 10s. 6d.

The *Daily Chronicle* says: "Compiled with so much knowledge, so much care."

THE COLLIE OR SHEEP DOG: Its history and description in its British Varieties, with full-page wood engravings and exquisite tail pieces by ARTHUR WARDLE. Price 3s. 6d. ; a few copies on large paper, price 10s. 6d.

The *Saturday Review* says: "Filled with accurate information as to the various strains, and valuable suggestions as to their rearing and management."

THE FOX TERRIER: Its history and description, with reminiscences. Illustrated by wood engravings and many typical tail pieces by ARTHUR WARDLE. Third Edition, price 5s.

The *Westminster Gazette* says: "Apart from its great value as a record of all that is worth knowing about Fox Terriers, its present cheap and elegant form is a delightful, historical, typographical, and artistic addition to the literature of dogology."

PUBLISHED BY HORACE COX,
WINDSOR HOUSE, BREAM'S BUILDINGS, LONDON, E.C.

www.ingramcontent.com/pod-product-compliance
Lightning Source LLC
Chambersburg PA
CBHW051245300426
44114CB00011B/890